From Participants in the
TEXT READING PROGRAM

If it were not for these enlightening Text commentaries, we would still be floundering in an intellectual soup. The soup was mighty tasty, but was difficult to get our teeth into without these brilliant observations, comparisons, and analogies. We know this is a vast body of work that has been given us and we are grateful from the bottom of our hearts.
—SYLVIA AND CAP LYONS

A very powerful tool to keep me on track, reading and absorbing just a few pages each day. This process has been an invaluable source of inner peace during this past year.
—CONNIE PORTER

Robert Perry and Greg Mackie are experts at making the sometimes challenging Text not just understandable, but rich with meaning and poignancy. This is a priceless gift to anyone who wants to fully understand the awesome teachings of *A Course in Miracles*. I can think of no better form of support than this!
—JULIA SIMPSON

The Text commentaries offer insights I could not have had alone, because of the deep understanding Robert and Greg have.
—DIETRUN BUCHMAN

An amazing journey into the genius and magnitude of this material. Don't miss this opportunity.
—SHARON EDWARDS

Robert and Greg's insights illuminate Text principles like never before.
—LORETTA M. SIANI, PH.D

I have studied the Text and read it through at least once a year for the last 19 years. I thought I knew it pretty well. However this year has been a real eye-opener. Many of those little question marks I made in the margins have been erased. I shall be forever grateful for this year of Text study.
—WENDY FINNERTY

After 20 years with the Course, I now understand it on a much different level.
—ULLA WALLIN

Robert and Greg's intelligence, insight, and wit, create a fun climate of spiritual scholarship that helps make the Text more intelligible and alive. They're extraordinarily gifted.
—AMY ELLISON

The clear and down-to-earth commentary has helped me connect with the Text as never before.
—NANCY NEVITT

Robert and Greg have a tremendous comprehension of the Course and provide down-to-earth explanations. I know of no better way to learn the message of the Text than this program.
—JAN WORLEY

Translates the beautiful poetry of the Course's Text into everyday common language, making the valuable meaning of each sentence easily understood.
—KATHERINE LATORRACA

Previously, I had never succeeded in completely reading the Text. Participating was the best thing that I did for myself this year.
—DAVID COLWELL

There is nothing else in my years of studying the Course that has helped me so much!
—GEORGE PORTER

I can honestly say I'll finally complete the reading of the entire Text—and I've been at this for 20 years!
—BARBARA OLSON

Robert and Greg's insights helped me understand and assimilate the Course's otherwise complex and difficult passages. I will do this again next year, and the next, and the next. This program is amazing.
—JO CHANDLER

Your program has been a revelation.
—DON DE LENE

I would like to say that this year has been too amazing to actually put into words.
—KATHY CHOMITZ

Having studied the Course faithfully for 28 years, I never imagined the insights and miracles I would receive from these commentaries on the Text!
—MIRKALICE GORE

I can truly say that this program has made an incredible difference to my life. I wholeheartedly recommend it.
—DAVID FLEMING

Nothing less than totally inspiring.
—REV. JERRY CUSIMANO

THE ILLUMINATED TEXT

Commentaries for Deepening Your Connection with
A Course in Miracles

Robert Perry & Greg Mackie

VOLUME 3

CIRCLE PUBLISHING

Published by Circle Publishing
A division of the Circle of Atonement
P.O. Box 4238 * West Sedona, AZ 86340
(928) 282-0790 * www.circleofa.org
circleoffice@circleofa.org

Cover design by Thunder Mountain Design and Communications
Design & layout by Phillips Associates UK Ltd
Printed in the USA

ISBN 978-1-886602-34-2

Library of Congress Cataloging-in-Publication Data

Perry, Robert, 1960-
  The illuminated text : commentaries for deepening your connection with A course in
miracles / Robert Perry & Greg Mackie.
      p. cm.
  Includes bibliographical references.
  Summary: "Provides in-depth analysis of the Text of A Course in Miracles"--
Provided by publisher.
  ISBN 978-1-886602-34-2
  1. Course in Miracles. 2. Spiritual life. I. Mackie, Greg, 1963- II. Title.
  BP605.C68P455 2010
  299'.93--dc22

                                2009039354

CONTENTS

Commentaries on Chapter 12: THE HOLY SPIRIT'S CURRICULUM

Commentaries on Chapter 13: THE GUILTLESS WORLD

FOREWORD

The Text is the foundation of *A Course in Miracles*. Doing the Course is simply a process of learning and internalizing its thought system, and the Text is where that thought system is laid out. It is an unparalleled spiritual tour de force. Careful study of it will change your outlook in ways that perhaps nothing else can.

Many students, however, find the Text to be very hard going. Many do not finish it, and even those who make it through, perhaps repeatedly, wish they had a deeper grasp of what they were reading.

For this reason, in 2006, the Circle of Atonement offered the Text Reading Program. This was a year-long tour through the Text of *A Course in Miracles* with commentary on each paragraph, written by myself and Greg Mackie, both teachers for the Circle. Before each weekday, we would send out to all the participants via e-mail the reading for that day. This would usually consist of a single section from the Text, accompanied by our commentary as well as practical exercises.

We often supplemented these sections with material from the Urtext, the original typescript of the Course. Our experience was that, especially in the early chapters of the Text, material from the Urtext that was eventually edited out was very helpful and clarifying. So when we felt it was useful, we included this Urtext material in brackets, and let it inform our commentary. We also indicated where a word had been emphasized in the Urtext, as this too often added clarity.

Note: In this volume, words that were originally emphasized in the Urtext are <u>underlined</u>. So when you see an underlined word here, know that that word was emphasized in the Urtext, but that emphasis was not included in the eventual published Course, which included fewer emphasized words. Again, we did this because quite often that emphasis from the Urtext would add clarity.

The reason we developed this program has a bit of history to it. In 2000, we offered a local program in Sedona that included a daily Text class, using a schedule that took us through the entire Text in a year of weekday readings. (On the sixth and seventh days, we rested!) Our friend, student, and colleague John Perry attended that program. When it ended, he began guiding people through the Text using the same schedule, only doing so online. He sent out the Text material for a given day and interspersed it with his own clarifying comments. In fall 2005 he felt guided to suggest we do something similar. Our guidance told us to go ahead, and so that's what we did. Without John's suggestion, however, it is safe to say we never would have done this.

2006, the year of the program, was an intense one. I would write commentaries for three weeks. Then I got a breather for a week while Greg wrote the commentaries. And then the schedule started over. Each day we wrote the commentary that needed to go out the next day. In addition, we led a weekly phone class for participants, in which we summarized the previous week's sections. (The recordings are still available to students who sign up for the online version of the Text Reading Program.)

The response to our program far exceeded our expectations. We have included a few edited comments at the front of the book, but if you want to read the unadulterated student reactions, straight from the various horses' mouths, then go to www.circlepublishing.org and click on the link for the Text Reading Program. During the year of the program, and actually ever since, we have had consistent requests that we put this material into published form.

So here it is, presented in book form as a multi-volume set. We hope you find these commentaries illuminating, and that they do indeed deepen your understanding of the spiritual masterpiece, *A Course in Miracles*.

ROBERT PERRY
SEPTEMBER 2009
SEDONA, ARIZONA

Commentaries on Chapter 10

THE IDOLS
OF SICKNESS

Introduction
Commentary by Robert Perry

1. <u>Nothing</u> beyond yourself can make you fearful or loving, because nothing *is* beyond you. Time and eternity are both in your mind [not beyond you], and <u>will</u> conflict until you perceive time <u>solely</u> as a means to <u>regain</u> eternity. You cannot do this as long as you believe that <u>anything</u> happening [Ur: that happens] to you is caused by factors <u>outside</u> yourself. You must learn that time is solely at <u>your</u> disposal, and that nothing in the world can take this responsibility <u>from</u> you. You can <u>violate</u> God's laws [which give you this responsibility] in your imagination, but you cannot escape from them. They were established for your protection and are as inviolate as your safety.

The impression I get from this paragraph is that the entire world of time is inside my mind, just as in a nighttime dream. In our dreams, we see a world that seems so obviously outside us, but in fact, it is all inside our mind, which means that everything that happens is being secretly controlled by our mind.

Normally, of course, we believe all sorts of things happen to us outside our will. This makes our use of time appear to be partly a product of our will yet largely a product of outside pressures. We try to walk a straight line, but outside winds keep knocking us off balance. Yet this paragraph is saying that there is only *one* force at work in our lives: our own will. Therefore, we can use time for whatever we want. We have it within our power to use time solely as a means to regain eternity, and we have no excuses not to.

Application: If you had total freedom to use your time for whatever you wanted, what would you use it for?

After you come up with your answer, realize that you *do* have that total freedom, and you *are* using it for what you want to. Would you like to change what you are using it for?

2.   God created nothing beside you and nothing beside you exists, for you are part of Him. What except Him <u>can</u> exist? Nothing <u>beyond</u> Him can happen, because nothing <u>except</u> Him is real. <u>Your</u> creations add to Him as <u>you</u> do, but nothing is added that is different because everything has always <u>been</u>. What can upset you except the ephemeral, and how can the ephemeral be real if you are God's <u>only</u> creation and He created you eternal? Your holy mind [Ur: will] establishes <u>everything</u> that happens to you. Every response you make to everything you perceive is up to you, because your mind [Ur: will] <u>determines</u> your perception of it.

Application: The opening lines are mind-blowing. Let's repeat an altered version of them to ourselves:

Nothing besides me exists.
For I am part of God.
And nothing except God exists.

This idea that there is nothing beyond me has two very different implications in this paragraph. First, it means that nothing in this world happens to me outside my will. My will is moving each thing I see. Further, my will is determining my perception of it and thus my response to it.

Second, it means that nothing happens to me at all! For all happenings here are ephemeral, transient. Yet if I am the only thing that exists, and I am eternal, then the non-eternal does not exist. Try repeating these lines:

Nothing besides me exists.
I am eternal.
Hence, the non-eternal does not exist.
The happenings of this world are not eternal.
Therefore, nothing happens to me here at all.

3.   God does not change His Mind about <u>you</u>, for He is not uncertain of <u>Himself</u>. And what He knows <u>can</u> be known [by you], because He does not know it only for Himself [He knows it for you, too]. He <u>created</u>

4

you for Himself, but He gave you the power to create for yourself so you would be like Him. That is why your mind [Ur: will {by which you create}] is holy. Can anything exceed the Love of God? Can anything, then, exceed your will? Nothing can reach you from beyond it because, being in God, you encompass everything. Believe this, and you will realize how much is up to you. When anything threatens your peace of mind, ask yourself, "Has God changed His Mind about me?" Then accept His decision, for it is indeed changeless, and refuse to change your mind about yourself. God will never decide against you, or He would be deciding against Himself.

When God created you, He endowed you with eternalness (paragraph 2), which means you are changeless and last forever. He endowed you with the power to create ("He gave you the power to create"), which means your will contains all power. And He made you co-extensive with Him ("being in God, you encompass everything"), which means that there is nothing outside you, and that nothing can reach you from beyond your will. Try to believe this, and then spend a moment thinking about "how much is up to you."

You can know all of this, because God knows it for you. And He never changes His Mind about you, no matter what happens to you, no matter what you do.

Application: Notice the practice towards the end of the paragraph: "When anything threatens your peace of mind, ask yourself..." This is what will later be called a response to temptation practice. Begin by thinking about something that is compromising your peace of mind right now. Then say,

Has God changed His Mind about me?

Then accept His decision about you, which is indeed changeless. And then actively refuse to change your mind about yourself.

I. At Home in God
Commentary by Robert Perry

1. [Ur: The reason] You do not know your creations [Ur: is] simply because you would decide against them as long as your mind is split, and to attack what you have created is impossible. But remember that *it is as impossible for God.* The law of creation is that you love your creations as yourself [a take-off on the biblical "love your neighbor as yourself"], because they are part of you. Everything that was created is therefore perfectly safe, because the laws of God protect it by His Love. Any part of your mind that does not know this has banished itself from knowledge, because it has not met its conditions. Who could have done this but you? Recognize this gladly, for in this recognition lies the realization that your banishment is not of God, and therefore does not exist.

If you think that God could decide against you (referring to the preceding paragraph), think again. For the whole law of creation is that the creator (any creator) loves his creations as himself, for they are literally part of him. God will always love you in just this way. And you will always love *your* creations in just this way.

But not in the conscious part of your mind. That part of your mind is so attack-prone that, were it aware of your creations, it would naturally attack them. This banishes knowledge of them from your conscious mind, for otherwise you would violate the law of creation (that you have only love for what you created). You have therefore banished yourself from knowledge. You need to own this, and own it "gladly," because it means that *God* didn't banish you. How could He, when the law of creation dictates that He forever love you as He loves Himself?

2. You are at home in God, dreaming of exile but perfectly capable of awakening to reality. Is it your decision to do so? You recognize [Ur: know] from your own experience that what you see in dreams you think is real while [Ur: as long as] you are asleep. Yet the instant you waken you realize [Ur: *know*] that everything that seemed to happen in the dream did not happen at all. You do not think this strange [Ur:

mysterious], even though <u>all</u> the laws of what you awaken to <u>were</u> violated while you slept [which could lead you to believe that your dream reality overturned and blotted out your waking reality]. Is it not possible that you merely shifted from one dream to another, without really waking?

I dreamt the other night that my wife's handbag had been stolen and with it our credit and debit cards. I was in a bad part of some nameless town. I couldn't get to a phone to cancel the cards, knowing that at that moment they were being used. It seemed so real. Yet as I woke up, it occurred to me that parts of it might not be real. Then, as I fully awoke, I realized with surprise and relief that the whole thing was a dream. The problem I was trying to solve had never occurred.

What I didn't realize is that I had just shifted from one dream to another, without really waking. In this larger dream, I have a much bigger problem. I am in exile from my home. I appear to have been banished by God. Why can't I get back? How do I undo whatever shameful thing got me banished in the first place? I can't seem to solve this gigantic problem.

The irony is that I am having this dream while *in* God. He is the "room" in which I sleep. So while asleep in God, I am dreaming of being banished by God. While asleep at home, I am dreaming of being exiled from my home. The problem I am trying to solve has never occurred.

Application: Imagine for a moment that the scene you see before your eyes really is a dream. Take a moment and make that real to you. The things you see are only mental images, nothing more. Try to let that sink in. And since it's a dream, you are not really here. Are you literally inside your dreams at night? No more are you inside *this* dream. While looking about, say to yourself,

I am not here.
I am somewhere else.
I am at home in God
dreaming I'm exiled in this world.
But I am perfectly capable of awakening to reality.
When I awaken, I will realize that none of this happened,
That I have always been at home in God.

7

> 3.   Would you bother to reconcile what happened in conflicting <u>dreams</u>, or would you dismiss <u>both together</u> if you discovered that <u>reality</u> is in accord with neither? You do not remember being awake. When you hear the Holy Spirit you may [Ur: you merely] feel <u>better</u> because loving then seems <u>possible</u> to you, but you do <u>not</u> remember yet that it once was so. And it is in this remembering that you will know it can be so again. What is possible has not yet been accomplished. Yet what has once been is so now, if it is eternal. When you remember, you will know that what you remember <u>is</u> eternal, and therefore is <u>now</u>.

The only game we play here is Dream Ping-Pong. We bounce back and forth between sleeping dreams and waking dreams. We don't wake up, and we don't remember being awake.

I find the third and fourth sentences so poignant. One of the truly wonderful things about hearing the Holy Spirit or reading the Course is that it kindles a hope in us, a hope we dare not utter: "Maybe I could be *loving*." Our dream of exile is a dream of lovelessness, and the idea that we could actually be loving is like the glow of paradise on the horizon. How we long to reach that glow! What we don't remember, though, is "that it once was so." *It once was so.* Once, it made no sense to *hope* to be loving. Once, we loved. What we further don't realize is that this "once upon a time" wasn't a point in time. It was outside of time. It was eternity. And being eternal, it is forever. It is *now*. Thus, while we feel trapped in this dream of lovelessness, there is a waking state that has continued uninterrupted. That promise of being loving, that paradise on the horizon, is actually the daylight of wakefulness that shines in us right now.

> 4.   You will remember everything the instant you <u>desire it wholly</u>, for if to desire wholly is to create, you will have willed away the separation, returning your mind simultaneously to your Creator and your creations. Knowing them you will have no wish to sleep, but only the desire [Ur: will] to waken and be glad. Dreams will be impossible because you will <u>want</u> only truth, and being at last your will, it will be yours.

We need to remember that waking state in which love is a present reality, not a future potential. Then "you will know it can be so again" (paragraph 3). How do we remember? We simply "desire it wholly." The whole spiritual journey is one of reaching that place where our desire is whole, without a trace of conflict. Then, being at last our will, waking will be ours. And when we open our eyes in Heaven and see our Creator and our creations again, the wish to sleep will leave us forever. We will be awake, and we will be glad.

II. The Decision to Forget
Commentary by Robert Perry

1.   Unless you first <u>know</u> something you <u>cannot</u> dissociate it. Knowledge must precede [Ur: therefore *precedes*] dissociation, so that dissociation is nothing more than a <u>decision to forget</u>. What has been <u>forgotten</u> then appears to be fearful, but <u>only</u> because the dissociation is an <u>attack on truth</u>. You are fearful *because* you have forgotten. And you have <u>replaced</u> your knowledge by an awareness of dreams because you are afraid of your dissociation, <u>not</u> of what you have dissociated. When what you have dissociated is accepted, it ceases to be fearful. [Ur: Even in this world's therapy, when dissociated material is *accepted*, it ceases to be fearful, for the laws of mind always hold.]

Obviously, if we have dissociated something—if we have separated it off from our awareness—it must have been in our awareness in the first place. Just as obviously, once we have dissociated it, we become afraid of letting it back into our awareness. What is not obvious is *why*. We assume it's because we're afraid of whatever that thing is. Not so, says Jesus. He points out that, in therapy, once dissociated material is accepted back into awareness, it ceases to be fearful. Actually, he says, we are afraid to let it back in because we are afraid of *our act of dissociation*, which was "an attack on truth." Thus, letting this thing back into our awareness means facing our attack, and facing ourselves as an attacker. And that's why we are afraid to let heavenly knowledge back in.

2.   Yet to give up the dissociation of <u>reality</u> brings more than merely lack of fear. In <u>this</u> decision lie joy and peace and the glory of creation. Offer the Holy Spirit only your willingness [Ur: will] to remember, for He retains the knowledge of God and of yourself <u>for</u> you, waiting for your acceptance. Give up gladly <u>everything</u> that would stand in the way of your remembering, for God is in your memory. [Ur: and] His Voice will tell you that you are part of Him when you are willing to remember Him and know your own reality again. Let nothing in this world delay your remembering of Him, for in this remembering is the knowledge of <u>yourself</u>.

II. The Decision to Forget

Since knowledge is not fearful in itself, remembering it is not fearful (as the previous paragraph said). Yet remembering it is not just an experience of absence of fear. It is an experience of "joy and peace and the glory of creation." For what lies there in our memory, waiting for us, is God. And with Him comes the knowledge of our own reality. Why would we ever want to delay this memory? Let us therefore give up every thought and every belief that stands in its way, and give them up gladly. Let us muster all the will we have to remember this, and then offer that will to the Holy Spirit, Who holds this memory in trust for us.

> 3. To remember is merely to restore to your mind *what is already there*. You do not make what you remember; you merely accept again what is already there, but was rejected [Ur: accept again what has *been* made *and rejected*]. The ability to <u>accept</u> truth in this world is the perceptual counterpart of creating in the Kingdom. God <u>will</u> do His part if you will do yours, and <u>His</u> return in exchange for yours <u>is</u> the exchange of knowledge for perception. <u>Nothing</u> is beyond His Will for you. [There is no treasure so great that He does not will it for you.] But signify your will to remember Him, and behold! He will give you everything but for the asking.

Our part is merely to want truth back in our minds. This wanting happens on the level of perception, but it *calls* upon the level of knowledge. On that level is God, Who will do His part once we have done ours. His part is to restore to our mind what is already there. To give us knowledge in exchange for perception. To return us to the joy of creating. In short, He will give us everything but for the asking. If He has not done His part yet, it because we have not yet done ours. Is it too much to ask for us to simply *want truth*?

> 4. When you attack [in the form of dissociating or denying knowledge], you are denying <u>yourself</u>. You are specifically teaching yourself that you are <u>not</u> what you are. <u>Your</u> denial of reality precludes the <u>acceptance</u> of God's gift, <u>because you have accepted something else in its place</u>. If you understand that this is always [Ur: If you understand that the misuse of defenses {in this case, the defense of dissociation} always constitutes] an attack on truth, and truth is God, you will realize why it is <u>always</u> fearful. If you further recognize that you are <u>part</u> of God, you will understand why it is that <u>you always attack yourself first</u>.

11

This paragraph explains further why we are afraid not of the knowledge we have dissociated, but of our *act* of dissociating it. Like the first paragraph, it says that we are afraid of this because it was an attack on truth. This paragraph expands this saying that it is also an attack on God—and taking on God is always a fearful thing. It also says that since we are part of God, this is also an attack on ourselves. What else could it be? In pushing knowledge out of our mind, we are pushing away the knowledge of our own reality. We are denying ourselves.

As an analogy, imagine that you had a doll that was a magical doll. It was actually alive and possessed great wisdom. It loved you deeply and never harmed you. Then let's say that one day, on a whim, you got mad at this doll and buried it in the back yard. At this point, you might understandably be afraid to dig it up, because doing so would mean facing the awful thing you did, and perhaps facing the doll's wrath (even if the doll is not wrathful, you might expect it to be). Your fear of digging up the doll is the same as your fear of remembering God.

> 5.   All attack is self attack. It cannot be anything else. Arising from your own decision not to be what you are, it is an attack on your identification. Attack is thus the way in which your identification is lost, because when you attack, you must have forgotten what you are. And if your reality is God's, when you attack you are not remembering Him. This is not because He is gone, but because you are actively choosing not to remember Him [Ur: *actively willing not to remember Him*].

Attack in this paragraph seems to have broadened from dissociation to "*all* attack," so that it now includes attack on our brothers. All attack, including attack on others, "is self-attack." All attack is a denial of what we are, an attack on our own identification, a decision to forget our reality. And since our reality is God's, it is a decision to forget God.

Application: Think of recent attacks on your part, obvious or subtle, covert or overt, and with each one say:

> *My attack on [name] was self-attack.*
> *It was a decision to forget my reality,*
> *And a decision to forget God.*

6.   If you realized the complete havoc this makes of your peace of mind you <u>could</u> not make such an insane decision. You make it only because you still believe it can <u>get you something you want</u>. It follows, then, that you want something <u>other</u> than peace of mind, but you have not considered what it must be. Yet the logical outcome of your decision is perfectly clear, if you will only <u>look</u> at it. By deciding <u>against</u> your reality, you have made yourself vigilant *against* God and His Kingdom. And it is <u>this</u> vigilance that makes you afraid to remember Him.

Attacking others wreaks havoc on our peace of mind. We do it because we think it gets us something we want, yet this can only mean that we *don't* want peace of mind. Have we really considered what we are hoping to get that is more precious than our peace of mind? And have we considered the real logical outcome of our attack? Since our attack drives our reality out of our mind, it also drives God and His Kingdom out of our mind. Through our attack, we have become vigilant *against* God and His Kingdom (a reverse of the third lesson of the Holy Spirit). This attack on God makes us afraid to remember Him. To use my earlier metaphor, we are afraid to dig up the doll.

III. The God of Sickness
Commentary by Robert Perry

What is the god of sickness? It is an image of ourselves that we made to replace our reality as God created us. It is an image of ourselves as autonomous, drained of power, attacking, and sick. It is the image we show up as in this world.

> 1.   You have <u>not</u> attacked God and you <u>do</u> love Him. Can you change your reality? No one can will to destroy himself. When you think you are attacking your<u>self</u>, it is a sure sign that you hate what you *think* you are. And this, and <u>only</u> this, can <u>be</u> attacked by you. What you <u>think</u> you are <u>can</u> be very hateful, and what this strange image makes you do can be very destructive. Yet the destruction is no more real than the image, although those who make idols <u>do</u> worship them. The idols are nothing, but their worshippers are the Sons of God in sickness. God would have them released from their sickness and returned to His Mind. He will not limit your power to help them, because He has given it <u>to</u> you. Do not be afraid of it, because it is your salvation.

As the previous section said, we scared ourselves by attacking God. We now see ourselves as hateful attackers. We hate ourselves for becoming such destructive creatures. What we don't realize is that the hateful thing we look upon as ourselves is just an image we made. It is a lifeless idol, which we worship. It is unreal, and what it does is also unreal. This puts us in a strange position: We, the Sons of God Himself, are worshipping an unreal, hateful image of ourselves, thinking this is who we are. What can this mean but that we are sick?

This is the condition of everyone we know. Yet God has given us the power to release them from their sickness.

Application: Think of someone you know. Realize that the image this person presents to you as an attacker is just that: an image. Behind the image, this person is the Son of God who needs release from this sick image. Say,

I have the power to release [name] from his/her sick image.
God gave this power to me and will not limit it.
Let me not be afraid of it, because it is my salvation.

2.   What Comforter can there be for the sick children of God except
His power through you? Remember that it does not matter where in
the Sonship He is accepted. He is always accepted for all, and when
your mind receives Him the remembrance of Him awakens throughout
the Sonship. Heal your brothers simply by accepting God for them.
Your minds are not separate, and God has only one channel for healing
because He has but one Son. God's remaining communication link with
all His children joins them together, and them to Him. To be aware of
this is to heal them because it is the awareness that no one is separate,
and so no one is sick.

Previous sections have talked about us healing our brothers through our
interactions with them. This paragraph talks about a more mystical way
to heal our brothers: We simply accept God for them. Since all minds are
joined through the Holy Spirit, the remembrance that we accept into our
own mind ripples through the Sonship, sparking awakening in everyone.
Indeed, simply being aware of this oneness of minds allows healing into
our mind and thus spreads healing to our brothers. Awareness of oneness
heals, for at root sickness is really a soul-sickness which stems from
feeling separate.

3.   To believe that a Son of God can be sick is to believe that part
of God can suffer. Love cannot suffer, because it cannot attack. The
remembrance of love therefore brings invulnerability with it. Do not
side with sickness in the presence of a Son of God even if he believes
in it, for your acceptance of God in him acknowledges the Love of God
he has forgotten. Your recognition of him as part of God reminds him
of the truth about himself, which he is denying. Would you strengthen
his denial of God and thus lose sight of yourself? Or would you remind
him of his wholeness and remember your Creator with him?

Application: This paragraph is a stirring call to refuse to acknowledge
the reality of sickness in a brother. Think of someone you know who is or

recently was ill. Imagine being with this person and saying the following to him or her in your mind:

> *You cannot be sick, for a part of God cannot suffer.*
> *You are love, and love cannot suffer, for it cannot attack.*
> *I accept God in you.*
> *I acknowledge God's Love for you, which you have forgotten.*
> *I remind you of your wholeness so that I can remember God with*
>   *you.*

4.   To believe a Son of God is sick is to worship the same idol he does. God created love, <u>not</u> idolatry. <u>All</u> forms of idolatry are caricatures of creation, taught by sick minds too divided to know that creation <u>shares</u> power and <u>never</u> usurps it. Sickness is idolatry, because it is the belief that <u>power can be taken from you.</u> Yet this is impossible, because you are part of God, Who <u>is</u> all power. A sick god <u>must</u> be an idol, made in the image of what its maker thinks <u>he</u> is. And that is exactly what the ego <u>does</u> perceive in a Son of God; a sick god, self-created, self-sufficient, very vicious and very vulnerable. Is this the idol you would worship? Is this the image you would be vigilant to <u>save</u>? Are you <u>really</u> afraid of losing <u>this</u>?

When you believe in a brother's sickness, you are worshipping "the same idol he does." You are worshipping his false image of himself. "All forms of idolatry" try to replace our reality as created by God with images we have made. These images are twisted caricatures of our real identity; they depict a limitless spirit as a weird hunk of flesh. By making these images, then, we are trying to make ourselves. We are attempting to wrest the creative process from God's Hands. We are trying to take power away from Him. That is the essence of idolatry—the attempt to take power from God.

Believing we have taken power from God, we now believe that power can be taken from us. That is what sickness is, isn't it—the experience of being drained of power. Yet how can this really be? We are part of God. Can power *really* be taken from God?

When we agree with a brother's perception that he is sick, this is what we are seeing in him. We are seeing him as "a sick god," an idol. But we only see him that way because that is what we think *we* are—a sick god, who has stolen fire from Heaven and is now all on his own. Just as he took power from God, so power has now been taken from him. He must look out for himself, yet he is constantly drained, constantly weakened, and thus constantly on the defensive. Doesn't this describe the creature we seem to be in this world?

This is not who we are. This is an image we made. This is a lifeless idol that we worship. This is what we are vigilant to protect from all threats, earthly and heavenly. Why? Do we really want to protect *this*?

> 5.   Look calmly at the logical conclusion of the ego's thought system and judge whether its offering is really what you want, for this *is* what it offers you. To obtain <u>this</u> you are willing to attack the Divinity of your brothers, and thus lose sight of <u>yours</u>. And you are willing to keep it hidden, to protect an idol you think will save you from the dangers for which it stands [Ur: the dangers *which the idol itself stands for*], but which do not exist.

Application: Look calmly at the image you show up as in this world. According to this image:

> *I define myself; I craft my image to suit my purposes* ("self-created").
> *I take care of myself; God's not going to do it for me* ("self-sufficient").
> *I am continually under threat of having my power stolen* ("very vulnerable").
> *As a result, I am always ready to attack* ("very vicious").

Then ask yourself the following questions, as deeply and genuinely as you can:

> *Is this the idol I would worship?*
> *Is this the image I would be vigilant to save?*
> *Do I really want to attack the Divinity of my brothers to protect*
>   *this idol?*
> *It cannot save me from the dangers I see—it is part of them.*

All this image can do is keep my Divinity hidden.
*Am I really afraid of losing **this**?*

6.   There are no idolaters in the Kingdom, but there is great appreciation for everything [Ur: every Soul] that God created, because of the calm knowledge that each one is part of Him. God's Son knows no idols, but he <u>does</u> know his Father. Health in this world is the counterpart of value in Heaven. It is not my merit that I contribute to you* but my love, for you do not value yourself. When you do not value yourself* you become sick, but <u>my</u> value of you can heal you, * because the value of God's Son is one. When I said, "My peace I give unto you," I meant it*. Peace comes [Ur: came] from God through me to <u>you</u>*. It is <u>for</u> you although you may not ask for it [Ur: It was *for* you*, but you did not ask].

Application: Reread the fourth through eighth sentences very slowly, inserting your name at every asterisk, and imagining that Jesus is speaking directly to you.

In the Kingdom, no one worships idols. Instead, everyone appreciates the limitless value of every Soul that God created, knowing that each one is part of Him. As an awake member of the Kingdom, Jesus can bring a taste of it to us, through his appreciation of our Soul. His gift to us is not his exemplary merit that trickles down from on high due to his great spiritual feats. Rather, his gift is simply his love. He knows we are part of God. He knows our true value. And so he loves us. He values us so deeply, so far beyond what we think we deserve, that his love for us can actually heal us. It can heal us because our sickness comes from not valuing ourselves.

7.   When a brother is sick it is because <u>he is not asking for peace</u>, and therefore does not know he <u>has</u> it. The <u>acceptance</u> of peace is the <u>denial</u> of illusion, and sickness *is* an illusion. Yet every Son of God has the power to deny illusions <u>anywhere</u> in the Kingdom, merely by denying them completely in himself. I <u>can</u> heal you because I <u>know</u> you*. I know your value <u>for</u> you, and it is this value* that makes you whole. A whole mind is not idolatrous, and does not know of conflicting laws. I will heal you* merely because I have only <u>one</u> message, and it is true.

III. The God of Sickness

Your faith in it* will make you whole when you have faith in me.

Application: Reread the fourth through eighth sentences slowly. Insert your name at each asterisk and imagine that Jesus is speaking directly to you. Then try to open your mind and heart to his valuing of you. Try to set aside your sense of littleness. Realize you don't know who you are, and open yourself to his knowledge of your real worth. Trust that he knows better than you do.

When you are sick, it is because you feel that you are so valueless that you don't deserve peace, and so you don't really ask for peace. Yet your sickness is an illusion, and any Son of God can dispel this illusion in you by denying all illusions in himself. That is the place Jesus is in. He has no more illusions, and thus has no illusions about you. He knows your value, and this value is what makes you whole in truth. It makes you forever impervious to all sickness. Thus, if you let him reveal your value to you, you will be healed.

> 8.   I do not bring God's message with deception, and you will learn this as you learn that you <u>always</u> receive as much as you <u>accept</u>. You could accept peace <u>now</u> for everyone [Ur: you meet], and offer them perfect freedom from <u>all</u> illusions because you heard His Voice [Ur: *because you heard*]. But have no other gods before Him or you will <u>not</u> hear. God is not jealous of the gods you make, but <u>you</u> are. You would save them and serve them, because you believe that <u>they made you</u>. You think they are your father, because you are projecting onto them the fearful fact that <u>you made them to replace God</u>. Yet when they seem to speak to you, remember that <u>nothing</u> can replace God, and whatever replacements you have attempted <u>are</u> nothing.

We don't *really* trust Jesus. We think that his promises are deceptions, that he doesn't really keep them. Yet it only *appears* that he doesn't give us what he said he would. His giving is not limited; the problem is our limited willingness to accept his gift.

If our acceptance wasn't so limited, we could accept peace for everyone, right now. We could offer them perfect freedom from all their illusions of sickness. What a promise! But to do this, we would have to

19

renounce our false gods—our false images of who we are and who our brother is. Right now, we jealously protect these gods. We listen to their every whisper and in the process, tune out God and become deaf to His Voice. We think they made us, simply because they are our replacements for our real Creator. Yet nothing can replace Him. We need to remember this when they speak to us. We will then realize that we are like a crazy person, listening to the voices of those who are not there.

> 9. Very simply, then, you may <u>believe</u> you are afraid of nothingness, but you are <u>really</u> afraid of <u>nothing</u>. And in <u>that</u> awareness you <u>are</u> healed. You <u>will</u> hear the god you listen to. You <u>made</u> the god of sickness, and <u>by</u> making him you made yourself <u>able</u> to hear him. Yet you did <u>not</u> create him, because he is <u>not</u> the Will of the Father. He is therefore not eternal and will be <u>un</u>made for you the instant you signify your willingness to accept <u>only</u> the eternal.

What is the fear of nothingness Jesus is talking about here? It must be fear of being annihilated, probably for the sin of replacing God with our idols. But we are really afraid of nothing, because nothing can replace God. Our task is simply to realize this, realize that the images we made of ourselves are like the Emperor's new clothes—they are not there. If we could realize that single thing, then the voice of our image would stop speaking to us. It would stop acting like our god and ordering us around. All ephemeral images would be gone and we would be left with nothing but the eternal.

> 10. If God has but one Son, there is but one God. You share reality with Him, <u>because</u> reality is not divided. To accept other gods before Him is to place other images before <u>yourself</u>. You do not realize how much you listen to your gods, and how vigilant you are on their behalf. Yet they exist only because you honor them. Place honor where it is due, and peace <u>will</u> be yours. It is your inheritance from your <u>real</u> Father. You cannot make your Father, and the father you made did <u>not</u> make you. Honor is not due to illusions, for to honor them is to honor nothing. Yet fear is not due them either, for nothing cannot be fearful. You have chosen to fear love <u>because</u> of its perfect harmlessness, and because of this fear you have been willing to give up your own perfect helpfulness and your own perfect Help.

We and God share one undivided reality. When we make an idol, when we craft an image of ourselves, we aren't just making a graven image that we place before God; we are placing this image before ourselves. We are hiding our Divinity behind a false image of who we are.

This image becomes our god. It issues its commandments: "Make sure you have the perfect shoes; you don't want to look plain." "Don't forget your medication; you are very vulnerable." "Make sure you keep abreast of the latest information; you don't want to be caught looking ignorant." We listen to this god's dictates all the time. Yet it only exists because we honor it. Our task is to withdraw all honor as well as all fear from this cruel god. After all, it is only an illusion.

We must instead give honor where honor is really due, to our Father. Then we will have His peace, the inheritance He has set aside just for us. And then we will have His help, the perfect Help we have so needed.

> 11. Only at the altar of God will you find peace. And this altar is in you because God put it there. His Voice still calls you to return, and He will be heard when you place no other gods before Him. You can give up the god of sickness for your brothers; in fact, you would <u>have</u> to do so if you give him up for yourself. For if you see the god of sickness anywhere, <u>you</u> have accepted him. And if you accept him you <u>will</u> bow down and worship him, because <u>he was made as God's replacement</u>. He is the belief that <u>you can choose which god is real</u>. Although it is clear this has nothing to do with <u>reality</u>, it is equally clear that it has <u>everything</u> to do with <u>reality as you perceive it</u>.

We have to make a choice: Which god will we acknowledge? We can kneel at the altar of our true Father, the altar He placed forever inside us. Or we can bow down and worship a false image of who we are, an image of ourselves as autonomous, disempowered, sick, hateful, and attacking. This image contains the belief that we have a choice about which god is real. Yet that is the ultimate illusion. In truth, we have no choice. God is God, period. The false god we made is nothing. When we are finally willing to lay down our false god, our god of sickness, we will at last hear our Father's Voice. We will at last find peace at His altar. And we will heal all our brothers. As we pluck the false god from our own mind, we will be simultaneously plucking him from everyone's mind. What are we waiting for?

IV. The End of Sickness
Commentary by Robert Perry

This is a very difficult section to interpret, being extremely abstract. I have had to take some guesses as to the meaning of some of the passages and have also allowed myself more space to describe what I think the paragraphs mean. The single biggest key to the section is the awareness that it is continuing the same discussion begun in yesterday's section, which focused on the false image of ourselves that we have made.

> 1.   All magic is an attempt at [Ur: is a form of] reconciling the irreconcilable. All religion is the recognition that the irreconcilable cannot be reconciled. Sickness and perfection are irreconcilable. If God created you perfect, you *are* perfect. If you believe you can be sick, you have placed other gods before Him. God is not at war with the god of sickness you made, but you are. He is the symbol of deciding [Ur: willing] against God, and you are afraid of him because he cannot be reconciled with God's Will. If you attack him, you will make him real to you. But if you refuse to worship him in whatever form he may appear to you, and wherever you think you see him, he will disappear into the nothingness out of which he was made.

Magic in the Course is not a simple concept. My best understanding can be boiled down to two points:

1.   Magic is any unreal power, any power apart from God's will—such as the power believed to be in medicine, in the mind of the ego-based healer, or in our own separate will.
2.   Being unreal, this power can't really do what it claims to do. Like stage magic, it can only produce an illusion of the promised feat.

In terms of this paragraph, my guess is that magic is the power we see residing in the god of sickness, the image of ourselves (as autonomous, vicious, sick) that we made to replace the identity God gave us. Our very

22

belief in this image gives it power (making it a power apart from God—point #1), yet it has no real power (point #2). It's just an image.

Here, then, is my understanding of the first sentence: Endowing our false god (the false image we've made of ourselves) with power means that we now believe in a power apart from God's, a magical power. So now there seem to be two things that are real. One is our false god (our false image of ourselves as sick) and the other is the real God. Now we see both existing, side by side. We thus see them as somehow compatible with each other. Yet they are not. And so we are attempting to reconcile the irreconcilable.

All true religion (the Course would classify itself as an example of this) is about letting go of that which can't be reconciled with God. It is about letting go of the false gods we have placed before the true God. It is about letting God *be* God. Sickness—which is part of our false image of ourselves—is an example of what true religion lets go of. Sickness can't be reconciled with the perfection that God gave us.

How, then, do we engage in true religion in relation to this idol we've made, this image of ourselves as autonomous, vicious, and sick? We cast aside the idol, which means we give the image no power. We don't fear it, seeing it as a demonic power in opposition to God. We don't attack it, thinking that if we hate it enough, we'll chase it from our mind. We just refuse to acknowledge it as a second power. We simply refuse to worship it, and it disappears.

> 2.   Reality can dawn only on an unclouded mind. It is always <u>there</u> to <u>be</u> accepted, but its acceptance depends on your <u>willingness to have it</u>. To know reality <u>must</u> involve the willingness to judge unreality <u>for what it is</u>. [Ur: This is the *right* use of selective perception.] To overlook nothingness is merely to judge it correctly, and because of your ability to evaluate it truly, to <u>let it go</u>. Knowledge cannot dawn on a mind full of illusions, because truth and illusions are irreconcilable. Truth is whole, and <u>cannot</u> be known by <u>part</u> of a mind.

Application: Look at the image you hold of yourself. On the surface, it has many details—talents, abilities, hair color, height, weight. But look beneath that at its basic characteristics: It is autonomous. It is vulnerable. It can be disempowered. It can get sick. It is attacking. It can even get vicious. Aren't all these things true of the image you hold of yourself? Then think to yourself:

> *The only way to judge this image correctly is to overlook it, because it is not there and I am not that.*
> *It is nothing.*
> *The only honest thing to do with it is to let it go.*
> *While half of my mind is filled with it, I cannot know the wholeness of truth.*
> *When its unreal clouds are gone from my mind, reality will dawn upon me.*

3.   The Sonship cannot be perceived as <u>partly</u> sick, because to perceive it that way is not to perceive it at all. If the Sonship is <u>one</u>, it is one in <u>all</u> respects. <u>Oneness cannot be divided.</u> If you perceive other gods <u>your</u> mind is split, and you will not be able to <u>limit</u> the split, because it <u>is</u> the sign that you have removed part of your mind from God's Will. This <u>means</u> it is out of control. To be out of control is to be out of <u>reason,</u> and then the mind <u>does</u> become unreasonable [Ur: unreasonable without reason. This is merely a matter of *definition*.]. By <u>defining</u> the mind wrongly, you perceive it as <u>functioning</u> wrongly.

Here is my best guess as to what this paragraph means: When it says, "Oneness cannot be divided," this applies to the oneness (and sameness) of all members of the Sonship. It also applies to the oneness of our mind. Yet when we believe in the false image of ourselves, we seem to divide our mind. We seem to split it between the *image* and the *truth*. Once we do, we will project this split everywhere. We will see it in everyone. We will see everyone as having a split nature, as being a walking war between light and darkness, sickness and health. We would like to believe that we can see only some people this way, but we can't limit it to some. The reason is that the split gets out of control. It goes on a wild rampage, projecting itself everywhere. It does this because the part of our mind that believes in the false image is removed from God's control and is thus *out* of control.

4.   God's laws will keep your mind at peace because peace <u>is</u> His

Will, and His laws are established to uphold it. His are the laws of freedom, but yours are the laws of bondage. Since freedom and bondage are irreconcilable, their laws cannot be understood together. The laws of God work only for your good, and there are no other laws beside His. Everything else is merely lawless and therefore chaotic. Yet God Himself has protected everything He created by His laws. [Ur: Therefore,] Everything that is not under them does not exist. "Laws of chaos" is a meaningless term [Ur: are meaningless, by definition]. Creation is perfectly lawful, and the chaotic is without meaning because it is without God. You have "given" your peace to the gods you made, but they are not there to take it from you, and you cannot [Ur: you are *not* able to] give it to them.

We may think that freedom lies in keeping part of our mind outside of God's control, yet we've got it backwards. Freedom and peace lie in placing our whole mind *under* God's control, under His laws. These laws work only for our good. When we place part of our mind outside these laws, we enter into the realm of lawlessness, of chaos. There, nothing really makes sense. Our lives simply hurtle forward, without true direction and devoid of meaning. Ironically, in this state of chaos we are also in bondage. For we have placed ourselves under the bondage of our false gods, gods who are like mad kings, making crazy demands based on their erratic whims. Think about how the image you hold of yourself orders you around, constantly telling you what you have to do to maintain the image. Aren't a lot of these demands just pure whims on the spur of the moment, without any rhyme or reason? All in all, we have handed our peace over to our false gods, yet ironically, there's nothing there to hand our peace *to*.

5. You are not free to give up freedom, but only to deny it. You cannot do what God did not intend, because what He did not intend does not happen. Your gods do not bring chaos; you are endowing them with chaos, and accepting it of them. All this has never been. Nothing but the laws of God has ever been [Ur: operated], and nothing but His Will will ever be. You were created through His laws and by His Will, and the manner of your creation established you a creator. What you have made [the idol, the false self-image] is so unworthy of you that you could hardly want it, if you were willing to see it as it is. You will see nothing at all. And your vision will automatically look beyond it,

to what is <u>in</u> you and all <u>around</u> you. Reality cannot <u>break through</u> the obstructions you interpose, but it <u>will</u> envelop you completely <u>when you let them go</u>.

By worshipping our false god (our image of ourselves as autonomous, vulnerable, vicious, sick), we think we have thrown away the freedom God gave us, along with the order and meaning He gave us. We think we have sold ourselves into slavery to our idols, where chaos rules our existence and where there's no going back. But in fact none of it ever happened. We are still free. If we will just look at the image of ourselves that we've made, we will see how unworthy it is, and we will cease to want it. And if we look really deeply, we'll see nothing at all. And with our gaze uprooted from the idol, we'll look all around us and within us. Shaken out of our unreal dream, we will find ourselves enveloped by the warm light of reality.

Application: Look again at your image of yourself. Look at how on your own you are, according to the image. Look at how vulnerable you are in its eyes. Look at how defensive you are. Look at how weak and powerless you are. See how undesirable this image really is. Then look even more deeply and see that it's just an image. *It's just an image.* And images are not real. Thus, the only way to see this image for what it is is to see it disappear from view. Imagine the image of yourself doing just that—vanishing, in an acknowledgment of the nothingness that it really is. Now there is no image. Nothing is there, which has been the truth all along. And now you can look all around you and within. Now you are free to see reality.

6. When you have experienced the protection of God, the making of idols becomes inconceivable. There are no strange images in the Mind of God, and what is not in His Mind <u>cannot</u> be in yours, because you are of one mind and that mind belongs to <u>Him</u>. It is yours *because* it belongs to Him, for to Him ownership is sharing. And if it is so for Him, it is so for you. His definitions *are* His laws, for by them He established the universe as what it is. No false gods you attempt to interpose between yourself and your reality affect truth at all. Peace is yours because God created you. And He created nothing else.

When God's protection dawns on our mind, the need to clothe ourselves in this phony image drops away. We step forth, imageless. Now we share God's Mind (for He shares with us *all* that is His), and in that Mind there are no strange images. How could idolatry exist within God Himself? In that Mind, we realize that our false gods never existed in the first place. And therefore we never handed our peace over to them. Peace is still ours because in reality there is only God and us.

> 7.   The miracle is the act of a Son of God who has laid aside all false gods, and calls on his brothers to do likewise. It is an act of faith, because it is the recognition that his brother <u>can</u> do it. It is a call to the Holy Spirit in his mind, a call [Ur: to Him] that is strengthened by [Ur: this] joining. Because the miracle worker has heard God's Voice, he strengthens It in a sick brother by weakening his belief in sickness, which he does <u>not</u> share. The power of one mind <u>can</u> shine into another, because all the lamps of God were lit by the same spark. It is everywhere and it is eternal.

After all the abstractness of this section, this paragraph is a beautiful description of giving the miracle, of giving a healing to a sick brother. First, the miracle worker is one who has laid aside his false gods, his self-images. He knows that he is not an image. From this place, he calls on his brothers to do what he has done. He joins with them in the faith that they can do it, they can give up their idols. He is appealing not just to their conscious mind, but to the presence in them of the true Healer, the Holy Spirit. The power of his mind shines into theirs, weakening their belief in sickness and strengthening the Holy Spirit's Voice. This puts them in a place where they can realistically lay aside their internal voices of sickness and choose the Voice for God.

To think that one mind can actually reach in and effect a healing in another mind goes against much conventional Course wisdom, yet this paragraph ends with an explanation of why it works: The light in every person was lit by the same divine spark. That is why one mind's light can shine into another mind and brighten it: It's all the same light.

> 8.   In many only the spark remains, for the Great Rays are obscured. Yet God has kept the spark alive so that the Rays can never be completely forgotten. If you but see the little spark you will learn of the

greater light, for the Rays are there unseen. Perceiving the spark will heal, but knowing the light will create. Yet in the returning the little light must be acknowledged first, for the separation was a descent from magnitude to littleness. But the spark is still as pure as the great light, because it is the remaining call of creation. Put all your faith in it, and God Himself will answer you.

To understand this paragraph, you need to understand its image. We are each like a lamp, a source of light. A good image would be a kerosene lamp with a wick. The same spark from God lighted each lamp. Once lit, the lamp, of course, throws off light. In this case, it produces vast rays of light called the Great Rays. The Great Rays, then, don't shine to us from God (as students often seem to visualize it), but rather shine out from us, shining out to infinity from the divine spark in us.

In Heaven, the Great Rays are plain as day. But here on earth, the Rays are mostly obscured. They are somewhat visible in great saints but mostly invisible in the rest of us. The miracle worker's task is to see the spark, the spark that lit the lamp from which the Rays shine. "Perceiving the spark will heal." His task is to put all of his faith in the divine spark in his brother, and none of his faith in his brother's false gods.

Application: Think of someone you know who is sick. Look at your view of this person. Is your view centered on a body that is sick? In your image, is she vulnerable and disempowered? Is she attacking at times, perhaps even capable of viciousness?

If you have answered "yes" to any of these questions, your faith is in the idol, the false image of her that she presents to the world. Try to withdraw your faith from this image. This is not who she is. She is not an image.

See the image become transparent, in acknowledgment of its unreality. Behind it, see a spark, shining with rarefied beauty and perfect purity. This spark, you realize, is holy. It is divine. It is so lovely you can't take your eyes off it.

Now, as you gaze at the spark, see rays of light begin to stream out from it. See them shine out in all directions and reach to infinity. These are the Great Rays. Notice how holy they make her appear. Only a being of magnificent holiness and divine grandeur would have such Rays shining from her. See these Rays grow brighter and extend farther, until they fill your vision with an intense and unearthly brilliance.

Now you see before you a faint transparent image, barely visible. Behind this, you see the divine spark and emanating from it, the Great Rays. If you put all your faith in the beautiful light (spark + Rays) that she is, and withdraw all your faith from the image, your realization will reach into her mind, and she will be healed.

V. The Denial of God
Commentary by Robert Perry

1. The rituals of the god of sickness are strange and very demanding. Joy is never permitted, for depression is the sign of allegiance to him. Depression <u>means</u> that you have forsworn God. Many [Ur: Men] are afraid of blasphemy, but they do not understand [Ur: know] what it means. They do not realize that to deny God is to deny their own Identity, and in this sense the wages of sin *is* death. The sense is very literal; denial of life [your Identity is your life] perceives its opposite [death], as <u>all</u> forms of denial replace what <u>is</u> with what is <u>not</u>. No one can really <u>do</u> this, but that you can <u>think</u> you can and <u>believe you have</u> is beyond dispute.

We all belong to a religious cult, the cult of the ego. The worship services are our daily lives. The hymns are the things we continually repeat, silently and out loud. The rituals of this cult are demanding as well as joyless. What do we do in these rituals? We forswear God. We blaspheme. (Apparently, it's a bit of a satanic cult.) What we don't realize is that in God lie our Identity, our life, and our joy. This means that forswearing God means affirming death and depression. This, therefore, is not a very happy cult—as you can see if you just look around you at the other members.

2. Do not forget [see 6.In.1:2 and 7.VII.8-9], however, that to deny God will inevitably result in projection, and you will believe that others <u>and not yourself</u> have done this <u>to</u> you. You must [Ur: *will*] receive [from others] the message you give [to others] because it is the message you <u>want</u>. You may believe that you judge your brothers by the messages they give <u>you</u>, but you <u>have</u> judged them by the message you give to <u>them</u>. Do not attribute your denial of joy to them, or you cannot see the spark in them that would bring joy to <u>you</u>. It is the <u>denial</u> of the spark that brings depression, for [Ur: and] whenever you see your brothers <u>without</u> it, you <u>are</u> denying God.

An odd thing about our strange religion is that spending our time in rituals in which we repeat over and over "I renounce God and all His works" causes us to naturally feel without God, but then we blame this on other people. We project onto them our decision to throw God away, so that now we see them as taking God from us. We hear them say to us, "I'm stealing God (life, joy, love) away from you," even though all they really said was "Hi, how are you doing?" Then, once we hear this message come from them, we judge them for it. We see them as God-stealers. Yet seeing them this way is yet another one of our rituals in which we deny God and deny joy. For this blinds us to the divine spark in them, and seeing this spark is how we acknowledge God and accept His joy.

> 3.   Allegiance to the denial of God is the ego's religion. The god of sickness obviously demands the denial of health, because health is in direct opposition to its own survival. But consider what this means to you. Unless you are sick you cannot keep the gods you made, for only in sickness could you possibly want them [you have to be sick in the head to want them]. Blasphemy, then, is *self-destructive*, not God-destructive. It means that you are willing not to know yourself in order to be sick. This is the offering your god demands because, having made him out of your insanity, he is an insane idea. He has many forms, but although he may seem to be many different things he is but one idea;— the denial of God.

The god of sickness is the image we have made of ourselves. In short, he is the ego. He is the idol we worship. He is the image we pray to, whether we are Course students, or Christians, or pagans, or atheists. We all kneel at his shrine. His altars dot the landscape. They are in every home, in every store, even out in nature. His religion has one central tenet: the denial of God. It is, therefore, a blasphemous religion. Yet as with all idols, we made this god of sickness ourselves. And being made out of our insanity, he is totally insane. He therefore makes insane deals: "If you'll agree to sacrifice the knowledge of who you are, then I'll grant you the reward of sickness." And we say, "OK." Yet this blasphemy doesn't offend God in the slightest. All it accomplishes is to deprive us— of health, of joy, of life.

> 4.   Sickness and death seemed to enter the mind of God's Son against

His Will. The "attack on God" made His Son think he was fatherless, and out of his depression he made the god of depression. This was his alternative to joy, because he would not accept the fact that, although he was a creator, he had been created. Yet the Son *is* helpless without the Father, Who alone is his Help.

This paragraph contains one of the most important statements about the motive behind the separation: We had a problem with being the "created." We wanted to be First Cause. We didn't want the dependency of being the child. So we decided to strike out on our own, to be autonomous. This attack on God left us feeling fatherless and helpless. We had just left our eternal Love and our only Help. And in our depression, we made a replacement for Him. Like the Israelites in the wilderness, we fashioned our own god. Being made from our depression, he was a god of depression. Being made from our denial of God's joy, he was the absence of joy. And as we began to worship him, he required us to undergo sickness and death as two of his foremost commandments.

> 5.   I said before that of yourself you can do nothing, but you are not *of* yourself. If you were, what you have made would be true, and you could never escape. It is because you did not make yourself that you need be troubled over [Ur: by] nothing. Your gods are nothing, because your Father did not create them. You cannot make creators who are unlike your Creator, any more than He could have created a Son who was unlike Him. If creation is sharing, it cannot create what is unlike itself. It can share only what it is. Depression is isolation, and so it could not have been created.

In this ancient, dark place inside us, we think that being autonomous from God is the road to power and to freedom. Yet we are wrong, in two ways. First, apart from God, we just get ourselves into trouble, like the boys in *Lord of the Flies*. Our dreams of power turn into nightmares of enslavement to insane gods that exist only in our mind. Second, the dependency on the God of our being and our nature doesn't disempower us; it saves us. For it means that all of the self-destructive games we play are, in the end, just games. They have no effect. It's as if the adults show up at the end of *Lord of the Flies* and tell the boys that their nightmarish experience was just a game in which no one got hurt.

32

The latter part of the paragraph is an argument against the reality of the idols we made. The key principle is "creation is sharing." The creator creates by sharing his being with the created. As a result, both now share the being of the creator. Yet depression is isolation. It is a state of non-sharing. Since creation is sharing and depression is non-sharing, depression could not have been created. And therefore, the god of depression was not created and does not exist.

> 6. Son of God, you have not sinned, but you have been much mistaken. Yet this can be corrected and God will help you, knowing that you could not sin against Him. You denied Him <u>because</u> you loved Him, knowing that if you <u>recognized</u> your love for Him, you <u>could</u> not deny Him. Your denial of Him therefore <u>means</u> that you love Him, and <u>that you know He loves you</u>. Remember that what you deny you <u>must</u> have once known. And if you accept denial, <u>you can accept its undoing</u>.

Application: Say to yourself,

By leaving God, I have not sinned.
But I have been much mistaken.
I was mistaken in thinking that leaving God meant gaining power.
I was mistaken in thinking that leaving God was possible.
Yet this mistake can be corrected, and God will help me.

This paragraph depicts our departure from God in poignant terms. As an analogy, think of a son who feels that, in order to become a man, he has to strike out on his own. He has to leave his father's house. Yet he loves his father deeply, and he knows his father loves him. Because of this love, he can't bear to leave. So, in order to leave, he denies his love for his father. He denies his father's love for him. He makes up the lie that he hates his father, just to get himself out the door. Now, does he really hate his father, or is his supposed hatred actually *proof* of his love?

The good news is this: God knows that *you* are this son. He knows you had to put on an act of not loving Him in order to follow through with what you had decided. And even though you have kept the act up for a long time, He knows that you still love Him, and will always love Him.

Thus, if it seems like you don't care about God, or are angry at God, that is all just an act you put on to keep your separated world intact. For if you really let yourself feel how intensely you love God, you would instantly throw your world away and leap back into His Arms.

> 7.   Your Father has not denied you. He does not retaliate, but He <u>does</u> call to you to return. When you think He has not answered your call, <u>you have not answered His</u>. He calls to you from every part of the Sonship, because of His Love for His Son. If you hear His message He <u>has</u> answered you, and you will learn [Ur: what you are] of Him if you hear aright. The Love of God is in everything He created, for His Son [the Son He loves] is everywhere. Look with peace upon your brothers, and God will come rushing into your heart in gratitude for your gift to Him.

When that son we talked about left his father's house, the father didn't retaliate. He did not say, "I hate you, too." Instead, he calls his son every day and asks him to return. Unfortunately, the son never picks up his messages, and so he thinks his father has forgotten him. Yet this is a very determined father, so he makes contact with the people around his son and has them deliver his messages for him. Each message says simply, "I love you, son. Come home." This, of course, is what our Father is doing through all the people around us, whether we hear the messages or not.

Application: Think of someone you have judged and say,

> *I will look with peace upon you, [name].*
> *And God will come rushing into my heart in gratitude for my gift*
> *to Him.*

> 8.   Do not look to the god of sickness for healing but only to the God of love, for healing is the acknowledgment of Him. When you acknowledge Him you will <u>know</u> that He has never ceased to acknowledge you, and that in His acknowledgment <u>of</u> you lies your being. You are not sick and you cannot die. But you <u>can</u> confuse yourself with things that do. Remember, though, that to do this <u>is</u> blasphemy, for it means that you are looking without love on God and His creation, from which He cannot be separated.

No matter how much we pray to our false god, he will never answer our prayers with healing, for he is the god of *sickness*. Instead, we need to acknowledge the true God. If our basic stance in life is *denial* of God, then *acknowledgment* of God is no isolated thing. It is a sea change in our overall posture of mind.

And when we at last acknowledge God, we will realize that He has never ceased to acknowledge us. If He ceased for one second, *we* would cease to be, for our very being flows continually from His acknowledgment of us. When we acknowledge Him, we will also remember who we are, and we will rediscover the perfect health and eternal life He placed in us. We will realize we can't really get sick and die. We only seem to when we identify with the body. Yet identifying with the body is blasphemy, for we cannot genuinely love ourselves if we are a body, and refusal to love ourselves is blasphemy against our Creator.

> 9.   Only the eternal can be loved, for love does not die. What is of God is His forever, and you <u>are</u> of God. Would He allow Himself to suffer? And would He offer His Son anything that is not acceptable to Him? If you will accept yourself as God created you, you will be incapable of suffering. Yet to do this you must acknowledge Him as your Creator. This is not because you will be punished otherwise. It is merely because your acknowledgment of your Father <u>is</u> the acknowledgment of yourself as you <u>are</u>. Your Father created you wholly without sin, wholly without pain and wholly without suffering of any kind. If you deny Him you bring sin, pain and suffering into your <u>own</u> mind because of the power He gave it. Your mind is capable of creating worlds, but it can also <u>deny</u> what it creates because it is free.

We can't truly love our body. Only what is eternal can be loved, because love is eternal. *We* are eternal, because we are of God. He created us not only beyond time, but also beyond suffering. He would no more allow His Son to suffer than allow *Himself* to suffer. All we need to do, then, is accept our being as God created it, and we will be literally incapable of suffering. Think about that.

To accept our true nature, however, we must acknowledge God, for our nature lies *in* God. If we deny Him, we deny the gifts He placed in us: freedom from suffering, sin, and pain. If we acknowledge Him, all the treasures that He placed in our being come tumbling into our experience.

10. You do not realize how much you have denied yourself, and how much God, in His Love, would not have it so. Yet He would not interfere with you, because He would not know His Son if he were not free. To interfere with you would be to attack <u>Himself</u>, and God is not insane. When you deny Him *you* are insane [Ur: When you denied *Him*, you *were* insane]. Would you have Him <u>share</u> your insanity? God will never cease to love His Son, and His Son will never cease to love Him. That was the condition of His Son's creation, fixed forever in the Mind of God. To know that is sanity. To deny it is insanity. God gave <u>Himself</u> to you in your creation, and His gifts <u>are</u> eternal. Would you deny yourself to Him [Would you deprive Him of yourself?]?

Let's return to that son who left home. The son, by putting on this act of hating his father, also blocks out the memory of how joyful it was to be in his father's house. Thus, he doesn't let himself realize how much he has lost in leaving home, nor how much his father must want to restore him to joy. But why doesn't his father just intervene, just twist his son's arm to come back home? Because for the father to compromise his son's freedom would be to attack himself. Because to interfere with his son would be to engage in the same kind of insanity his son did when he left. Therefore, the father simply waits, and calls, and loves. Which is what our Father does with us.

Application: Repeat,

> *God will never cease to love me, and I will never cease to love Him.*
> *God gave Himself to me forever.*
> *Why would I not give myself to Him?*

11. Out of your gifts to Him the Kingdom will be restored to His Son. His Son removed himself from His gift by refusing to accept what had been created <u>for</u> him, and what he had created in the Name of his Father. Heaven waits for his return, for it was created as the dwelling place of God's Son. You are not at home anywhere else, or in any other condition. Do not deny yourself the joy that was created <u>for</u> you for the misery you have made for yourself. God has given you the means for undoing what you have made. Listen, and you <u>will</u> learn how to

remember what you are.

We think of Heaven as the domain that God lives inside. Actually, God *created* Heaven to be our dwelling place, a home of infinite happiness. But we decided to go somewhere else, a place where we could be god, a place of endless misery. We thought as the Devil thought in *Paradise Lost*: "Better to reign in hell than serve in Heaven"—forgetting, of course, that hell is *hell*.

Yet Heaven still waits for us. Our Father has kept our room exactly as it was when we left. All we have to do is acknowledge Him. All we have to do is give ourselves to Him once again.

> 12. If God knows His children as wholly sinless, it is blasphemous to perceive them as guilty. If God knows His children as wholly without pain, it is blasphemous to perceive suffering anywhere. If God knows His children to be wholly joyous, it is blasphemous to feel depressed. All of these illusions, and the many other forms that blasphemy may take, are refusals to accept creation as it is. If God created His Son perfect, that is how you must learn to see him to learn of his reality. And as part of the Sonship, that is how you must see yourself to learn of yours.

The previous paragraph ended with "Listen, and you will learn how to remember what you are." This paragraph describes how.

Application: Let's apply this way "to remember what you are." Think of something you feel guilty over and say,

> *If God knows me as wholly sinless, it is blasphemous to perceive myself as guilty.*

Think of some kind of pain you are experiencing and say,

> *If God knows me as wholly without pain, it is blasphemous to see myself as suffering.*

Think of something you are feeling depressed about and say,

> *If God knows me as wholly joyous, it is blasphemous to feel depressed.*

Now switch over to others. Think of someone you perceive as sinful and say,

> *If God knows [name] as wholly sinless, it is blasphemous to perceive him/her as guilty.*

Now think of someone you think of as suffering and say,

> *If God knows [name] as wholly without pain, it is blasphemous to see him/her as suffering.*

13. Do not perceive <u>anything</u> God did not create or you <u>are</u> denying Him. His is the <u>only</u> Fatherhood, and it is yours only because <u>He</u> has given it to you. Your gifts to <u>yourself</u> are meaningless, but your gifts to <u>your</u> creations are like His, because they are given in His Name. That is why your creations are as real as His. Yet the real Fatherhood must be acknowledged if the real Son is to be known. You believe that the sick things you have made are your real creations, because you believe that the sick images you perceive are the sons of God. Only if you <u>accept</u> the Fatherhood of God will you have anything, because His Fatherhood <u>gave</u> you everything. That is why to deny Him <u>is</u> to deny yourself.

The way to acknowledge God (which the whole section has been telling us to do) is to accept ourselves as He created us. And the way to accept ourselves as He created us is to acknowledge His Fatherhood (referred to four times in this paragraph). These are both the same thing. This does not mean to bow down and be submissive to God and sing praise hymns all day. We are being asked to accept His *Fatherhood*, which means His absolute Authority in determining our nature, even now. This Authority is a very good thing, for only God would create us wholly free of sin, pain, and depression. The sick images we make of ourselves will never have those qualities. They are full of sin, pain, and depression. To love ourselves, then, we have to give over to God the power to determine what we are, letting go all claim to that power ourselves.

14.   Arrogance is the denial of love, because love shares and arrogance withholds. As long as both appear to you to be desirable the concept of choice, which is not of God, will remain with you. While this is not true in eternity it *is* true in time, so that while time lasts in your mind there will be choices. Time itself is [Ur: *was*] your choice. If you would remember eternity, you must [Ur: learn to] look only on the eternal. If you allow yourself to become preoccupied with the temporal, you are living in time. As always, your choice is determined by what you value. Time and eternity cannot both be real, because they contradict each other. If you will accept only what is timeless as real, you will begin to understand eternity and make it yours.

Arrogance in the Course is usually associated with denying God's Authority—thinking you know better than Him. Obviously, the whole religion of the ego does this and is therefore the height of arrogance. Since we belong to this religion yet are also children of God, we feel torn between arrogance and love. This places us in the realm of choice. Choice is an illusion that only exists in time. In eternity, there are no alternatives to choose between.

In fact, the choice before us is always a choice between time and eternity. We choose time by being preoccupied with the temporal, with the things of time. We choose eternity by looking past the physical to the eternal. Think over your typical day. How much of it is spent preoccupied with the things of time? How much of it is spent looking past time to the eternal in your brothers and in yourself? This simple test can tell you what you really value. Yet even if now you mainly value time, you can change that. You can value anew.

Commentaries on Chapter 11

GOD OR THE EGO

Introduction
Commentary by Robert Perry

1.   Either God or the ego is insane. If you will examine the evidence <u>on</u> <u>both sides</u> fairly, you will realize this <u>must</u> be true. Neither God nor the ego proposes a partial thought system. Each is internally consistent, but they are diametrically opposed in all respects so that partial allegiance is impossible. Remember, too, that their results are as different as their foundations, and their fundamentally irreconcilable natures <u>cannot</u> be reconciled by [Ur: *your*] vacillations between them. Nothing alive is fatherless, for life is creation. Therefore, your decision is always an answer to the question, "Who is my father?" And you <u>will</u> be faithful to the father you choose.

God puts forward a thought system which is internally consistent and covers everything. The ego puts forward a thought system which is internally consistent and covers everything. These two thought systems, however, are diametrically opposed, in their content and their results. Which leads us to a sobering conclusion: One of them is stark raving mad. This is extremely uncomfortable, because if God is mad then reality itself is madness. There is nowhere to go to find sanity and meaning. Yet if the ego is mad, then we ourselves are insane, since we identify primarily with the ego.

Our attachment to both makes us want to vacillate between them. We even think that by doing so we are essentially reconciling them. Yet instead we have to decide between them. The only logical option is to choose one or the other. We do so by answering the question, "Which one is my father?" Our being must have come from somewhere. Did it come from God or the ego?

2.   Yet what would you say to someone who [Ur: *really*] believed this question really involves [Ur: this question involves] conflict? If <u>you</u> made the ego, how can the ego have made <u>you</u>? The authority problem is still the <u>only</u> source of [Ur: perceived] conflict, because the ego was <u>made</u> out of the wish of God's Son to father <u>Him</u>. The ego, then, is nothing more than a delusional system in which <u>you made</u>

your own father. Make no mistake about this. It sounds insane when it is stated with perfect honesty, but the ego never looks on what it does with perfect honesty. Yet that is its insane premise, which is carefully hidden in the dark cornerstone of its thought system. And either the ego, which you made, *is* your father, or its whole thought system will not stand.

Try asking yourself, "Did God father me or did my ego father me?" It is a no-brainer, isn't it? After all, you made your ego. How could it turn around and make you? Yet the crazy belief that the ego we made made us is the foundation of its whole thought system. For we made the ego out of our wish to create God. Remember, we didn't want to be the created (10.V.4:3). We in essence said to God, "You're not the boss of me!" The natural extension of this, of course, is for us to want to be the boss of Him. We didn't want Him to be our Creator, we wanted to be *His*.

We therefore made the ego out of the thought, "I want to be the creator of my Creator." Consequently, at the very core of the ego is a version of this same thought: "I (the ego) am the maker of my maker." The ego is not honest about this belief. It hides it very carefully from view. If its whole thought system rests on this belief, and if the belief is patently absurd, then the ego will do everything in its power to keep us from seeing it.

> 3.   You make by projection, but God creates [Ur: has created] by extension. The cornerstone of God's creation is you, for His thought system is light. Remember the Rays that are there unseen. The more you approach the center of His thought system, the clearer the light becomes. The closer you come to the foundation of the ego's thought system, the darker and more obscure becomes the way. Yet even the little spark in your mind is enough to lighten it. Bring this light fearlessly with you, and bravely hold it up to the foundation of the ego's thought system. Be willing to judge it with perfect honesty. Open the dark cornerstone of terror on which it rests, and bring it out into the light. There you will see that it rested on meaninglessness, and that everything of which you have been afraid was based on nothing.

The cornerstone of God's creation is you, and you shine with the light of the Great Rays. Thus, the closer you get to the heart of His system, the brighter the radiance and clarity grow. With the ego, however, it is just the opposite. The closer you come to its foundation, the darker and foggier things get, for its existence depends on keeping its foundation hidden from us. Yet we need to expose the cornerstone on which its entire edifice was built, open it up (probably a reference to the practice of placing things like time capsules inside of cornerstones), and expose it to reason. We may not be aware of the Great Rays in us, but we are aware, at least to some degree, of the little spark, and the little spark is the spark of *reason*. We need to hold this light up to what is inside the ego's cornerstone, and see the utter senselessness of it.

> 4.   My brother, you are part of God and part of me. When you have at last looked at the ego's foundation without shrinking you will also have looked upon ours. I come to you from our Father to offer you everything again. Do not refuse it in order to keep a dark cornerstone hidden, for <u>its</u> protection will not save you. I <u>give</u> you the lamp and I will go with you. You will not take this journey alone. I will lead you to your true Father, Who hath need of you, as I have. Will you not answer the call of love with joy?

Application: The following is a visualization based on paragraphs 3 and 4:

You are walking down a dark, dank corridor, underneath some massive stone building—the thought system of the ego.

The way is becoming ever "darker and more obscure" because the ego keeps its foundations hidden from your view.

You feel that you are approaching some nameless horror. You almost can't bear the thought of looking at the ego's foundation.

But Jesus is with you, walking beside you, leading you along the way.

You feel your hand in his.

He hands you a lamp, the lamp of pure reason within you, which illuminates the way.

The way now seems not so dark and fearful.

Looming up ahead, you see the cornerstone on which the ego's whole edifice is built, the dark cornerstone of terror.

With Jesus still at your side, you bend down and break the cornerstone open, not knowing what awful thing you will find inside.

What you find is a stone tablet with ancient letters carved on it, letters you cannot quite make out in the dim light.

You take a deep breath and bravely hold up your lamp, illuminating the tablet.

It says simply, "I, the ego, made [your name], and you made me."

It sounds like the ravings of a mad person.

You think, "This is nothing to be afraid of. This is nonsense!"

After all your fear, you actually laugh in relief.

"The ego's whole thought system rests on *this*?" you laugh.

The building around you starts to fade, while Jesus, standing beside you, remains.

You turn to him and say,

"Show me my real foundation.

Take me to my real Father."

I. The Gifts of Fatherhood
Commentary by Robert Perry

1. You <u>have</u> learned your need of healing. Would you bring anything <u>else</u> to the Sonship, recognizing your need of healing for yourself? For in this [bringing healing to the Sonship] lies the beginning of the return to knowledge [Ur: the beginning of knowledge]; the foundation on which God will help build again the thought system you share <u>with</u> Him. Not one stone you place upon it but will be blessed by Him, for you will be restoring the holy dwelling place of His Son, where He wills His Son to be and where he <u>is</u>. In whatever part of the mind of God's Son you restore this reality, you restore it to <u>yourself</u>.

If you want to be healed, if you want to build a new thought system with God, then bring only healing to the Sonship. This (bringing healing to others) will be the foundation of your new thought system. What a different foundation than "I made my own father"! Then on this firm foundation, you will lay one stone after another. Like St. Francis, you will rebuild the temple; only in this case it will be the temple of your mind. The stones you are placing are God-inspired beliefs, and they will build a holy home for your mind to live in. Every time you place one of these stones in a brother's mind, you add another stone to your growing inner temple. And when this temple is complete, it will be transformed into the Kingdom of God, the holy home that God created for His Son, the home in which you will live forever.

You dwell in the Mind of God <u>with</u> your brother, for God Himself did not will to be alone.

2. To be alone is to be separated from infinity, but how can this be if infinity has no end? No one can <u>be</u> beyond the limitless, because what has <u>no</u> limits must be everywhere. There are no beginnings and no endings in God, Whose universe is Himself. Can you exclude yourself from the universe, or from God Who *is* the universe? I and my Father are one with <u>you,</u> for you are part of us. Do you <u>really</u> believe that part of God can be missing or lost to Him?

The ancient philosopher Plotinus wrote movingly of our return to the One as "the flight of the lone to the Alone." This, obviously, is not how the Course conceives of things. From its standpoint, God created us because He "did not will to be alone" (a line which occurs four times in this section). Given that that was our origin, is it likely that He would create us alone, without Him or without our brothers? And how *could* we be alone if God is infinite? How could we not be inside God if we are part of God? How can part of Him be missing?

This faces us with two opposing bodies of evidence. Our experience tells us that we are alone, yet the Course's logic tells us that we aren't. This leaves us with an interesting proposition: If the Course's logic is true, then our experience (of being separate) is not.

> 3. If you were not part of God, His Will would not be unified [since you are His Will]. Is this conceivable? Can part of His Mind contain nothing? If your place in His Mind cannot be filled by anyone <u>except</u> you, and your filling it <u>was</u> your creation, <u>without</u> you there would be an empty place in God's Mind. Extension cannot be blocked, and it has no voids. It continues forever, however much it is denied. Your <u>denial</u> of its reality may arrest [Ur: arrests] it in time, but not in eternity. That is why your creations have not ceased to be extended, and why so much is waiting for your return.

Application: Begin by thinking about your experience of being a separate individual. You make your own choices, you think your own thoughts, you have your own body. Your experience in life seems to prove that you are separate. Yet we have experiences all the time that we don't take as true, such as our dream experiences at night. So mull over the following lines and use their logic to overrule or at least cast doubt on your experience of being separate:

> *I am a piece of God's Will.*
> *If I am not part of God*
> *Then His Will is split, not unified.*
> *Is this conceivable?*

I. The Gifts of Fatherhood

My place in God's Mind cannot be filled by anyone else.
Without me there would be an empty place in God's Mind.
Yet how can part of His Mind contain nothing?
How can He be without me?

Just as our current denial doesn't affect the fact that we remain God's extension, so this denial doesn't affect our own extension in Heaven, which produces our creations. This is "why so much is waiting for your return."

> 4. Waiting is possible <u>only</u> in time, but time has no meaning. You who made delay can leave time behind simply by recognizing that neither beginnings nor endings were created by the Eternal, Who placed no limits on His creation or upon those who create like Him. You do not know this simply because you have tried to limit what <u>He</u> created, and so you believe that <u>all</u> creation is limited. How, then, could you know <u>your</u> creations, having <u>denied</u> infinity?

It seems that we will have to wait a long time until we can return home to our creations (see end of previous paragraph). This is exactly why we made time in the first place, to procrastinate, to delay. Now that it's here, it seems convenient to use it to delay things, like paying our bills. But we actually *put* it here to delay our coming home.

We can leave all this behind by remembering that the Eternal created neither beginnings nor endings, for they are limits. They are tiny prison cells in which we seem to be trapped. When we are trapped in the beginning, the ending seems outside our reach. Yet God would never put limits on us or on our creations. We don't know this, because we've tried to limit *His* creations—by putting ourselves in the boxes of time. And this has blocked from awareness *our* creations, for they are limitless, and we won't accept the limitless into our minds.

> 5. The laws of the universe do not permit contradiction. What holds for God holds for you. If you believe <u>you</u> are absent from God, you <u>will</u> believe that He is absent from you. Infinity is meaningless <u>without</u> you, and <u>you</u> are meaningless without God. There <u>is</u> no end to God and His Son, for we *are* the universe. God is not incomplete, and He is not

childless. Because He did not will to be alone, He created a Son like Himself. Do not deny Him His Son, for your unwillingness to accept His Fatherhood has denied you yours. See His creations [your brothers and yourself] as <u>His</u> Son, for yours were created in honor of Him. The universe of love does not stop because you do not see it, nor have your closed eyes lost the ability to see. Look upon the glory of His creation, and you will learn what God has kept for <u>you</u>.

If you believe that you are absent from God, you are really saying that God is incomplete and that He is childless. You are saying that His infinity is meaningless, for it is missing a crucial ingredient: *you*. You are also implying that He is absent from you, that He is not your Father, and that you are not His Son. And this naturally implies that your creations are absent from you, their creator. In this one decision, then, you lose everything.

Yet this hasn't changed the truth one bit. God and His Son are still endless. The universe of love has not stopped. You have simply closed your eyes. How do you open them? You look on the glory of God's creation, the glory of your brothers.

Application: Repeat,

> *Infinity is meaningless without me.*
> *And I am meaningless without God.*

6.   God has given you a place in His Mind that is yours forever. Yet you can keep it only by giving it, as it was given you. Could <u>you</u> be alone there, when [Ur: if] it was given you because <u>God</u> did not will to be alone? God's Mind cannot be lessened. It can <u>only</u> be increased, for [Ur: and] <u>everything</u> He creates has the function of creating. <u>Love does not limit</u>, and what it creates is not limited. To give without limit is God's Will for you, because only this can bring you the joy that is His and that He wills to share with <u>you</u>. Your love is as boundless as His because it *is* His.

We all seek continually for our place in life, because we have left our true place—the place in God's Mind that He gave us for eternity. In this place, all our beloved brothers surround us and we bask forever in God's Smile. As long as we are absent from this place, we will live in search of it. How, then, do we find it? By giving it to our brothers.

Application: First repeat,

To give without limit is God's Will for me.
Only this can bring me the joy He has willed for me.
*My love is as boundless as His because it **is** His.*

Now express this love by thinking of someone who seems undeserving of God and saying to him or her,

I welcome you [name] into the place you have been searching for,
   the place in God's Mind that is yours forever.
I welcome you there with all my heart.

7.   Could any part of God be <u>without</u> His Love, and could any part of His Love be contained? God is your heritage, because His one gift is Himself. How can you give except <u>like</u> Him if you would know His gift to <u>you</u>? Give, then, without limit and without end, to learn how much <u>He</u> has given <u>you</u>. Your ability to <u>accept</u> Him depends on your willingness to give as He gives. Your fatherhood and your Father are one. God wills [Ur: willed] to create, and your will is His. It follows, then, that <u>you</u> will to create, since your will follows from His. And being an extension of <u>His</u> Will, yours <u>must</u> be the same.

This paragraph has a simple message: If we want to know God's gift to us, we must give as He gives. We cannot reflect enough on this simple idea. Its corollary is that if we *don't* know God's gift to us, it's because we *haven't* yet given as He gives. What has He given us? All of Himself. And what must we give? All of ourselves to our brothers. This may sound hard, but this is our true will. We were built to do this. It is more natural for us than breathing.

Application: Think of someone you have been withholding from, and repeat these lines:

God has given me Himself.
If I would know His gift to me,
I must give myself to [name] as He gives Himself to me.

8.   Yet what you will you do not know. This is not strange when you realize that to deny is to "not know." God's Will is that you are His Son. By denying this you deny your own will, and therefore do not know what it is. [Ur: The reason] You must ask what God's Will is in everything, [Ur: is merely] because it is yours. You do not know what it is, but the Holy Spirit remembers it for you. Ask Him, therefore, what God's Will is for you, and He will tell you yours. It cannot be too often repeated that you do not know it. Whenever what the Holy Spirit tells you appears to be coercive, it is only because you have not recognized your will [Ur: *you do not recognize your own will*].

The previous paragraph told us that it is our will to give without limit and without end. Yet our will seems to be to be something else entirely: to *get* without limit and without end. This puts us in a strange situation: What we automatically assume to be our will is *not* our will. How did we get into this mess? By denying God's Will. This meant denying our own will since our will is the same as His.

Now, when we receive guidance from the Holy Spirit, it often sounds challenging and foreign, even coercive. Yet what we are hearing is actually our own true will, being relayed to us by the Holy Spirit.

Imagine, for instance, that you noticed yourself gradually slipping into a deep amnesia. Seeing this, you left instructions for a loved one to take you to your childhood home, where you would live your remaining days in happiness. Once the amnesia set in, you might resent this person putting you and your belongings in the car and driving you to some unknown place. You would feel that this was an outside will being imposed on you. You wouldn't realize it was your own will being put into action.

Application: Think of a situation where you need guidance. Remind yourself,

In this situation, I don't know what my will is.

I have to trust the Holy Spirit to remember it for me.

9.   The projection of the ego makes it appear as if God's Will is <u>outside</u> yourself, and therefore <u>not yours</u>. In <u>this</u> interpretation it seems possible for God's Will and yours to conflict. God, then, may seem to demand of you what you do <u>not</u> want to give, and thus <u>deprive</u> you of what you want. Would God, Who wants <u>only</u> your will, be capable of this? Your will is His life, which He has <u>given</u> to you. Even in time you cannot live apart from Him. Sleep [the sleep of time] is not death. What He created can sleep, but <u>cannot</u> die. Immortality is <u>His Will</u> for His Son, and His Son's will for <u>himself</u>. God's Son cannot will death for himself because his Father is Life, and <u>His Son is like Him</u>. Creation is your will *because* it is His.

Projection throws outside of you something that is really in you, but that you don't want to *admit* is in you. That's what we have done with God's Will and our true will. We have projected them both outside of us. Now, when God speaks to us, His will seems to an outside will that conflicts with ours. It seems that He is demanding of us what we don't want to give. Think about the Workbook lessons, for instance. God keeps asking so much of us in those instructions. Shouldn't we assert our own will and say, "Enough is enough"? Shouldn't we affirm our own wisdom about how we should be practicing the Course? Shouldn't we do it *our* way?

These questions, however, assume that God's Will is actually outside of us. That is what projection does—makes the inside seem to be outside. In truth, what is coming at us through the Workbook instructions is our *own* true will, which we projected outward. The will that we call ours, the will that wants to "do it my way"—is not our will at all. It is the ego's will.

Application: Think of a time when some expression of God's Will came to you, some bit of guidance or spiritual teaching that you know came from God, yet which seemed to go against your best interests. Then say,

This was my own true will speaking to me.

It only seemed to come from outside me,
because I have projected my will outward.

10.   You cannot be happy unless you do what you will truly, and you cannot <u>change</u> this because it is immutable. [Ur: But] It is immutable by God's Will <u>and yours</u>, for otherwise His Will would not be [Ur: have been] extended. You are afraid to know God's Will, because you believe it is <u>not</u> yours. This belief is your whole sickness and your whole fear. Every symptom of sickness and fear arises here, because this is the belief that makes you *want* not to know. Believing this you hide in darkness, denying that the light is in <u>you</u>.

The idea that God's Will is at odds with our own is our whole sickness and our whole fear. This, then, is no small issue! Once we assume the two wills are different, we don't want to know His Will, which means we don't want to know our own. And this means that we don't know that a pure, loving will beats inside our heart. We think there is no light in us. Now, our only options are to ignore His Will and assert our own, or to "surrender" to His Will in the belief that we'll score points with Him. At this point, who would guess that the most lofty calls to selfless giving are actually our own natural will?

11.   You are asked to trust the Holy Spirit only because He speaks for <u>you</u>. He is the Voice for God, but never forget that God did not will to be alone. He <u>shares</u> His Will with you; He does not thrust it <u>upon</u> you. Always remember that what He gives He keeps [Ur: holds], so that nothing He gives <u>can</u> contradict Him. You who share His Life must share it [with others] to <u>know</u> it, for sharing *is* knowing. Blessed are you who learn that to hear the Will of your Father is to know your own. For it is <u>your</u> will to be <u>like</u> Him, Whose Will it is that it be so. God's Will is that His Son be one, and united with Him in His Oneness. That is why healing is the beginning of the recognition that <u>your will is His</u>.

Clearly, it is no small feat to trust that the Holy Spirit's guidance is actually our own true will being relayed to us. I can almost imagine a scale of trust:

1.   There is no Holy Spirit. I am on my own.

2. The Holy Spirit's guidance asks me to be good at the expense of my happiness. I better protect myself from Him.
3. The Holy Spirit's guidance asks for sacrifice, but I suppress my will and follow it, to gain His rewards and avoid His punishments.
4. The Holy Spirit has my best interests in mind. I will be happier in the long run if I follow His guidance.
5. The Holy Spirit's guidance is really just my own true will being passed on to me, the holy will that I have denied. Following His guidance means following my own natural will, and doing this is my happiness.

And when we follow His guidance, what do we learn about this buried will that we have forgotten? We learn that it is our will to be like God. We learn that it is our will to give ourselves as God gives Himself. More specifically, we learn that it is our will to heal our brothers. Try to imagine a day when these things feel like the most natural, unforced expression of your own will, when they feel more authentically "you" than anything else.

II. The Invitation to Healing
Commentary by Robert Perry

1.   If sickness is separation [10.III.2:7], the decision [Ur: will] to heal and to <u>be healed</u> is the first step toward <u>recognizing what you truly want</u>. Every <u>attack</u> is a step <u>away</u> from this, and every healing thought brings it closer. The Son of God *has* both Father and Son, because he *is* both Father and Son. To unite *having* and *being* is [Ur: only] to unite your will with His, for He wills you [to have] <u>Himself.</u> And you will yourself to <u>Him</u> because, in your perfect understanding of Him, you <u>know</u> there <u>is</u> but one Will. Yet when you attack <u>any</u> part of God and His Kingdom your understanding is <u>not</u> perfect, and what <u>you</u> really want is therefore lost to you.

The previous section told us that we have no clue what our will is. This section opens by saying that the first step toward discovering our will is healing, both giving healing and accepting healing. This is because healing unites us with our brothers and with God (as the last two sentences of the previous section said), and only in this state of unity do we discover our true will. Each healing thought, then, brings the discovery of our will closer, while each attack thought pushes it away, making us lose touch with what we really want.

In Heaven, having is being—what we *have* is what we *are*. Because we *are* both a father (of our creations) and a Son (of God), we *have* both a Father (God) and a Son (our creations). The focus here, though, is specifically on *being* a Son and *having* a Father. To unite these two would mean realizing that the Father we *have* is not outside us but is part of our very *being*. And this is true, because He has bequeathed His Being to us ("He wills you Himself"). Now His Being is ours as much as it is His. Since His Being is ours, His Will must be ours, too. The same thing is true in the reverse: The Son that God *has* is part of God's *being*, because we, the Son, give our being to God ("you will yourself to Him"). Thus, there is only one Will, the Will of both Father and Son to give Themselves to Each Other, so that the Father or Son that one *has* becomes the being that one *is*.

2.   Healing thus becomes <u>a lesson in understanding</u>, and the more you practice it the better teacher <u>and learner</u> you become. If you have <u>denied</u> truth, what better witnesses to its reality could you have than those who have been healed <u>by</u> it? But be sure to count yourself among them, for in your willingness to <u>join</u> them is your healing accomplished. Every miracle that you accomplish speaks to you of the Fatherhood of God. Every healing thought that you <u>accept</u>, either <u>from</u> your brother or in your <u>own</u> mind, teaches you that you are God's Son. In every hurtful thought you hold, wherever you perceive it, lies the denial of God's Fatherhood and of your Sonship.

You only attack because you perceive competing wills, clashing wills. This means you don't understand that there is only one Will. Only when you heal, when you give miracles, do you understand the one Will. Those you heal therefore become the witnesses to the one Will in you, the truth in you. The miracles you give them are a case of God's Will flowing through you, thus proving that He is your Father. The miracles you receive (from your own thoughts or from a brother) become the testament to God's Will flowing *to* you, thus proving that you are His Son. Every attack thought denies both His Fatherhood and your Sonship, because it is a rejection of Him flowing either *through* you or *to* you.

Application: Pick someone you are judging and say,

When I attack [name] in my mind,
I assert that God is not my Father
And I am not His Son.

3.   And denial <u>is</u> as total as love. You cannot deny <u>part</u> of yourself [a brother], [Ur: simply] because the rest [Ur: remainder] will seem to be separate [Ur: unintegrated] and therefore without meaning. And being without meaning <u>to you</u>, you will not understand it. To deny meaning is [Ur: *must* be] to fail to understand. You can heal only yourself, for only God's Son [who is both you and everyone else] <u>needs</u> healing. You need [Ur: He needs] it because you do [Ur: he does] not understand yourself [Ur: himself], and therefore know not what you do [Ur: knows not what he does]. Having forgotten your [Ur: his] will, you do not know what you really want [Ur: he does not know what he *wants*].

When you have hurtful thoughts about one brother, you deny your identity as a whole. You deny the entire Sonship which *is* your identity. Even the remainder that you haven't attacked seems split off, unintegrated, and therefore fragmented and meaningless. The Sonship's meaning lies in all of its parts forming one cohesive whole. By denying this wholeness, you deny the Sonship's meaning. You fail to understand what it is.

This entire constellation (the Sonship) is yourself and needs healing. The Son needs healing because he does not understand what he is. As a result, he has forgotten his will, doesn't know what he wants, and, like those who crucified Jesus, has no idea what he is doing.

> 4.   Healing is a sign that you want [Ur: *he wants*] <u>to make whole</u>. And this willingness opens your ears [Ur: *his own* ears] to the Voice of the Holy Spirit, Whose message <u>is</u> wholeness. He will enable you to go far beyond the healing <u>you</u> would undertake, for beside your small willingness to make whole He will lay His Own <u>complete</u> Will and make <u>yours</u> whole. What can the Son of God <u>not</u> accomplish with the Fatherhood of God in Him? And yet the invitation must come from you, for you have surely learned that whom you invite as your guest <u>will</u> abide with you.

When you heal, it is a sign that you want to restore the wholeness of the Sonship. You want all the fragments to be united once again. And this desire invokes the Holy Spirit, for restoring this wholeness is what He's all about. Now your ears are open to His Voice. And now He will strengthen your small willingness (to restore the Sonship's wholeness) by adding to it His Own perfect Will. With Him in you, there is nothing you cannot do. Yet for Him to come, you must invite Him. You do this by simply wanting to restore the wholeness of the Sonship.

> 5.   The Holy Spirit cannot speak to an unwelcoming host, <u>because He will not be heard</u>. The Eternal Guest remains, but His Voice grows faint in alien company. He needs your protection, only because your care is a sign that you <u>want</u> Him. Think like Him ever so slightly, and the little spark becomes a blazing light that fills your mind so that He becomes your only Guest. Whenever you ask the ego to enter, you lessen His welcome. <u>He</u> will remain, but <u>you</u> have allied yourself <u>against</u> Him. Whatever journey you choose to take, He will go with you, waiting.

You can safely trust His patience, for He <u>cannot</u> leave a part of God. Yet you need far more than patience.

A parable of the two guests in our mind

Imagine that you have a house, and outside a storm is blowing. You see a little old man out there, and so you ask him to come in. You sense that he doesn't actually need your protection, but offering it to him is a sign that you want him inside, which you do, because you sense something about him. He comes in and you make him feel at home. You get him some dry clothes and prepare him a hot drink. He begins to speak to you. His wisdom is astonishing, like nothing you have ever heard. You feel as if a holy man has graced you with his presence. You feel profoundly honored to be his host.

But just then this renter of yours that lives in your basement (though he never pays his rent) comes into the room. He is both cunning and domineering. He begins to talk loudly and quickly, and the old man grows quiet. He still has much to offer, but he knows he won't be heard. Eventually, he leaves the room, heading for the stairs. In the meantime, you make exciting plans with your renter. The two of you go into a home business together, but he becomes so controlling and manipulative that he, the renter, takes over. You feel like a hostage in your own home. After years of living under his thumb, one day you go up the stairs to the attic to try to find something. When you get to the attic, you find, to your total surprise, that the old man is sitting there, waiting patiently for you. He has been sitting there this entire time, simply waiting for you. Throughout all your misadventures, he never left you. Seeing him sitting there, you realize for the first time in ages that you have a choice. What will you do?

6.   You will never rest until you know your function <u>and fulfill it</u>, for only in this can your will and your Father's be wholly joined. To <u>have</u> Him is to be <u>like</u> Him, and He has <u>given</u> Himself to you. You who have God <u>must</u> be as God, for <u>His</u> function became <u>yours</u> with His gift. Invite this knowledge back into your mind, and let nothing that obscures it enter. The Guest Whom God sent you will teach you how to do this, if you but recognize the little spark <u>and are willing to let it</u>

grow. <u>Your</u> willingness need not be perfect, because His <u>is</u>. If you will merely offer Him a little place, He will lighten it so much that you will gladly let it be increased. And by <u>this</u> increase [Ur: extending], you will begin to remember creation.

We need more than the Holy Spirit's patience. We need His help in resuming our function, for our function represents the union of our will and God's Will, and remembering this union is our goal. Only in that remembering will we find rest. God gave Himself to us, and that means we are like Him. And being like Him, we must function as He does. We must give ourselves as He does. We must create like Him.

Our only goal on this earth is to invite this glorious knowledge back into our mind. The Holy Spirit will teach us how to do this. We need only offer Him a place in our mind, and in that place recognize the little spark in us. All we need do is see that it's there and be willing to let it expand. We will be somewhat ambivalent about this, but that's OK. He will make up for our ambivalence, and under His care our spark will grow into a blazing light. And the brighter the light gets, the closer we will come to remembering our true function of creation.

> 7.   Would you be hostage to the ego or host to God? You will accept only whom <u>you</u> invite. You are free to determine who shall be your guest, and how long he shall remain with you. Yet this is not <u>real</u> freedom, for it still depends on how you see it. The Holy Spirit is <u>there</u>, although He cannot help you without your invitation. And the ego is nothing, whether you invite it in or not. Real freedom depends on welcoming <u>reality</u>, and of your guests only the Holy Spirit [Ur: only He] <u>is</u> real. Know, then, Who abides with you merely by recognizing <u>what is</u> there already [Ur: *already there*], and do not be satisfied with imaginary comforters, for the Comforter of God is in you.

Let's go back to that parable of the two guests. We are free to determine which one shall be our guest —the evil renter or the wise old man. Yet this is not real freedom, for we don't see things as they are. We don't realize that the renter is not actually there. He is an hallucination, like the college roommate in *A Beautiful Mind* (if you saw that movie). Only the old man in the attic (the Holy Spirit) is actually real. Until we really see this, we are likely to use our so-called free will to choose enslavement.

As long as we think the imaginary renter is a real person, are we actually free?

Application: Realize that the story of the two guests is the story of your life. You've got your ego running the show, making you a hostage in your own mind. And you have the Holy Spirit waiting in the attic, a Guest so holy that anyone would feel eternally privileged to be His host. Yet there He sits mostly forgotten, among your dusty memories. With this in mind, take a couple of minutes and ask yourself this all-important question again and again:

Would I be hostage to the ego or host to God?

III. From Darkness to Light
Commentary by Robert Perry

1.   When you are weary, remember you have hurt yourself. Your Comforter will rest you, but <u>you</u> cannot. <u>You do not know how,</u> for if you did you could never have grown weary. Unless you hurt yourself you could never suffer in <u>any</u> way, for that is not God's Will for His Son. Pain is not of Him, for He knows no attack and His peace surrounds you silently. God is very quiet, for there is no conflict in Him. Conflict is the root of all evil, for being blind it does not see whom it attacks. Yet it <u>always</u> attacks the Son of God, and the Son of God is <u>you</u>.

We see weariness as a natural consequence of expending lots of energy. Not so, says this paragraph. We only get weary when we hurt ourselves. We don't have to get weary at all, ever. It is not God's Will for us. Imagine never being weary! How, then, do we weary ourselves? The clear implication is through attack, through conflicting with others. This "conflict is the root of all evil." When you attack, have you ever felt blinded by your anger and upset? That is a clue to the nature of attack. It is always blind, so blind that when you attack you don't realize you are really attacking the Son of God—in the other person and in yourself.

We are too caught up in this blindness. That's why we need the Holy Spirit. That's why only He can rest us. We will find out how He does at the end of the section.

2.   God's Son is indeed in need of comfort, for he knows not what he does, believing his will is not his own. The Kingdom is his, and yet he wanders homeless. At home in God he is lonely, and amid all his brothers he is friendless. Would God let this be real, when He did not will to be alone Himself? And if your will is His it <u>cannot</u> be true of you, <u>because</u> it is not true of Him.

What a poignant description of our condition. We don't know what we are doing. When we attack, we think we are following our own will, when actually we have been hypnotized and are obeying an alien will. We are like a king who has an entire kingdom, yet, under the influence of this alien will, chooses to wander homeless and penniless. Worse yet, this king is actually in his palace, surrounded by his loving father and brothers, yet in his delirium he feels totally alone. While lying in his bed safe at home, he merely *imagines* himself to be a homeless wanderer.

That is our condition. That is why we need comforting. And the core of our comfort is this single fact: God would not let this be real.

> 3.   O my child [Ur: children], if you knew what God wills for you *, your joy would be complete! And what He wills <u>has</u> happened, for it was <u>always</u> true. When the light comes * and you have said, "God's Will is mine," you will see such beauty that you will <u>know</u> * it is not of you. Out of your joy you will create beauty in His Name, for <u>your</u> joy * could no more be contained than His. The bleak little world will vanish into nothingness, and your heart will be so filled with joy * that it will leap into Heaven, and into the Presence of God. I cannot tell you what this will be like, for your heart is not ready *. Yet I <u>can</u> tell you, and remind you often, that what God wills for Himself He wills for <u>you</u>, and what He wills for you * <u>is</u> yours.

Application: Please read the paragraph again, very slowly, inserting your name at the asterisks.

We are that king, lying in our palace, caught in a nightmare in which we wander alone and homeless. In this paragraph, Jesus is telling us the good news—news that is good beyond our wildest dreams. If we will only accept God's will as our own, we will pass into a state of uncontainable joy, a state of wonder at the beauty of His transcendental Kingdom. Our heart will be unable to restrain itself; it will abandon the world and leap into God's Presence. Jesus sounds so rapt as he tells us this. He knows exactly what this is like, but he can't tell us—our hearts are not ready. So he has to reduce his description to tantalizing hints and to the simple (but stunning) statement that what God wills for Himself is ours.

> 4.   The way is not hard, but it *is* very different. Yours is the way of pain, of which God knows nothing. <u>That</u> way is hard indeed, and very lonely. Fear and grief are your guests, and they go with you and abide with you on the way. But the dark journey is not the way of God's Son.

> Walk in light and do not see the dark companions, for they are not fit [worthy] companions for the Son of God, who was created *of* light and *in* light. The Great Light <u>always</u> surrounds you and shines out <u>from</u> you. How can you see the dark companions in a light such as this? If you see <u>them</u>, it is only because you are denying the light. But <u>deny them instead</u>, for the light is here and the way is clear.

As soon as we hear that the way home is "very different," we assume that it's going to be a lot harder, filled with sacrifice and loneliness. Yet ironically, that describes the way we are on *now*. It is "the way of pain," the "dark journey," the lonely wandering, in which our only companions are fear and grief. This sounds like such a downer, yet does it not describe the typical human journey? In the midst of all our friends and family, there remains within us an aloneness, an unsettling isolation. Is there anyone that we can truly count on no matter what challenge may come? Well, yes, we can count on our emotions—our anxiety, our dread, our loneliness, and our grief. No matter who else may leave us, they never will. They are our constant companions—"the dark companions."

Who wouldn't jump off this path the instant they could? That is exactly what Jesus asks us to do. "Walk in light and do not see the dark companions." Come on—you are God's Son; such companions are not worthy of you. Deny the dark companions and turn your eyes to the Great Rays shining out from you, illuminating your way. There *is* a different way to walk through life, "for the light is here and the way is clear."

> 5. God hides nothing from His Son, even though His Son would hide himself. Yet the Son of God cannot hide his glory, for God wills him to be glorious, and gave him the light that shines in him. You will never lose your way, for God leads you. When you wander, you but undertake a journey that is not real. The dark companions, the dark way, are all illusions. Turn toward the light, for the little spark in you is part of a Light so great that it can sweep you out of all darkness forever. For your Father *is* your Creator, and you *are* like Him.

Application: Say to yourself,

I cannot hide my glory.

For God wills me to be glorious.
He gave me the light that shines in me.

We can't turn off the Great Rays. It is God's Will that they shine from us forever. They illuminate our way. And God Himself leads us along it. Therefore, we can't ever really lose the way. We can only temporarily wander off. Yet when we do, we don't really go anywhere. When we step off the path, we embark on an illusory journey, into a dark forest that is not real. Why do that when we can turn toward the light in us, the light that can sweep us out of darkness forever?

Application: Try to think of some way in which you feel that you've recently stepped off the path. See yourself heading into a dark forest that you now realize is illusory. Instead, see yourself turning toward the light and asking God, "How can I set foot back on my right path?"

6.   The children of light cannot abide in darkness, for darkness is <u>not</u> in them. Do not be deceived by the dark comforters, and never let them enter the mind of God's Son, for they have no place in His temple. When you are tempted to deny Him remember that there *are* no other gods to place before Him, and accept His Will for you in peace. For you <u>cannot</u> accept it otherwise.

We were taught that our body is God's temple, but the truth is that our *mind* is His temple. And would we set up false gods in His temple? Yet that is what we are doing when we invite fear and grief into our minds.

Application: Think of something you are currently fearing, or grieving over. Picture your mind as God's holy temple, and your fear or grief as a dark companion that you are inviting in. Say,

I will not let this idol into the mind of God's Son,
For it has no place in God's temple.
*There **are** no other gods to place before Him.*

7.   Only God's Comforter <u>can</u> comfort you. In the quiet of His temple,

He waits to give you the peace that is yours. <u>Give</u> His peace, that you may enter the temple and find it waiting for you. But be holy in the Presence of God, or you will not know that you are there. For what is unlike God cannot enter His Mind, because it was not His Thought and therefore does not belong to Him. And <u>your</u> mind must be as pure as His, if you would know what belongs to <u>you</u>. Guard carefully His temple, for He Himself dwells there and abides in peace. You cannot enter God's Presence with the dark companions beside you, but you also cannot enter alone. All your brothers must enter <u>with</u> you, for until you have accepted them *you* cannot enter. For you cannot understand Wholeness unless <u>you</u> are whole, and no part of the Son can be excluded if he would know the Wholeness of his Father.

8. In your mind you can <u>accept</u> the whole Sonship and bless it with the light your Father gave it. Then you will be worthy to dwell in the temple <u>with</u> Him, because it is <u>your</u> will not to be alone. God blessed His Son forever. If you will bless him in <u>time</u>, you will <u>be</u> in eternity. Time cannot separate you from God if you use it on <u>behalf</u> of the eternal.

Application: Imagine your mind as some kind of building, a building that reflects the uses to which it is currently put.

What sort of building do you see?
Now see yourself inside this building.
Milling around inside with you are all sorts of dark characters—your negative emotions.
You see a character who clearly is your fear.
You see another who is your anger.
You see another who is your intolerance.
You see another who is your grief.
Now you look across the interior of the building, and see golden doors, the doors to the temple of God.
Your initial reaction is to go to those doors and bring all your dark companions with you.
But then you realize that they cannot enter with you.
You sense that, in order to enter, your thoughts must be as pure as God's.

66

So you send the dark companions away.

And instead you invite your brothers, all your brothers, even people you have alienated.

See them all standing with you, by your side, as you prepare with them to enter God's Presence.

Having accepted all of them, your thoughts *are* as pure as God's.

What a wonderful feeling!

You open the doors and survey the inside.

There you see (or sense or feel) God Himself waiting for you at the altar, waiting to give you His peace.

Yet first you look around and realize that this is the same building that you have just left,

only seen differently.

You realize that all along your mind has been the temple of God, and that God has always been there, waiting to give you His peace,

Only when you banished the dark companions and invited in your brothers did you realize the holy temple that you had been living in all along.

With that joyous thought, you, together with all your brothers, approach God to receive His everlasting consolation.

For this is how you let Him comfort you.

IV. The Inheritance of God's Son
Commentary by Robert Perry

This section is an extended argument as to why we cannot enter God's Presence if we hate our brothers or blame ourselves.

> 1.   Never forget that the Sonship is your salvation, for the Sonship is your Self [Ur: Soul]. As God's creation It is yours, and belonging to you It is His. Your Self [Ur: Soul] does not need salvation, but your mind needs to learn what salvation is. You are not saved *from* anything, but you <u>are</u> saved *for* glory. Glory is your inheritance, given you [Ur: your Soul] by your Creator that you might <u>extend</u> it. Yet if you hate part of your Self [Ur: your own Soul] <u>all</u> your understanding is lost, because you are looking on what God created <u>as yourself</u> without love. And since what He created <u>is</u> part of Him, you are denying Him His place in His Own altar.

Never forget that your salvation does not lie in redeeming your image of yourself. Your salvation lies in your brothers, in the Sonship as a whole. You need to look at the entire Sonship as your own Soul.

You are not saved *from* sinfulness. Rather, you are saved *for* glory. God created you to shine with His glory. Returning to that state is the goal of the journey we are on. Yet if we hate one brother, then we are looking on our own Soul without love, and we lose all our understanding. Not only that, we kick God out of His own altar, for the brother we are hating *is* His altar.

Application: Repeat these words to yourself,

*I am not saved **from** anything.*
*I am saved **for** glory.*
Glory is my inheritance from God.

2.   Could you try to make God homeless and know that <u>you</u> are at home? Can the Son deny the Father <u>without</u> believing that the Father has denied <u>him</u>? God's laws hold <u>only</u> for your protection, and they never hold in vain. What you experience when you deny your Father is still for your protection, for the power of your will cannot be lessened without the intervention of God <u>against</u> it, and <u>any</u> limitation on <u>your</u> power is <u>not</u> the Will of God. Therefore, look <u>only</u> to the power that <u>God</u> gave to save you, remembering that it is yours *because* it is His, and join with your brothers in His peace.

As I said above, when we hate a brother, we are throwing God out of His home (the brother). We will then conclude that God has thrown *us* out of *our* home. This is because the laws of God guarantee that our thoughts produce results after their own nature. This can feel scary, as if those laws are out to get us. Yet they are only for our protection. If our hateful thoughts didn't roll through our mind producing effects in their likeness, those thoughts would be powerless. And that would be a limitation on *our* power, which is not God's Will.

Therefore, the fantasy option is to keep on hating and hope that our hateful thoughts won't have any power, that God will bury them in lead-encased barrels. The more realistic option is to use our unlimited power constructively, use it to join with our brothers.

3.   Your peace [Ur: The peace of *your* Soul] lies in its limitlessness. Limit the peace you share, and your Self [Ur: your own Soul] <u>must</u> be unknown to you. Every altar to God is part of you [Ur: your Soul], because the light He created is one with Him. Would you cut off a brother from the light that is yours? You would not do so if you realized that <u>you can darken only your own mind</u>. As you bring <u>him</u> back, so will you [Ur: *your* mind] return. That is the law of God, for the protection of the wholeness of His Son [it keeps the parts of the Son together by guaranteeing that you can't return while your brother stays behind].

Have you ever felt a kind of defensive peace, as if you were an island of peace, superior to the unpeaceful ones and determined not to let them tear down your peace? If so, what you didn't realize was that you can only know the peace of your Soul if you let it be limitless, and it can only be limitless if you limitlessly *share* it. If you cut your brothers off from your light, "you can only darken your own mind" (3:5). Here again we see the laws of God at work. Only now there is *a* specific law: "As you bring him back, so will *your* mind return." This is mentioned elsewhere in the Course as the law of love. It can be rephrased in this way: as you give, so shall you receive.

> 4. *Only you can deprive yourself of anything.* Do not oppose this realization, for it is truly the beginning of the dawn of light. Remember also that the denial of this simple fact takes many forms, and these you must learn to recognize and to oppose steadfastly, <u>without exception</u>. This is a crucial step in the reawakening. The beginning phases of this reversal are often quite painful, for as blame is withdrawn from without, there is a strong tendency to harbor it within. It is difficult at first to realize that this is <u>exactly</u> the same thing, for there <u>is</u> no distinction between within and without.

Application: What is the main thing you are feeling deprived of today? Once you have identified it, repeat:

> *No one else has deprived me of [specify].*
> *Only I can deprive myself of anything.*

The hard part about this realization is that the guilt we had displaced onto our brothers (by blaming them for our deprivation) now comes home to roost. As we refuse to blame them and instead take responsibility ourselves, we can start feeling massively guilty. I am sure many of us are in this exact place—we've never felt so guilty as since we started on the spiritual path. The crucial thing now is to realize that blaming ourselves is no different from blaming others, for we are, of course, one.

> 5. If your brothers are part of <u>you</u> and you blame <u>them</u> for your deprivation, you <u>are</u> blaming yourself. And you cannot blame yourself <u>without</u> blaming them. That is why blame must be <u>undone</u>, <u>not</u> seen elsewhere [Ur: *not* re-allocated]. Lay it to yourself and you cannot <u>know</u> yourself, for <u>only the ego blames at all</u>. Self-blame is therefore ego identification, and as much an ego defense as blaming others. *You cannot enter God's Presence if you attack His Son.* When His Son lifts his voice in praise of his Creator, he <u>will</u> hear the Voice for his Father.

Yet the Creator cannot be praised <u>without</u> His Son, for Their glory is shared and They are glorified together.

Application: Briefly review the exercise you did for the previous paragraph. Then add these lines:

But I will not blame myself for this.
If I blame myself I blame my brothers, for they are part of me.
Only the ego blames at all.
Self-blame is just as much of the ego as blaming others.
I cannot enter God's Presence if I blame His Son,
only if I glorify him.

6.   Christ is at God's altar, waiting to welcome His [God's] Son. But come wholly without condemnation, for otherwise you will believe that the door is barred and you cannot enter. The door is <u>not</u> barred, and it is impossible that you cannot enter the place where God would have you be. But love yourself with the Love of Christ, for so does your Father love you. You <u>can</u> refuse to enter, but you <u>cannot</u> bar the door that Christ holds open. Come unto me who hold it open <u>for</u> you, for while I live it cannot be shut, and I live forever. God is my life and <u>yours</u>, and <u>nothing</u> is denied by God to His Son.

Application: This paragraph is clearly an expansion of the temple image from the previous section.

Imagine yourself approaching the door to God's temple.
It appears to have an iron bar across it, holding it shut.
Realize this is an hallucination produced by your desire to see it shut for others,
and the self-condemnation that results from that.
So say to yourself,

"I let go of all condemnation toward my brothers.
And I love myself with the love of Christ,

71

For so does my Father love me."

As you say these words, you see the scene before you transform.
You see that the door is not barred after all.
In fact, it is open.
And you see Jesus there, holding it open for you (Jesus as doorman!).
Through the doorway, you see inside the temple.
And there, at the altar, both God and Christ (your true Self) are waiting
    for you,
waiting to welcome you.
The whole scene is one of total welcome.
As you prepare to enter, you realize at last that God denies nothing to
    His Son.

> 7.   At God's altar Christ waits for the restoration of Himself in
> you. God knows His Son as wholly blameless as Himself, and He is
> approached through the appreciation of His Son. Christ waits for your
> acceptance of Him as yourself, and of His Wholeness as yours. For
> Christ is the Son of God, Who lives in His Creator and shines with His
> glory. Christ is the extension of the Love and the Loveliness of God, as
> perfect as His Creator and at peace with Him.

Why was Christ waiting for you at the altar? You are a part of His
universal Self, a part that has wandered off. Your return, therefore,
represents the restoration of His Wholeness. He will be restored when
you accept Him as yourself. And you can only accept a Being as lofty
and perfect as Christ as yourself when you are willing to see yourself as
wholly *blameless*.

> 8.   Blessed is the Son of God whose radiance is of his Father, and
> whose glory he wills to share as his Father shares it with him. There is
> no condemnation in the Son, for there is no condemnation in the Father.
> Sharing the perfect Love of the Father the Son must share what belongs
> to Him, for otherwise he will not know the Father or the Son. Peace be
> unto you who rest in God, and in whom the whole Sonship rests.

Application: Repeat these lines with as much feeling as you can:

Blessed am I, the holy Son of God.
My radiance is of my Father.
I will only to share this glory, as God shared it with me.
I have no desire to condemn, for my Father has none.
I will only to share His perfect Love.

V. The 'Dynamics' of the Ego
Commentary by Robert Perry

1.   No one can escape from illusions unless he looks at them, for not looking is the way they are <u>protected</u>. There is no need to shrink from illusions, for they <u>cannot</u> be dangerous. We are ready to look more closely at the ego's thought system because together we have the lamp that will dispel it, and since you realize you do not <u>want</u> it, you <u>must</u> be ready. Let us be very calm in doing this, for we are merely looking honestly for truth. The "dynamics" of the ego will be our lesson for a while, for we must look first at this to see beyond it, since you <u>have</u> made it real. We will <u>undo</u> this error quietly together, and then look beyond it to truth.

Who of us wants to look at our ego? We are all afraid of what we'll find there, so much so that relabeling our ego as wonderful and divine is rampant among spiritual seekers these days. Yet the only way to escape from the ego is to *look*. How often have you seen that real change in you only happened once you decide to look at what needed changing? Given this, not looking at the ego is an act of protecting it.

Aware of our fear, Jesus tries to reassure us in a number of ways. He tells us that looking at illusions is the "escape from" them, that they "cannot be dangerous," that "we are ready to look" now, that he will be with us as we look (third sentence), that "together we have the lamp that will dispel" them, that we can look calmly because all we want is the truth (fourth sentence), and that once we have looked at our illusions, we will look beyond them *to* the truth (final sentence). We must need lots of reassurance!

2.   What is healing but the removal of all that <u>stands in the way</u> of knowledge? And how else can one dispel illusions [remove the illusions that stand in the way of knowledge] <u>except</u> by looking at them directly, <u>without</u> protecting them? Be not afraid, therefore, for what you will be looking at <u>is</u> the source of fear, and you are beginning to learn that <u>fear is not real</u>. You are also learning [Ur: We have accepted the fact already] that its <u>effects</u> can be dispelled merely by denying

their reality. The next step is obviously to recognize that <u>what has no effects does not exist</u>. Laws do not operate in a vacuum, and what leads to nothing <u>has not happened</u>. If reality is recognized <u>by its extension</u>, what leads [Ur: extends] to nothing could not be real. Do not be afraid, then, to look upon fear, for it cannot <u>be</u> seen. Clarity undoes confusion by definition, and to look upon darkness through light <u>must</u> dispel it.

This paragraph continues explaining why we need not be afraid to look at our ego's illusions. Much of the paragraph is an elaboration on the third sentence. The Urtext version of the fourth sentence is crucial, for read properly, that sentence gives the first step in an elaboration on the third sentence, rather than stating an additional learning (as the edited version reads). Let me lay out the train of thought:

1. You are beginning to learn that fear is not real.
2. You've already learned that fear's effects can be dispelled by denying their reality.
3. The next step is to realize that what has no real effects cannot itself be real.
4. This is because something is recognized as real by its ability to produce effects.
5. Now you can finish what you've begun to learn and realize that, since fear has no real effects, fear cannot be real.

And being unreal, fear cannot be terrifying to look at. You would think that looking at the source of fear would be the most terrifying thing we could ever do. Yet if fear itself is not real, when we look at its source, there will be nothing there to see.

3. Let us begin this lesson in "ego dynamics" by understanding that the term itself does not mean anything. It contains the very contradiction in terms that <u>makes</u> it meaningless. "Dynamics" implies the power to <u>do</u> something, and the whole separation fallacy lies in the belief that the ego *has* the power to do <u>anything</u>. The ego is fearful to you <u>because</u> you believe this. Yet the truth is very simple:

<u>All power is of God</u>.
What is <u>not</u> of Him has <u>no power to do anything</u>.

"Ego dynamics," of course, refers to how the ego operates, to the various forces that swirl and contend within it and what they produce. Yet Jesus is saying that the term itself is an oxymoron, like "peaceful violence." Dynamics implies power to do something. It implies *dynamism*. Yet all power is of God, and so the ego has no power to do anything. Just as fear cannot produce real effects, the ego cannot, either. The ego has no dynamics. How, then, can looking at its "dynamics" be fearful?

It is strange to hear that the word "dynamic" applies only to God, isn't it? As Course students, we would probably assume that Heaven is not dynamic, but rather perfectly still. Yet this is saying that *only* Heaven is dynamic.

> 4.　When we look at the ego, then, we are <u>not</u> considering dynamics but delusions. You can surely regard a delusional system without fear, for it cannot have any effects if its source is not real. Fear becomes more obviously inappropriate if you recognize the ego's <u>goal</u>, which is so clearly senseless that any effort on its behalf is <u>necessarily</u> expended on nothing. The ego's goal is quite explicitly <u>ego autonomy</u>. From the beginning, then, its <u>purpose</u> is to be separate, sufficient unto itself and independent of any power <u>except its own</u>. This is <u>why</u> it is the symbol of separation.

We can look at the ego without fear because it is just a delusional system, a system of beliefs that flies in the face of reality. It is more zany than dangerous.

Being afraid of looking at the ego gets even more inappropriate if we see what the ego's goal is. Its goal is ego autonomy. Its whole aim is to be separate from God, from others, even from us. The first two go against our own instincts for togetherness. The third goes against all logic, for the ego depends directly on our mind. It has no independent existence. Its desire for autonomy from us, then, is like the image on the movie screen wanting to be autonomous from the projector. No projector, no image.

> 5.　<u>Every</u> idea has a purpose, and its purpose is always the natural outcome of what it <u>is</u>. <u>Everything</u> that stems from the ego is the natural outcome of its central belief, and the way to undo its <u>results</u> is merely to recognize that their <u>source</u> is <u>not</u> natural, being out of accord with

your <u>true</u> nature. I said before [7.X.4:9-10] that to will contrary to God is wishful thinking and not real willing. His Will is one *because* the extension of His Will <u>cannot</u> be unlike <u>itself</u>. The real conflict you experience, then, is between the ego's idle wishes and the Will of God, <u>which you share</u>. Can this be a real conflict?

The ego's effects are the *natural* outcome of an *unnatural* source. The ego is unnatural to us because it goes against our nature. Yet how can we will something that is contrary to our nature? How can we be wholehearted in going against our own innate character? Trying to do so can only be wishful thinking, such as when the gay man convinces himself he can be contented in a heterosexual marriage.

The ego is powerless because we simply can't put our power behind it. We can't put our heart into it. Our conflict, then, is not between our wayward will and God's holy Will, but between the ego's powerless wishes and our true will, which is joined with God's.

6. Yours is the independence of creation, <u>not</u> of autonomy. Your whole creative function lies in your complete dependence on God, Whose function He shares <u>with</u> you. By <u>His</u> willingness to share it, He became as dependent on you as you are on <u>Him</u>. Do not ascribe the ego's arrogance to Him Who wills <u>not</u> to be independent of <u>you</u>. He has included <u>you</u> in <u>His</u> Autonomy. Can <u>you</u> believe that autonomy is meaningful <u>apart</u> from Him? The belief in <u>ego</u> autonomy is costing you the knowledge of your dependence on God, <u>in which your freedom lies</u>. The ego sees <u>all</u> dependency as threatening, and has twisted even your longing for God into a means of establishing <u>itself</u>. But do not be deceived by <u>its</u> interpretation of your conflict.

What do we find so desirable about independence? Isn't it the idea that nothing can thrust itself upon us against our will? Yet that is exactly what we get when we acknowledge our dependence on God. His power flows to us, but *not* against our will. And then our power flows outward in the act of creation, in which nothing hinders our free self-expression. In God, then, there is absolutely nothing that can reach us against our will. Our will is totally unfettered, totally free. Try to imagine that. Dependence on God is a state of complete freedom.

Further, God completely includes us. We shouldn't see Him as arrogantly holding himself aloof from us. That is what the ego does. Rather, God envelops us in His Autonomy, in which we are independent of anything that is not of Him. Again, try to imagine that.

We long for this state of independence from all that would hurt us. This longing is part of our nature. Yet the ego tells us, "I am the one who can satisfy your longing for independence." And for some reason, we listen.

> 7.   The ego <u>always</u> attacks on behalf of separation. Believing it <u>has</u> the power to do this it does nothing else, because its goal of autonomy *is* nothing else. The ego is totally confused about reality, <u>but it does not lose sight of its goal</u>. It is much more vigilant than <u>you</u> are, <u>because</u> it is perfectly certain of its purpose. <u>You</u> are confused because you do <u>not</u> recognize [Ur: know] <u>yours</u>.

"The ego always attacks on behalf of separation." Think of the implications of this. When you are coming from your ego, that is all you are ever doing. You are in some (usually subtle) way attacking in order to establish the complete autonomy of your ego. This is hard to face, because you want to love and not attack. Yet it's as if you are in a marriage in which you are wishy-washy about your goals in life, yet your spouse is 100% committed to an unshakable goal every second of the day. Who is going to get his or her way in this scenario?

> 8.   You must recognize that the <u>last</u> thing the ego wishes you to realize is <u>that you are afraid of it</u>. For if the ego could give rise to fear, it would diminish [Ur: it is *diminishing*] your independence and weaken [Ur: *weakening*] your power. Yet its one claim to your allegiance is that it can <u>give</u> power to you. Without <u>this</u> belief you would not listen to it at all. How, then, can its existence continue if you realize that, by accepting it, you <u>are</u> belittling yourself and <u>depriving</u> yourself of power?

The ego sells itself to us by saying that, if we follow it, we can be independent. No more hanging onto Mommy's apron strings. No one will tell us what to do. No one can assail us. We can be powerful. Isn't that what our ego whispers in our ear? Yet that is what tyrants always say to get into power, and the ego is a tyrant. In fact, *it* wants to tell us what to do. It wants to threaten us into submission. It wants us to be its slave. This leaves the ego in an odd position: It promises us that we'll be so independent and so powerful that we'll never be afraid again, and yet the one promising us this scares the hell out of us. Clearly, the last part of that statement is the last thing the ego wants us to recognize.

> 9.   The ego can and does allow you to regard yourself as supercilious, unbelieving, "light-hearted," distant, emotionally shallow, callous, uninvolved and even desperate, <u>but not really afraid</u>. <u>Minimizing</u> fear, but <u>not</u> its undoing, is the ego's constant effort, and is indeed a skill at which it is <u>very</u> ingenious. How can it preach separation <u>without</u> upholding it through fear, and would you listen to it if you recognized this <u>is</u> what it is doing?

The ego has to constantly keep us afraid. It has to literally scare us into accepting something we don't really want: separation. But then it has to promise to take our fear away and actually appear to be minimizing our fear. What a juggling act! Again, a great analogy is a tyrant. How does it feel to consider that you are at the mercy of an inner tyrant?

The list in the first sentence I have always found extremely insightful and revealing. Jesus says that the ego allows us to regard ourselves as everything on this list, but *not* really afraid. Let's see if he's right.

Application: Which of the following have you secretly accused yourself of being (put a check by the ones you have):

_____supercilious (coolly and patronizingly haughty, haughtily contemptuous)

_____unbelieving (overly skeptical, refusing to believe even when you should)

_____ "light-hearted" (not in touch with the real gravity of situations; irresponsibly free of care)

_____distant (reserved or aloof in personal relationship)

_____emotionally shallow (lacking depth of feeling)

_____callous (lacking appropriate inner response to the needs of others)

_____uninvolved (not getting appropriately absorbed in situations, not committing oneself emotionally)

_____desperate (intensely needy yet also despairing)

Do you sense a running theme here? Don't all of these add up to a *lack of connection*? You are standing apart from others (supercilious, callous, distant) and from situations (uninvolved). You are standing mentally apart from what you should believe (unbelieving), from what you should feel (emotionally shallow), and from the real gravity of the situation ("light-hearted").

Oddly enough, standing apart means *autonomy*. This means that you are constantly accusing yourself of being inappropriately autonomous.

And this suggests that you must have a powerful attachment to being autonomous. Because even though part of you doesn't *like* being autonomous (hence, the negative accusations), you are still OK about labeling yourself as autonomous.

Let's switch gears. Now imagine announcing to your spiritual friends at a spiritual gathering, "I'm afraid all the time." How does that feel?

Imagine telling people at a social gathering, "I'm afraid all the time. In situations in which other people wouldn't feel afraid, I do." How does that feel?

Imagine telling your parents (if they are still around), "I've never managed to stop being afraid all the time." How does that feel?

In light of your answers, is being afraid all the time something you want to admit to? If not, why not?

If it fits your answers above, acknowledge to yourself the following,

> *I am deeply attached to being autonomous (as shown by the list).*
> *Yet I don't want to admit to being really afraid.*

Try this alternative version:

> *I'd rather feel guilty over being too autonomous*
> *than feel humiliated by admitting to being too afraid.*

This is the evidence that the ego is in charge.

Remaining Commentary by Greg Mackie

10. <u>Your</u> recognition that whatever seems to separate you from God is <u>only</u> fear, regardless of the form it takes and quite apart from <u>how the ego wants you to experience it</u>, is therefore the basic ego threat. Its dream of autonomy is shaken to its foundation by this awareness. For though you may countenance a false idea of independence, you will <u>not</u> accept the cost of fear <u>if you recognize it</u>. Yet this <u>is</u> the cost, and the ego <u>cannot</u> minimize it. [Ur: For] If you overlook love you are overlooking <u>yourself</u>, and you <u>must</u> fear <u>un</u>reality *because* you have denied yourself [Ur: *because you have denied yourself*]. By believing that you have successfully attacked truth, <u>you are believing that attack has power</u>. Very simply, then, <u>you have become afraid of yourself</u>. And no one wants to find [Ur: wills to learn] what he believes would <u>destroy</u> him.

The previous two paragraphs said that the ego doesn't want us to realize how afraid we are. We have convinced ourselves that ego autonomy gives us independence and power, and thus gives us freedom from fear. We tell ourselves that safety lies in pumping our ego up to Superman proportions. If we saw that ego autonomy causes us to feel more like Chicken Little than Superman and therefore *diminishes* our independence and power, we would send the ego packing.

So, the ego tries to minimize our fear. But try as it might, it can't really do this, because ego autonomy is a truly terrifying thing. Deep down, we think we have successfully attacked truth and thus permanently corrupted our loving nature. In our eyes, we "have made a devil of God's Son" (W-pI.101.5:3). So, when the Course comes along and says it will get us in touch with who we really are, we say, "Get thee behind me, Satan!"

11. If the ego's goal of autonomy <u>could</u> be accomplished <u>God's</u> purpose could be defeated, and this <u>is</u> impossible. Only by learning what fear <u>is</u> can you finally learn to distinguish the possible from the impossible and the false from the true. According to the ego's teaching, *its* goal <u>can</u> be accomplished and <u>God's</u> purpose can *not*. According to the Holy Spirit's teaching, *only* God's purpose can be accomplished, and it is accomplished already [Ur: *only* God's Purpose *is* accomplishment and it is *already* accomplished].

81

We're terrified of what our ego autonomy has wrought, but in fact ego autonomy is *impossible*. How could we defeat God? He is God, after all—not only does He have the power to accomplish whatever He wills, but He's already done it. While this is awful news for the ego, it is incredibly good news for *us*, because it means we have *not* made a devil of God's Son. Our fear is really a fear of nothing—that is "what fear is." How can nothing be fearful?

> 12. God is as dependent on you as you are on Him, because His Autonomy <u>encompasses</u> yours, and is therefore incomplete <u>without</u> it. You can only <u>establish</u> your autonomy by identifying <u>with</u> Him, and <u>fulfilling your function as it exists in truth</u>. The ego believes that to accomplish <u>its</u> goal <u>is</u> happiness. But it is given <u>you</u> to know that <u>God's</u> function <u>is</u> yours, and happiness <u>cannot</u> be found apart from your joint Will. Recognize only that the ego's goal, which you have pursued so [Ur: quite] diligently, has merely brought you <u>fear</u>, and it becomes difficult to maintain that <u>fear</u> is happiness. <u>Upheld</u> by fear, this <u>is</u> what the ego would have you believe. Yet God's Son is not insane, and <u>cannot</u> believe it. Let him but <u>recognize</u> it and he will <u>not</u> accept it. For only the insane would choose fear <u>in place</u> of love, and only the insane could believe that love can be gained by <u>attack</u>. But the sane realize [Ur: *know*] that only attack <u>could</u> produce fear, from which the Love of God <u>completely</u> protects them.

The ego believes that autonomy means declaring independence from God. This, it tells us, will free us to do whatever we want and will therefore make us happy. But true autonomy is sharing God's Autonomy. His Autonomy makes us dependent on Him, but His decision to share it with us makes Him equally dependent on us. Paradoxically, this mutual dependence gives us the freedom to do what we *really* want: to share in God's function of creation, the only function that can truly make us happy. To rediscover this happiness, we must call upon our inherent sanity to help us recognize that striving for ego autonomy is an attack on God. As such, it brings us nothing but fear, and fear is most definitely not happiness.

Application: Bring to mind an ego-oriented goal you have pursued. You have believed that to accomplish this goal—which serves the ego's ultimate goal of ego autonomy—would bring you happiness. Yet if you look closely, you'll realize that this goal has really brought you fear. Get in touch with this fear, and then say: *"I recognize that this goal has merely brought me fear. How can fear be happiness?"*

13. The ego analyzes; the Holy Spirit <u>accepts</u>. The appreciation of wholeness comes <u>only</u> through acceptance, for to analyze <u>means</u> to break down or to separate out. The attempt to understand totality by breaking it down [Ur: *breaking it up*] is clearly the characteristically contradictory approach of the ego to everything. [Ur: Never forget that] The ego believes that power, understanding <u>and truth</u> lie in separation, and to <u>establish</u> this belief it <u>must</u> attack. Unaware that the belief cannot <u>be</u> established, and obsessed with the conviction that separation <u>is</u> salvation, the ego attacks everything it perceives by breaking it into small, disconnected parts, without meaningful relationships and therefore without meaning. The ego will <u>always</u> substitute chaos for meaning, for if separation is salvation, harmony is threat.

Course students often use the first line here as an argument against the intellect, but I think it should be read in light of earlier sections. In Chapter 9, Jesus said that instead of pointing out our brothers' errors (T-9.III), analyzing their egos as the psychoanalyst does (T-9.V.6:3; see also T-12.I.1-2, which speaks of analyzing motivations), and thereby making their errors real (T-9.IV.4:6), we should accept our brothers as the holy Sons of God they really are (T-9.III.6:4; T-9.IV.1:4; T-9.VI.7:8). I think the discussion here continues this theme: The ego analyzes and the Holy Spirit accepts *our brothers*. Through accepting our brothers as the Holy Spirit does, we come to accept ourselves as well.

The previous section said that we come to know God through our appreciation of His Son, through the acceptance of Christ's Wholeness as ours (T-11.IV.7:2-3). But the ego wants nothing to do with God, so it shatters wholeness by analyzing God's Son to death, reducing him to little more than a catalog of errors. A psychoanalyst diagnoses a patient and concludes that he is a neurotic with delusions of grandeur and unresolved Oedipal issues. An office worker sizes up the guy in the next cubicle and concludes that he's an ignorant jerk who can't be trusted—oh, and he has bad breath and could stand to lose a few pounds. Even those we love (like our spouses) don't escape the microscope. This process goes on with everyone we see, so in the end we see our brothers and ourselves not as holy Sons of God united in a shared Identity as Christ, but as weak and fallible bodies and personalities in constant conflict with one another in a chaotic world. This is just the way the ego likes it.

14. The ego's interpretations of the laws of perception are, and would <u>have</u> to be, the exact opposite of the Holy Spirit's. The ego <u>focuses on error</u> and <u>overlooks truth</u>. It makes real every mistake it perceives, and with characteristically circular reasoning concludes that <u>because</u> of the mistake consistent truth must be meaningless. The next step, then, is obvious. If consistent truth is meaningless, <u>inconsistency</u> must be true [Ur: if truth has meaning]. Holding error clearly in mind, and protecting what it has made real, the ego proceeds to the next step in its thought system: [Ur: that] Error is real and <u>truth is error</u>.

15. The ego makes no attempt to <u>understand</u> this, and it is clearly not understandable, but the ego does make <u>every</u> attempt to <u>demonstrate</u> it, and <u>this</u> it does constantly. Analyzing to <u>attack</u> meaning the ego succeeds [Ur: *does* succeed] in overlooking it, and is left with a series of fragmented <u>perceptions</u> [Ur: *in*] <u>which it unifies on behalf of itself</u>. This, then, becomes the universe it perceives. And it is this universe which, in turn, becomes its demonstration of its own reality.

These paragraphs lay out a string of insane ego logic that ends up "demonstrating" the ego's reality. It all starts with analyzing our brothers' errors, focusing on errors and ignoring truth. This makes those errors real: We see them as the "truth" about what our brothers really are. We now regard people as so inherently error-prone that there couldn't possibly be any consistent truth in them, anything pure and holy and stable that transcends their errors. In other words, inconsistency is true; the only constant is change. We've turned things completely upside down, so that now, in our minds, "Error is real and truth is error." This chaotic, changeable, error-filled, separate world is now seen as real, while the truth of our changeless, pure, unified nature as Sons of God is now seen as error, a pipe dream of fuzzy-headed idealists. Finally, if this world is real, the ego is real. After all, this is a world of separation, so the idea of separation—the ego—must be real.

In short: If we make our brothers' errors real, we will inevitably lose sight of the truth and see everything as tainted by error: our brothers, ourselves, and the world we live in. If you think about it, isn't this what we actually believe? The belief that error is at the heart of existence is reflected in "laws" like Murphy's Law ("Everything that can go wrong, will"), in statements like "Nobody's perfect," and in the acronym that gave us the word "snafu" (G-rated version): "Situation Normal, All Fouled Up." The perfection of God's creation has been replaced by the chaos of the ego's cobbled-together world.

> 16. Do not underestimate the appeal of the ego's demonstrations to those who would listen. Selective perception chooses its witnesses carefully, and its witnesses are consistent. The case for insanity is strong to the insane. For reasoning ends at its beginning, and no thought system transcends its source. Yet reasoning without meaning cannot demonstrate anything, and those who are convinced by it must be deluded. Can the ego teach truly when it overlooks truth? Can it perceive what it has denied? Its witnesses do attest to its denial, but hardly to what it has denied. The ego looks straight at the Father and does not see Him, for it has denied His Son.

It's crucial that we don't underestimate just how much we've bought into the ego's insane logic. We're like a paranoid whose entire life is based on the premise "Everyone is out to get me." Everything that happens to him, even the most benign and ordinary of events, is interpreted through the filter of that premise and thus seen as evidence of the conspiracy against him. His reasoning ends at its beginning: It starts with the belief that everyone is out to get him and ends with "proof" that everyone is out to get him. In like manner, we start with the belief that error is real, and end with "proof" that error is real, in the form of the ego's chaotic, error-filled world.

We need to wake up to the fact that this is simply nuts. The ego's bogus evidence only shows how clueless it is. This evidence doesn't demonstrate the truth of the ego's views; it only demonstrates how vigorously the ego has denied truth. If the ego denies truth, how can it teach us anything that's true? If it overlooks God's Son, how can it see the Father?

> 17. Would *you* remember the Father? Accept His Son and you will

remember Him. Nothing can demonstrate that His Son is unworthy, for nothing can prove that a lie is true. What you see of His Son through the eyes of the ego is a demonstration that His Son does not exist, yet where the Son is the Father <u>must</u> be. Accept what God does <u>not</u> deny, and it [Ur: *He*] will demonstrate its truth. The witnesses for God stand in His Light and behold what <u>He</u> created. Their silence is the sign that they have beheld God's Son, and in the Presence of Christ <u>they</u> need demonstrate nothing, for Christ speaks to them of Himself and of His Father. They are silent because Christ speaks to them, and it is His words <u>they</u> speak.

Now we come to the acceptance side of "The ego analyzes; the Holy Spirit accepts." If we want to stop denying our Father and remember Him, we must replace our obsession with our brothers' errors with *acceptance* of our brothers as the Sons of God they really are. We must refuse to listen to the ego's strident witnesses that seem to demonstrate the unworthiness of God's Son. We must reject the ego's denial and accept the Son whom God does not deny. If we do so, we will see our brothers as witnesses for Christ instead of the ego, witnesses through whom Christ speaks and tells us of Himself and His Father.

18. Every brother you meet becomes a witness for Christ or for the ego, depending on what you perceive in him. Everyone convinces you of <u>what you want to perceive</u>, and of the reality of the kingdom you have chosen for your vigilance. Everything you perceive is a witness to the thought system <u>you want to be true</u>. Every brother has the power to release you, if you choose to be free [Ur: *if you will to be free*]. You cannot accept false witness of him unless you have evoked false witnesses <u>against</u> him. If <u>he</u> speaks not of Christ to <u>you,</u> <u>you</u> spoke not of Christ to him. You hear but your own voice, and if Christ speaks through you, <u>you</u> will hear Him [in your brother].

Here's how we apply this section's teaching in a practical way. It all comes down to what we *want*. Do we want the ego or Christ? Do we want the kingdom of chaos or the Kingdom of God? Do we want bondage or freedom? Whichever we choose, every single brother we encounter will bear witness to that choice—he will provide evidence in support of that choice. If we want the ego, we will call forth witnesses for the ego in him (his errors) and accept their testimony without question. But if we want Christ, we will call forth witnesses for the Christ in him (his loving thoughts) and accept *their* testimony without question. We will let Christ speak through us and hear Him respond to us through each and every brother. Is this not a Voice you want to hear?

Application: Whenever you meet another person today, remember that this person is a witness to the ego or Christ, depending on which one you *want* to see. Affirm your desire to see Christ by saying to this person in your mind: *"I speak of Christ to you, so that I may hear you speak of Christ to me."*

VI. Waking to Redemption
Commentary by Greg Mackie

This section speaks of choosing to join the crucifixion or the resurrection. What does this mean? Literally, the words "crucifixion" and resurrection" refer to those events in Jesus' life, of course, but they also have a broader meaning. Crucifixion is the ego's way of life. The ego's world crucifies us constantly, inflicting suffering and ultimately killing us for our "sin" of separating from God. The ego goads us to crucify our brothers for their seeming "sins" against us, which compounds our suffering even more. Resurrection is escape from all this, rising up to everlasting life by recognizing the perfect innocence and holiness of everyone. Jesus recognized this in his resurrection, and by identifying with his resurrection through forgiving our brothers, we too will be resurrected. We will wake to redemption.

> 1.   It is impossible not to believe what you see, but it is equally impossible to see what you do <u>not</u> believe. Perceptions are built up on the basis of experience, and experience leads to beliefs. It is not until <u>beliefs</u> are fixed that perceptions stabilize. In effect, then, what you believe you *do* see. That is what I meant when I said, "Blessed are ye who have not seen and still believe" [John 20:39], for those who believe in the resurrection <u>will</u> see it. The resurrection is the complete triumph of Christ over the ego, not by attack but by transcendence. For Christ <u>does</u> rise above the ego and all its works, and ascends to the Father and <u>His</u> Kingdom.

"Seeing is believing," as the saying goes, but it also works the other way around: "Believing is seeing." If we add the third element of "experience," the result is a loop that goes like this: Our experiences lead to beliefs, and those beliefs lead to what we perceive. What we perceive then loops us back to the beginning of the cycle, because perceptions themselves are experiences, which reinforce our beliefs, which lead again to perceptions, etc. For instance, if I *experience* tourists who are slow drivers (a common occurrence in Sedona), I'll come to *believe* tourists are slow drivers, which will lead me to *see* slow-driving tourists. (I'll tend to notice those tourists who are driving slowly and overlook those who aren't.) This *experience* of slow-driving tourists will reinforce my belief about slow-driving tourists, etc.

This loop will be repeated endlessly unless something from outside it can inject a new element into it. This seems to be suggested by Jesus' reference to John 20:39, which speaks of believing in the resurrection *before* seeing it, which will then lead to *actually* seeing it. (One way this belief can come about is suggested in the third paragraph below.) This Bible quotation was originally addressed to "doubting Thomas," and is traditionally taken to mean that blessed are those future generations who, unlike Thomas, have not seen the resurrected Jesus in the flesh and yet still believe in his resurrection (and therefore believe he is Christ). I think Jesus is saying something similar here, but with an important difference: blessed are those who believe in the resurrection not only of Jesus but of Christ in *all* of us, our shared Self. Believing this is a blessing because it means we will see the Christ in everyone transcend the ego. We will awaken to God and His Kingdom.

> 2. Would you join in the resurrection or the crucifixion? Would you condemn your brothers or free them? Would you transcend <u>your</u> prison and ascend to the Father? [Ur: For] These questions are all the same, and are answered together. There has been much confusion about what perception means, because the [Ur: same] word is used both for awareness and for the <u>interpretation</u> of awareness. Yet [Ur: But] you cannot <u>be</u> aware without interpretation, for [Ur: and] what you perceive *is* your interpretation.

We normally think perception has two aspects: awareness of raw sense data and interpretation of that data. My eyes report a particular configuration of color, size, mass, and shape, and then I interpret it: "That's my wife, and I'm happy to see her." But here, Jesus says there is no such thing as raw sense data. Everything I see is filtered through my mind's interpretation: "what you perceive is your interpretation."

The idea behind the first three sentences here is that what we want to see will guide the interpretation that determines what we do see. If we really want to see Christ's resurrection and awaken to God, we will interpret our brothers as innocent rather than condemned for "crucifying" us. Interpreting them as innocent will lead to perceiving the resurrection of Christ in them, and this will enable us to perceive the resurrection of Christ in us.

Application: With this in mind, ask yourself the three questions in this paragraph:

> Would I join in the resurrection or the crucifixion?
> Would I condemn my brothers or free them?
> Would I transcend my prison and ascend to the Father?
> Let me recognize that these questions are all the same, and are answered together.

3. This course is perfectly clear. If you do not see it clearly, it is because [Ur: You do not see it clearly, because] you are interpreting against it, and therefore do not believe it. [your interpreting against it shows that you do not believe it.] And since [Ur: if] belief determines perception, you do not perceive what it means and therefore do not accept it. Yet different experiences lead to different beliefs, and with them different perceptions. For perceptions are learned *with* beliefs, and experience does teach [Ur: experience teaches]. I am leading you to a new kind of experience that you will become less and less willing to deny. Learning of Christ is easy, for to perceive with Him involves no strain at all. His perceptions are your natural awareness, and it is only the distortions you introduce that tire you. Let the Christ in you interpret for you, and do not try to limit what you see by narrow little beliefs that are unworthy of God's Son. For until Christ comes into His Own, the Son of God will see himself as Fatherless.

Why does the Course seem so muddy at times? It isn't just because of the iambic pentameter and fuzzy pronouns. The explanation here is a bit tricky, but here is what I think Jesus is saying: Because we resist the Course, we don't believe it. Our lack of belief leads us to interpret against it, to give ourselves convenient "reasons" to dismiss it. This leads to us perceiving its words as a muddle, which gives us the perfect excuse not to accept it.

Jesus' solution, as I hinted at in my commentary on the first paragraph, is to inject something new into the loop. The new element is a new *experience*—an experience of Christ—because this leads to different beliefs and therefore a new interpretation, a new way of seeing. Our resistance comes from trying to learn the Course under the ego's tutelage, which is a huge strain because the ego is fighting the Course's new way of seeing every step of the way. But learning it under Christ's tutelage is easy, because His way of seeing *is* the Course's and is totally natural to us. As we let Him be our Interpreter and the eyes through which we see the world, the Course will indeed become "perfectly clear."

Note: We can now add "interpretation" to the loop described in paragraph 1, making our cycle of perception complete:

1. What we *experience* teaches our beliefs.
2. Our *beliefs* guide our interpretations.
3. Our *interpretations* become what we perceive.
4. What we *perceive* becomes what we experience, and the cycle starts over.

> 4. I am *your* resurrection and *your* life. You live in me because you live in God. And everyone lives in you, as you live in everyone. Can you, then, perceive unworthiness in a brother and not perceive it in yourself? And can you perceive it in yourself and not perceive it in God? Believe in the resurrection because it has been accomplished, and it has been accomplished in you. This is as true now as it will ever be, for the resurrection is the Will of God, which knows no time and no exceptions. But make no exceptions yourself, or you will not perceive what has been accomplished for you. For we ascend unto the Father together, as it was in the beginning, is now and ever shall be, for such is the nature of God's Son as his Father created him.

We all feel crucified by the ego and the painful world it made, but Easter is our destiny. Our resurrection is the Will of God. What's more, our resurrection is already accomplished; when Jesus arose from the tomb two thousand years ago, "you were with me" (T-19.IV(B).6:5). Our task now is to "join in the resurrection," to believe in what has already been accomplished in us. To do this, we must see it as accomplished in our *brothers*. If we see *any* of our brothers as unworthy of resurrection, we will see ourselves the same way and even see God Himself as unworthy. But if we see the infinite worthiness of every Son of God without exception, we will ascend to our Father together.

I can't resist pointing out the brief reference to the traditional Christian "Doxology," which in its full form says, "Glory be to the Father and to the Son and to the Holy Spirit, as it was in the beginning, is now, and ever shall be, world without end, Amen." As is so common in the Course, a traditional formula that is normally applied to the divine is applied to *us*.

> 5.   Do not underestimate the power of the devotion of God's Son, nor the power the god he worships has over him. For he places <u>himself</u> at the altar of his god, whether it be the god <u>he</u> made or the God Who created <u>him</u>. That is why his slavery is as complete as his freedom, for he will obey <u>only</u> the god he accepts. The god of [Ur: the] crucifixion demands that he crucify, and his worshippers obey. In his name they crucify <u>themselves</u>, believing that the power of the Son of God is born of sacrifice and pain. The God of [Ur: the] resurrection demands nothing, for He does not will to <u>take away</u>. He does not require obedience, for obedience implies submission. He would only have you learn your [Ur: *own*] will and follow it, not in the spirit of sacrifice and submission, but in the gladness of freedom.

Here, Jesus gives us a strong incentive to join in the resurrection. Right now, we are fervently worshipping the "god of the crucifixion," the same "god of sickness" we read about in Chapter 10: our egoic self-image. This cruel god, like the crowd before Pilate in the Gospels, beholds the Son of God and demands, "Crucify him!" We dutifully obey by sacrificing our brothers at the altar of our precious self-image. But like those who crucified Jesus, we know not what we do: In crucifying our brothers, we crucify ourselves as well, condemning ourselves to a life of pain and suffering in this cruel world, sacrificing the happiness we had with God to the capricious demands of the ego that has enslaved us.

The "God of the resurrection," on the other hand, demands nothing. He merely asks that we learn our own will and do what we truly want: get down from the cross and celebrate together the resurrection of Christ in everyone. In doing this, we sacrifice nothing at all. Which of these options is more appealing to *you*?

> 6.   Resurrection must compel your allegiance gladly, because it is
> the symbol of joy. Its whole compelling power lies in the fact that it
> represents what <u>you</u> want to be. The freedom to leave behind everything
> that hurts you and humbles you and frightens you cannot be thrust upon
> you, but it <u>can</u> be offered you through the grace of God. And you can
> <u>accept</u> it <u>by</u> His grace, for God <u>is</u> gracious to His Son, accepting him
> without question as His Own. Who, then, is *your* own? The Father has
> given you all that is His, and He Himself is yours <u>with</u> them. Guard
> them in their resurrection, for otherwise you will not awake in God,
> safely surrounded by what is yours forever.

When we obey the god of crucifixion (the ego), it seems that things
that hurt us and humble us and frighten us are thrust upon us by the cruel
world we live in, a world created by a cruel god who demands sacrifice
of us. But the real God isn't like that at all. He offers us freedom from
this cruel world through resurrection, and the whole idea of freedom
being *thrust* upon us is an oxymoron. Resurrection doesn't need to be
forced down our throats anyway, because it is inherently compelling to
us. We truly *want* to be liberated from the pain of this cruel world. If you
offer a meal to a starving man, you don't have to force him to accept
it—he'll wolf it down on his own. Who would turn down something that
brings him joy?

What must we do to accept our resurrection? Accept all members of
the Sonship, from Jesus himself to Osama bin Laden, as our own dear
brothers who share the same Father and the same Self. Only by guarding
them in their resurrection, seeing the resurrected Christ in them, can we
experience our own resurrection to eternal life with God.

> 7.   You will not find peace until you have removed the nails from the
> hands of God's Son, and taken the last thorn from his forehead. The
> Love of God surrounds His Son whom the god of [Ur: the] crucifixion
> condemns. Teach not that I died in vain. Teach rather <u>that I did not die</u>
> by demonstrating that <u>I live in you</u>. For the <u>undoing</u> of the crucifixion
> of God's Son is the work of the redemption, in which everyone has a
> part of equal value. God does not judge His guiltless [Ur: blameless]
> Son. Having given <u>Himself</u> to him, how could it be otherwise?

In traditional Christianity, Jesus has a unique and supremely valuable role in the redemption: dying on the cross for our sins. But here, he tells us that all of us have an *equal* role in the redemption: to teach that Jesus did *not* die by demonstrating that he lives in us. We do this by letting Jesus' forgiving love shine through us, demonstrating to our brothers through our forgiveness that God does not judge his blameless Son, so there is no need for anyone to die for sins. Have you nailed someone to a cross recently with a hateful thought, a harsh word, an unloving act? Your part in the redemption is to take this person down from the cross of your condemnation and see him or her as the risen Christ.

> 8.   You have nailed <u>yourself</u> to a cross, and placed a crown of thorns upon your own head. Yet you <u>cannot</u> crucify God's Son, for the Will of God cannot die. His Son <u>has been</u> redeemed from his own crucifixion, and you cannot assign to death whom God has given eternal life. The dream of crucifixion still lies heavy on your eyes, but what you see in dreams is not reality. While you perceive the Son of God as crucified, you are asleep. And as long as you believe that <u>you</u> can crucify him, you are only having nightmares. You who are beginning to wake are still aware of dreams, and have not yet forgotten them. The forgetting of dreams and the awareness of Christ come with the awakening of others to <u>share</u> your redemption.

When we nail our brothers to a cross, we nail ourselves to our own cross. (I've always wondered how we nail the second hand down after we've nailed the first hand down.) But we can't *really* do this: It is only a nightmare. Just as Jesus did not really die on the cross, we can't really die either. God has given us all eternal life, so all these crucifixions are really attempts to accomplish the impossible. No matter how many times we try to kill the Christ in us, he'll keep rolling the stone away and leaving the tomb. And how do we awaken from the nightmare of crucifixion? Once again, by "the awakening of others to share your redemption," by seeing the risen Christ in our brothers.

> 9.   You will awaken to your own call, for the Call to awake is <u>within</u> you. If I live in you, you <u>are</u> awake. Yet <u>you</u> must see the works I do through you, or you will not perceive that I have done them unto <u>you</u>. Do not set limits on what you believe I can do <u>through</u> you, or you will

not accept what I can do *for* you. Yet [Ur: For] it is done <u>already</u>, and unless you give <u>all</u> that you have received you will not know that your redeemer liveth, and that <u>you</u> have awakened <u>with</u> him. Redemption is recognized <u>only</u> by sharing it.

Jesus lives within each of us, and has called us to awaken and be glad. His call is really our own call, the call of the Christ in us. Yet we won't hear this call unless we share it with everyone by letting Jesus work *through* us and seeing the effects of those works. In other words, we must extend miracles from Jesus to our brothers. He healed the sick and raised the dead two thousand years ago, and only by seeing him work equally limitless miracles *through* us can we recognize all that he has already done *for* us. Yet again, the familiar refrain: We must give redemption to recognize the redemption we have received.

> 10. God's Son *is* saved. Bring only <u>this</u> awareness to the Sonship, and you will have a part in the redemption as valuable as mine. For your part must be <u>like</u> mine if you learn it of me. If you believe that <u>yours</u> is limited, <u>you are limiting mine</u>. There is no order of difficulty in miracles because all of God's Sons are of equal value, and their equality <u>is</u> their oneness. The whole power of God is in every part of Him, and nothing contradictory to His Will is either great or small. What does not exist <u>has</u> no size and no measure. To God <u>all</u> things are possible. And to Christ it is given to be like the Father.

As I mentioned earlier, traditional Christianity teaches that Jesus had a unique and supremely valuable role in salvation. As the only begotten Son of God, he did things that we could never do in our wildest dreams. I recently read an article that emphasized this idea by taking aim at the popular slogan "What would Jesus do?" In the author's view, "We cannot do what Jesus would do because we are not divine."

Nonsense, Jesus says here. We are all God's Sons. We are all of equal value. We all have a part in salvation just like Jesus' part, a part that is just as valuable and unlimited as his, a part he is teaching us in the pages of his Course. Because we have all the power of God within us and everything that seems to oppose that power is nothing, we can perform limitless miracles just as Jesus did. Jesus rose from crucifixion to eternal life two thousand years ago, and we can do the same. By seeing the risen

Christ in everyone, we will join in Jesus' resurrection and ascend to the Father together.

Visualization: From the Cross to the Risen Christ

Think of a person you have condemned for his "sins" against you.

Your condemning him is an act of crucifying him, so visualize this person nailed to a cross with a crown of thorns on his head.

See the blood flowing from his wounds.

See the look of agony on his face.

How do you feel about seeing this person crucified?

Now you realize that in crucifying this person, you have crucified yourself as well.

You too are nailed to a cross, directly facing this person, with a crown of thorns on your own head.

You too have ghastly wounds with blood flowing from them.

You too are in agony.

The two of you are suffering together.

What can you do to alleviate this suffering?

There is only one way out of your shared agony.

Say, *"I will not find peace until I have removed the nails from the hands of [name], and taken the last thorn from his forehead."*

To end your agony, you must see this person whom you have crucified as the risen Christ, as pure and innocent and holy as Jesus himself.

Now, see this person facing you transform before your eyes.

See a radiant light of holiness, the Great Rays, extending from him.

See the nails disappear from his hands and feet.

See the crown of thorns disappear from his head.

See the bloody wounds fade away.

See the agony on his face melt into a beaming smile of gratitude and relief.

See him step down from the cross.

VI. Waking to Redemption

Notice that as you see this, you are transformed as well.
See the Great Rays of holiness shining forth from you.
See your nails and your crown of thorns disappear.
See your wounds fade away.
You too feel immense gratitude and relief as you step down from your
  cross.

Now, greet this person warmly as a brother in Christ, redeemed from
  crucifixion.
Smile, embrace him, and welcome him into your heart.
He is the risen Son of God, and so are you.
The nightmare of crucifixion is over.
You have both wakened to redemption.

VII. The Condition of Reality
Commentary by Greg Mackie

This section contains one of the Course's first extended discussions of what it calls the *real world*. In this section, to quote from Robert's Course glossary, the real world is said to be "composed of the loving thoughts that went into the making and maintaining of this world,…which are all that is *real* about the *world* we made."

> 1. The world as <u>you</u> perceive it cannot have been created by the Father, for the world is <u>not</u> as you see it. God created <u>only</u> the eternal, and everything <u>you</u> see is perishable. Therefore, there must be another world that you do <u>not</u> see. The Bible speaks of a <u>new</u> Heaven and a <u>new</u> earth [Rev. 21:1], yet this cannot be literally true, for the eternal are not <u>re</u>-created. To <u>perceive</u> anew is merely to perceive again, implying that before, or in the interval between [the phrase "or in the interval between" was apparently added by the editors], <u>you were not perceiving at all</u>. What, then, is the world that awaits your perception <u>when you see it</u>?

In the world we see with our physical eyes, everything is impermanent. Some things last longer than others, but all things perish eventually:

> What *seems* eternal all will have an end. The stars will disappear, and night and day will be no more. All things that come and go, the tides, the seasons and the lives of men; all things that change with time and bloom and fade will not return. (T-29.VI.2:7-9)

How can this be a world created by an eternal God, Whose creations are as eternal as Himself? To perceive such a world is to perceive nothing. Yet the Course insists there is a "new earth," something eternal within this world that we *can* behold if we'll just open our eyes—or better, open our minds. What exactly is this "new earth," this other world?

> 2. Every loving thought that the Son of God ever had is eternal. The loving thoughts his mind perceives [Ur: Those which his mind

98

perceived] in this world are the world's only reality. They are still perceptions, because he still believes that he is separate. Yet they are eternal because they are loving. And being loving they are like the Father, and therefore cannot die. The real world can actually be perceived. All that is necessary is a willingness to perceive nothing else. For if you perceive both good and evil, you are accepting both the false and the true and making no distinction between them.

That other world, the real world, consists of "loving thoughts." Even in our insanity, we couldn't shut love out entirely when we made this world; the loving thoughts the Holy Spirit inspires have slipped in under the ego's radar. Strictly speaking, loving thoughts in the world are only *reflections* of reality, since they are in the realm of perception. Yet since they are loving, the heart of them is eternal and will remain even when the world is undone.

To see these loving thoughts, all we must do is be willing to see *nothing else as real*. Notice that to do this, we must practice a form of judgment or discernment: We must (with the Holy Spirit's help) distinguish between good and evil, the true and the false, and commit ourselves fully to the good and the true.

> 3.   The ego may see [Ur: sees] some good, but never only good. That is why its perceptions are so variable. It does not reject goodness entirely, for that you could not accept. But it always adds something that is not real to the real, thus confusing illusion and reality. For perceptions cannot be partly true. If you believe in truth and illusion, you cannot tell which is true. To establish your personal autonomy you tried to create unlike your Father, believing that what you made is [Ur: believing what you made to be] capable of being unlike Him. Yet everything true [Ur: Yet everything in what you have made that *is* true,] is like Him. [Only this is the real world, and] Perceiving only the real world [Ur: this] will lead you to the real Heaven, because it will make you capable of understanding it.

We continue with the theme of discernment. Many Course students believe any form of distinguishing between good and evil is a judgment to be avoided. The Course does say elsewhere that our own thoughts are such a mixed bag that none of them could be called either "good" or "bad" (see, for instance, W-pI.4.1:6-7). Yet as we see here, the Course does want us to distinguish (again, with the Holy Spirit's help) between the *truly* good—loving thoughts, the real world—from the evil ego thoughts that obscure it. Of course, the evil is nothing but illusion, but that's the entire point: If we don't distinguish the evil from the good, we will believe in both truth *and* illusion and not be able to tell them apart.

Lack of such discernment is what keeps the ego going. It throws everything into one pot—good with evil, truth with illusion—so it can have, in its eyes, the best of both worlds. It keeps just enough good to convince us that ego life has its roses along with its thorns (who wants pure evil?), and just enough evil to keep us from figuring out that our true nature as Sons of God is pure goodness. To remember Heaven, we need to dump the illusory garbage we made as rebellious teenagers thumbing our noses at our Father, and recognize only the true things we made in spite of ourselves: the loving thoughts that make up the real world.

> 4. The perception of goodness is not knowledge, but the denial of the <u>opposite</u> of goodness enables you to recognize [Ur: perceive] a condition in which opposites do not exist. And this *is* the condition of knowledge. <u>Without</u> this awareness you have <u>not</u> met its conditions, and until you do you will not know it is yours already. You have made many ideas that you have placed between yourself [Ur: yourselves] and your Creator, and these beliefs are the world as <u>you</u> perceive it. Truth is not absent here, but it <u>is</u> obscure. You do not know the difference between what you have made and what God created, and so you do not know the difference between what you have made and what *you* have created. To believe that you can perceive the real world is to believe that you can know yourself. You <u>can</u> know God because it is His Will to <u>be</u> known. The real world is all that the Holy Spirit has saved for you out of what you have made, and to perceive only this is salvation, because it is the recognition that reality is <u>only what is true</u>.

We return to heavenly knowledge by perceiving only goodness and denying the reality of evil. This is the true denial the Course spoke of earlier (T-2.II.1-2). When we perceive only good, we no longer perceive opposites. And "no opposites" is the condition of knowledge in both senses of "condition": The *state* of knowledge has no opposites, and the *prerequisite* for recognizing knowledge is perceiving no opposites. We have made evil illusions that obscure the truth of pure goodness. They have blotted out awareness of both God's creations and our own. But we can choose to see only the loving thoughts that went into the making of this world, "all that the Holy Spirit has saved for you out of what you have made." Perceiving only the real world is the way to know ourselves and God again.

Application: Bring to mind a difficult situation you're facing, one in which you're seeing "evil" in some form (misbehaving people, pain, limitation, etc.). Now, ask the Holy Spirit for a new perception of this situation: *"Holy Spirit, help me to see only goodness here. Help me to deny the opposite of goodness. Help me to see only the real world, all the loving thoughts You have saved for me out of what I made. Help me to see only what is true."*

VIII. The Problem and the Answer
Commentary by Greg Mackie

1.   This is a very simple course. Perhaps you do not feel you need a course which, in the end, teaches that only reality is true. But do you believe it? When you perceive [Ur: have perceived] the real world, you will recognize that you did not believe it. Yet the swiftness with which your new and only real perception will be translated into knowledge will leave you but an instant to realize that this alone [Ur: that this judgment] is true. And then everything you made will be forgotten; the good and the bad, the false and the true. For as Heaven and earth become one, even the real world will vanish from your sight. The end of the world is not its destruction, but its translation into Heaven. The reinterpretation of the world is the transfer of all perception to knowledge.

If you saw a course in a college catalog called Truth 101, in which you would learn that "only reality is true," would you sign up for it? Most likely, you'd say, "Well, duh. I'm not throwing away good money for that." Yet oddly enough, we really need such a course, because we're so insane that we actually believe reality *isn't* true and illusion *is* true. Thank God Jesus has provided one for us. The vision that will come to us from taking his Course will convince us that all we believed about reality before was utter nonsense.

The last section talked about perceiving only what is good and true in what we made, and letting go of the evil and illusory. This is the vision of the real world. Now Jesus describes the transition from the real world into knowledge, a state in which "everything you made will be forgotten; the good and the bad, the false and the true." Traditional Christianity depicts the end of the world as a massive cataclysm full of blood and gore and pits of sulfur, but here it is merely the world's "translation into Heaven." As the Manual section on the end of the world puts it, the world "will not be destroyed nor attacked nor even touched. It will merely cease to seem to be" (M-14.2:11-12). In the twinkling of an eye, the dream will be over and we will awaken in our Father's Arms.

2.   The Bible tells you to become as little children [Matthew 18:3]. Little children recognize that they do not understand what they perceive, and so they <u>ask what it means</u>. Do not make the mistake of believing that <u>you</u> understand what <u>you</u> perceive, for its meaning <u>is</u> lost to you. Yet the Holy Spirit has saved its meaning <u>for </u>you, and if you will <u>let</u> Him interpret it [Ur: *for* you], He will restore to you what you have thrown away. Yet while [Ur: As long as] you <u>think you know</u> its meaning, you will see no need to ask it <u>of </u>Him.

The next couple of paragraphs emphasize how little we know, because if we think we're too advanced for that Truth 101 course, we'll never sign up for it. We must give up our notion that we're too smart for the room and "become as little children." This Bible verse is often taken to mean that children are innocent and wise, but here it means that they are *lacking understanding* and recognize that fact. Just as children humbly ask a trusted adult what things mean (at least until they become teenagers), we should do the same with the Holy Spirit.

3.   You do not know the meaning of <u>anything</u> you perceive. <u>Not one thought you hold is wholly true.</u> The recognition of this is your firm beginning. You are not misguided; you have accepted no [real] guide at all. Instruction in perception is your great need, <u>for you understand nothing</u>. <u>Recognize</u> this but do not accept it, for understanding is your inheritance. Perceptions are learned, and you are not without a Teacher. Yet your willingness to learn of Him depends on your willingness to question <u>everything</u> you learned <u>of yourself</u>, for you who [Ur: have] learned amiss should not be your own teacher [Ur: teachers].

We're all convinced that we know so much, but this paragraph throws a bucket of cold water on our pretensions. We do not know the meaning of *anything* we perceive. Not one thought we have is *wholly* true. Like Ferris Bueller, we've taken the day off—no, the *lifetime* off—from the school of the Holy Spirit.

It's not fun to find out that you're a complete ignoramus. Yet finding this out is a good thing. It is our "firm beginning." It will get us to sign up for Truth 101. It makes us willing to question all the nonsense we've taught ourselves. Best of all, it helps us to realize that being an ignoramus isn't our destiny. We are smart enough to graduate with honors from the school of the Holy Spirit, if we will simply let Him be our Instructor in perception.

Application: Take the opportunity now to let go of all you think you know and sign up for the Holy Spirit's Truth 101 course. Say, *"I do not know the meaning of anything I perceive. Not one thought I hold is wholly true. I understand nothing. Therefore, instruction in perception is my great need. Holy Spirit, I resign as my own teacher and accept You as my Teacher. Only You will give me the understanding that is my inheritance."*

4.   No one can withhold truth except from himself. Yet God will not refuse you the Answer He gave [Ur: you]. Ask, then, for what is yours, but which you did <u>not</u> make, and do not defend yourself <u>against</u> truth. <u>You</u> made the problem God <u>has</u> answered. Ask yourself [Ur: yourselves], therefore, but one simple question:

Do I want the problem or do I want the answer?

Decide for the answer and you <u>will</u> have it, for you will see it as it is, and it is yours already.

Application: Let's really ask this question. Think of how little you really know, how many problems you've made for yourself in your life, all the silly things you've taught yourself and furiously defended against truth. Realize that you don't have to keep wallowing in the problem. God has given you the Answer to all your apparent ignorance, all your problems, all the false things you taught yourself. With as much willingness as you muster, ask (repeatedly if you find it helpful):

Do I want the problem or do I want the answer?

"Decide for the answer and you will have it, for you will see it as it is, and it is yours already."

5.   You may complain [Ur: You complain] that this course is not sufficiently specific for you to understand and use [Ur: to understand

it *and use it*]. Yet perhaps you have not done what it specifically advocates. [Ur: Yet it has been *very* specific, and *you have not done what it specifically advocates.*] This is not a course in the <u>play</u> of ideas, but in their <u>practical application</u>. Nothing could be more specific than to be told [Ur: very clearly] that if you ask you <u>will</u> receive. The Holy Spirit will answer <u>every</u> specific problem as long as you believe that problems <u>are</u> specific. His answer is both many and one, as long as you believe that the One <u>is</u> many. You may be afraid of His specificity [Ur: Realize that *you are afraid of His specificity*], for fear of what you think it will <u>demand</u> of you. Yet only by asking will you learn that nothing [Ur: that is] of God demands <u>anything</u> of you. God <u>gives</u>; He does <u>not</u> take. When you refuse to ask, it is because [Ur: You are refusing to ask, because] you believe that asking is <u>taking</u> rather than [Ur: asking is *taking*, and you do not perceive it as] <u>sharing</u>.

Many Course students see the Course as primarily a *teaching* that doesn't provide practical means to actually live the teaching. For instance, I've heard Course teachers say that the Course teaches forgiveness but never gives us instructions for how to forgive. But this is simply not true. The Course is a complete *path* that provides not only teaching but "practical application." It gives us all sorts of specific instructions, including instruction in how to forgive.

Helen and Bill apparently also thought the Course was lacking in specific instructions for practical application. Jesus refuted this by reminding them of the specific instruction he had just given them in the last paragraph: "Ask, then, for what is yours," and "God will not refuse you the Answer He gave you." Not only has the Holy Spirit answered the ultimate problem of separation, but within that answer is the answer to every specific problem we have.

The real issue behind our complaint, then, is not that the Course isn't specific enough, but that we're afraid it's *too* specific. We don't do what the Course specifically advocates—we're afraid to ask the Holy Spirit for the answer to our problems—because we think that to ask Him is to take from Him, and therefore He will demand some sort of sacrifice from us in return. Yet only by asking will we recognize that asking is sharing, not taking, and so He will share His answer with us without demanding any sacrifice at all.

6.   The Holy Spirit will give you only what is yours, and will take nothing in return. For what is yours is everything, and you share it with God. That is its reality. Would the Holy Spirit, Who wills only to restore, be capable of misinterpreting the question you must ask to learn His answer? You *have* heard the answer, but you have misunderstood the question. You believe [Ur: You have believed] that to ask for guidance of the Holy Spirit is to ask for deprivation.

Our belief that the Holy Spirit will demand sacrifice when we ask for His answer to our problems is a profound misunderstanding of the question. He demands nothing. He only gives us what is already ours— He is the administrator of a limitless trust fund in which our Father has placed our inheritance. *We* misinterpret the question as a call for sacrifice, but *He* does not. And we will hear His answer once we understand the question as He does.

7.   Little child [Ur: children] of God, you do not understand your Father. You believe in a world that takes, because you believe that you can get by taking. And by that perception you have lost sight of the real world. You are afraid of the world as you see it, but the real world is still yours for the asking. Do not deny it to yourself, for it can only free you. Nothing of God will enslave His Son whom He created free and whose freedom is protected by His Being. Blessed are you who are willing to [Ur: you who will] ask the truth of God without fear, for only thus can you learn that His answer is the release from fear.

We think the Holy Spirit's answer will demand sacrifice because we're so wedded to our belief in getting by *taking*. In our world, no one gives anything without demanding his pound of flesh, so we naturally think God must be the biggest Butcher of all. The real world, however, is completely different. Since it consists only of loving thoughts, it is a world of pure giving that reflects God's pure giving. How can we perceive the real world if we're terrified of the price God will demand for it? We need to set aside our terror long enough to ask the truth of God with an open mind. Only by asking like "little children" will we learn that our Father's answer *frees* us from terror.

8.   Beautiful child of God, you are asking only for what I promised you. Do you believe I would deceive you? The Kingdom of Heaven *is*

within you. Believe that the truth is in me, for I <u>know</u> that it is in <u>you</u>. God's Sons have nothing they do not share. Ask for truth of any Son of God, and you have asked it of me. Not one of us but has the answer in him, to give to anyone who asks it <u>of</u> him.

Application: This is another beautiful message from Jesus. Read the paragraph as a personal message to you, inserting your name at appropriate points.

Asking for God's answer is asking not for sacrifice but for the Kingdom of Heaven, the priceless gift Jesus promised us, a gift he shares with all the Sonship. Since the gift of the Kingdom is *in* everyone, we can ask it *of* everyone. Each person we encounter thus gives us a precious opportunity. We so often see people as merely instruments to get our earthly needs met, but we can just as easily see them as holy messengers of God who can give God's answer to us, if we will only remember to ask.

9.   Ask anything of God's Son and his Father will answer you, for Christ is not deceived in [mistaken about] His Father and His Father is not deceived in Him. Do not, then, be deceived in your brother, and see only his loving thoughts as his reality, for by denying that his mind is split <u>you will heal yours</u>. Accept him as his Father accepts him and heal him [by giving him] unto Christ, for Christ is his healing <u>and yours</u>. Christ is the Son of God Who is in no way separate from His Father, Whose <u>every</u> thought is as loving as the Thought of His Father by which He was created. Be not deceived in God's Son, for thereby you <u>must</u> be deceived in yourself. And being deceived in yourself you <u>are</u> deceived in your Father, in Whom no deceit is possible.

The phrase "deceived in" essentially means "mistaken about," with the implication (in the word "deceived") that this is an *intentional* mistake. When this paragraph says we shouldn't be deceived in something, it means that we should stop fooling ourselves about it. We are willfully perceiving it falsely, and we need to stop doing that.

We are deceived in our brothers whenever we see them as Jekyll and Hyde mixtures of loving thoughts and (mostly) unloving thoughts. This is how we normally see people, right? Even those we love the most have their dark side in our eyes—we even speak of "love-hate relationships." This view of our brothers inevitably leads to a view of ourselves and even God as equally mixed bags. But to receive God's answer, we must see *only* loving thoughts as our brothers' reality. We must see the real world in them. Accepting them as God accepts them—seeing them as Christ, Whose love is as pure and limitless as his Father's—will heal their minds and ours.

> 10. In the real world there is no sickness, for there is no separation and no division. Only loving thoughts are recognized, and because no one is without <u>your</u> help, the Help of God goes with <u>you</u> everywhere. As you become willing to <u>accept</u> this Help <u>by asking for It</u>, you will give It <u>because you want It</u>. Nothing will be beyond your healing power, because nothing will be denied your simple request. What problems will not disappear in the presence of God's Answer? Ask, then, to learn of the reality of your brother, <u>because this is what you will perceive in him</u>, and you will see <u>your</u> beauty reflected in his [Ur: *Him*].

I see in this paragraph a picture of us as healers, the function we will assume once we stop pushing away God's answer and receive the real world from Him. Living in the real world, we will see no sickness as real and recognize only loving thoughts everywhere. Our only goal will be to be truly helpful to everyone, and therefore the Help of God will go with us everywhere. We will give this Help without reservation, because we want It and recognize that giving It is the way to receive It. The Holy Spirit will flow through us unimpeded, and so absolutely nothing will be beyond our healing power—we will be miracle workers just as Jesus was.

Application: We become this kind of healer by asking to learn of the reality of our brothers, so let's do that now. Think of a person whom you are seeing as less than totally loving, someone against whom you are nursing a grievance. Now, say to the Holy Spirit: *"Reveal the reality of this brother to me. Let me see only his loving thoughts. Let me see his beauty, in which I will see the reflection of my own."*

11. Do not accept your brother's variable perception of himself for his split mind is yours, and you will not accept your healing without his. For you share the real world as you share Heaven, and his healing is yours. To love yourself is to heal yourself, and you cannot perceive part of you [your brother] as sick and achieve your [Ur: *own*] goal. Brother, we heal together as we live together and love together. Be not deceived in God's Son, for he is one with himself and one with his Father. Love him who is beloved of his Father, and you will learn of the Father's Love for you.

Whatever they may say on the surface, virtually all people see themselves as those Jekyll and Hyde mixtures of loving and unloving thoughts. A person sees herself helping her friend through a crisis one moment and yelling at her kids the next, and concludes that she is a hopeless mess of conflicting impulses. Our job as healers is to not accept our brothers' "variable perception" of themselves, but instead share the real world with them, in which only their loving thoughts are real. We join with Jesus in seeing them this way: "Brother, we heal together as we live together and love together." And since we are all one, extending this loving perception of our brothers is how we recognize that *we* are not Jekyll and Hyde either. We, too, are beings of pure love. As we love those who are beloved of God, we recognize God's infinite love for us.

12. If you perceive offense in a brother pluck the offense from your mind, for you are offended by Christ and are deceived in Him. Heal in Christ and be not offended by Him, for there is no offense in Him. If what you perceive offends you, you are offended in yourself and are condemning God's Son whom God condemneth not. Let the Holy Spirit remove all offenses [Ur: offense] of God's Son against himself and perceive no one but through His guidance, for He would save you from all condemnation. Accept His healing power and use it for all He sends you, for He wills to heal the Son of God, in whom He is not deceived.

Jesus continues his discussion of our function as healers with a fascinating spin on a well-known saying from the gospels: "And if thine eye offend thee, pluck it out, and cast it from thee" (Matthew 18:9; cf. Matthew 5:29, Mark 9:47). There also seems to be a subtle reference to the story of the woman caught in adultery (John 8:2-11), where Jesus says to her after she tells him no man has condemned her, "Neither do I condemn thee."

We see once again a familiar refrain: how we see our brothers is how we see ourselves. If we are offended by what our brothers do and condemn them as unloving wretches, we are condemning ourselves. We are condemning Christ Himself, which is the height of arrogance. When we feel offended by anyone, we should "pluck the offense from [our] mind." We should let the Holy Spirit remove the offense and help us see the person truly. This frees *everyone* from condemnation.

Application: Think of someone who has "offended" you and say to the Holy Spirit: *"Help me pluck this offense from my mind. Help me to see that this person is Christ, in Whom there is no offense. Remove the offense for me and let me perceive this person only through your guidance, which will save me from all condemnation."*

Note: This is one of the places in the Course that states quite clearly that the Holy Spirit *sends* us people for healing. It can be helpful to remember this as we go through our day: The people we encounter don't come to us randomly, but are sent by divine appointment for a holy encounter. How would seeing all encounters this way transform your day?

13. Children perceive frightening ghosts and monsters and dragons, and they are terrified. Yet [Ur: But] if they ask someone they trust for the [Ur: *real*] meaning of what they perceive, and are willing to let their own interpretations go in favor of reality, their fear goes with them. When a child is helped to translate his "ghost" into a curtain, his "monster" into a shadow, and his "dragon" into a dream he is no longer afraid, and laughs happily at his own fear.

14. You, my child [Ur: children], are afraid of your brothers and of your Father and of yourself [Ur: *yourselves*]. But you are merely deceived in them. Ask what they are of the Teacher of reality, and hearing His answer, you too will laugh at your fears and replace them with peace. For fear lies not in reality, but in the minds of children who do not understand reality. It is only their lack of understanding that frightens them, and when they learn to perceive truly they are not afraid. And because of this they will ask for truth again when they are frightened. It is not the reality of your brothers or your Father or yourself that frightens you. You do not know what they are, and so you perceive

them as ghosts and monsters and dragons. <u>Ask</u> what their reality is [Ur: *Ask* of their reality] from the One Who knows it, and He will tell you what they are. For you do <u>not</u> understand them, and because you are deceived by what you see you <u>need</u> reality to dispel your fears.

We return to the image of children. If you'll recall, paragraph 2 said that the biblical injunction to become as little children meant that, like little children who don't understand what they perceive, we should ask someone we trust—the Holy Spirit—what things mean. Like little children, we are afraid of what we don't understand. We cower in a room shrouded in the ego's darkness, and so we see our beloved brothers, our loving Father, and ultimately ourselves as horrible ghosts and monsters and dragons, terrifying to behold. But when we let the Holy Spirit come in and turn on the light, we will see only love everywhere we look, and our fear will vanish. And this will be such a wonderful experience that we will ask for His help again the next time we are frightened.

What ghost or monster or dragon is terrifying you right now? Osama bin Laden? George W. Bush? Those people building nukes in Iran? Your spouse? "Ask what they are of the Teacher of reality, and hearing His answer, you too will laugh at your fears and replace them with peace."

15. Would you not exchange your fears for truth, if the exchange is yours for the asking? For if God is not deceived in you, you can be deceived only in <u>yourself</u>. Yet you can learn the truth about [Ur: of] yourself from [Ur: of] the Holy Spirit, Who will teach you that, as part of God, deceit in <u>you</u> is impossible. When you perceive yourself without deceit, you will accept the real world in place of the false one you have made. And then your Father will lean down to you and take the last step <u>for</u> you, by raising you unto Himself.

We think we're trapped by our fears because we think what we fear is *real*. If you're facing a real dragon, just saying "I'm not afraid" won't do the trick; you need some sturdy armor, a good sword, and more than a little luck. But in truth, our fears are only self-deceptions; all our dragons are dreams. Therefore, we can exchange our fears for truth whenever we want. Do we want the problem or the answer? If we want the answer, we can ask the Holy Spirit for the truth about ourselves. He will teach us that since we are of God, *true* self-deception is impossible. We can fool ourselves for a while, but our true nature can't be hidden forever. The Holy Spirit will give us a vision of ourselves that reveals the real world, and once the real world is all we perceive, God will lift us to Heaven by taking the last step Himself.

Commentaries on Chapter 12

THE HOLY SPIRIT'S
CURRICULUM

I. The Judgment of the Holy Spirit
Commentary by Greg Mackie

1. You have been told not to make error real [T-9.IV.4-5], and the way to do this is very simple. If you <u>want</u> to believe in error, you would <u>have</u> to make it real because it is not true. But <u>truth</u> is real in its <u>own</u> right, and to believe in truth *you do not have to do anything.* Understand that you do not respond to anything directly, but to your interpretation of it [Ur: Understand that you do not respond to stimuli, but to *stimuli as you interpret them*]. Your interpretation thus becomes the <u>justification</u> for the response. That is why analyzing the motives of others is hazardous to <u>you</u>. If you decide that someone is <u>really</u> trying to attack you or desert you or enslave you, you will respond as if he had actually <u>done</u> so, having [Ur: *because* you have] made his error <u>real</u> to you. To interpret error is to <u>give it power</u>, and having done this you <u>will</u> overlook truth.

Analyzing the motives of others is one of the great parlor games of the ego—even Course students seem to enjoy pointing out where people who disagree with them are "really" coming from. But this analysis is "hazardous" to us, because it inevitably leads to misinterpretation of others, which leads in turn to an inappropriate response to them.

What happens is this: We analyze other people's motives and conclude that those motives are dark to the core. Those slimeballs out there are truly bent on attacking and deserting and enslaving us. Therefore, in our minds, they are evil sinners. Of course, the motives of their egos *are* dark, but in truth people are not their egos and listening to their egos is only an error, not a sin. By misinterpreting others as *truly* evil sinners, we make their errors real, and this "justifies" our response to them: some form of attack.

We do this because we *want* to believe in error, so to stop doing this we must replace our desire for error with a commitment to the truth. "To believe in truth, *you do not have to do anything,*" which in this context means "You don't have to analyze the motives of others." We'll learn more about this as the section continues.

2.   The analysis of ego-motivation is very complicated, very obscuring, and <u>never</u> without [Ur: the risk of] your own ego-involvement. The whole process represents a clear-cut attempt to demonstrate <u>your own</u> ability to understand what you perceive. This is shown [Ur: demonstrated] by the fact that you <u>react</u> to your interpretations as if they <u>were</u> correct [Ur: and control your reactions behaviorally, *but not emotionally*]. You may then control your reactions behaviorally, <u>but not emotionally</u>. This would obviously be a split or an attack on the integrity of your mind, pitting one level within it against another. [Ur: This is quite evidently a mental split, in which you have attacked the integrity of your mind, and pitted one level within it against another.]

Analyzing other people's ego motivations is a complicated and confusing undertaking, as any psychologist can tell you. When we do this, our own egos are highly likely to get involved—recall the earlier statement that "The ego analyzes; the Holy Spirit accepts" (T-11.V.13:1). Our analysis is a way of "proving" to ourselves and to the world that we really understand what makes people tick. Our very reaction to our interpretations seems to demonstrate that they are not interpretations but facts: "How could I *not* get angry when she did that to me?" And once we've decided that our dark interpretations *are* facts, it seems impossible to change our emotional state. The best we can do is pretend everything is fine while we seethe inside. We put on a happy face while the smoke is coming out of our ears.

3.   There is but one interpretation of [Ur: *all*] motivation that makes any sense. And because it is the Holy Spirit's judgment it requires no effort at all on your part. Every loving thought is true. <u>Everything else</u> is an appeal for healing and help [Ur: That is what it *is*], regardless of the form it takes. Can anyone be justified in responding with anger to a brother's plea for help? No response can <u>be</u> appropriate <u>except</u> the willingness to give it <u>to</u> him, for this and <u>only</u> this is what he is <u>asking</u> for. Offer him anything <u>else</u>, and <u>you</u> are assuming the right to attack his reality by interpreting it <u>as you see fit</u>. Perhaps the danger of this to your <u>own</u> mind is not yet fully apparent. If you believe [Ur: maintain] that an appeal for help is something <u>else</u> you will <u>react</u> to something else. Your response will therefore be inappropriate to reality as <u>it</u> is, but <u>not</u> to your perception <u>of</u> it.

Giving up our analysis of other people's motivations opens our minds to the Holy Spirit's interpretation, which is one of the best-known ideas in the entire Course: everything they think, say, and do is either an expression of love or a call for help. This new interpretation completely transforms our response. When we think people are attacking or deserting or enslaving us, it seems perfectly natural for us to attack back. We even justify our attack by saying, "She asked for it!" But in fact, this response is totally inappropriate because attack is *not* what they have asked for. It is a gross misinterpretation of what they really want, as if a guy in a bar said "Give me a shot" and the bartender responded by blowing him away with a shotgun. But if we see other people's apparent attacks as calls for help, a whole different response logically follows: a willingness to *offer* help.

Application: Bring to mind someone you think is attacking or deserting or enslaving you in some way. Now repeat these words to help you see the Holy Spirit's interpretation of this person's motivation: *"Every loving thought [name] has is true. Everything else is an appeal for healing and help, including this apparent attack. Can I be justified in responding with anger to [name]'s plea for help? No response can be appropriate except the willingness to give it to him, for this and only this is what he is asking for."* Then ask the Holy Spirit how He would have you help this person, and do as He instructs.

4. There is nothing to prevent you from recognizing all calls for help as exactly what they are except your own imagined [Ur: *perceived*] need to attack. It is only this that makes you willing to engage in endless "battles" with reality, in which you deny the reality of the need for healing by making it unreal. You would not do this except for your unwillingness to accept reality as it is, and which you therefore withhold from yourself. [Ur: You would not do this except for your *unwillingness* to perceive reality, *which you withhold from yourself.*]

As I mentioned in my commentary on the last paragraph, when we think people are attacking us, it seems natural to attack back. In this paragraph, we see why we interpret others' actions as attacks instead of calls for help: we *want* to attack, and seeing others as attackers gives us the perfect justification. Committed to the ego and its illusions, we don't want to see the ultimate reality of our brothers or ourselves. Therefore, we deny the reality of our brothers' need for healing, because responding to that need with true helpfulness is what reveals ultimate reality to us.

> 5. It is surely good advice to tell you not to judge what you do not understand. No one with a personal investment is a reliable witness, for truth to him has become what he <u>wants</u> it to be. If you are unwilling to perceive an appeal for help <u>as what it is</u>, it is because <u>you</u> are unwilling to give help <u>and to receive it</u>. [Ur: The analysis of the ego's "real" motivation is the modern equivalent of the inquisition. For in both, a brother's errors are "uncovered," and he is then attacked *for his own good*. What can this be, *but* projection? For *his* errors lay in the minds of his *interpretors* {sic}, for which they punished *him*.] To fail to recognize a call for help is to refuse help. [Ur: Whenever you fail to recognize a call for help, you are *refusing* help.] Would you maintain that you do not <u>need</u> it? Yet this <u>is</u> what you are maintaining when you refuse to recognize a brother's appeal, for only by <u>answering</u> his appeal *can* [Ur: can *you*] you be helped. Deny him <u>your</u> help and you will <u>not</u> recognize [Ur: perceive] God's Answer to <u>you</u>. The Holy Spirit does <u>not</u> need your help in interpreting motivation, but you <u>do</u> need <u>His</u>.

If we're determined to attack, we're going to find justifications to attack, truth be damned. Like Spanish inquisitors determined to meet their quota of heretics, we'll find all the "evidence" we need to burn our brothers at the stake. Most of us these days regard the Spanish Inquisition as insane, but our inquisition of our brothers is equally insane because it is rooted in our stubborn refusal of the Holy Spirit's help. We *do* maintain that we do not need it. How crazy is that?

"Only by answering [your brother's] appeal for help can *you* be helped." This line belongs on everyone's bathroom mirror. We all say we want God, but are often reluctant to help others. We even have Course "justifications" for not helping others, like the oft-repeated idea that we don't need to help others because there's no one out there anyway. If we're serious about finding God, we need to turn over interpretation of our brothers' motivations to the Holy Spirit, so we can hear the calls for help we must answer to find God's Answer for ourselves.

> 6. Only appreciation is an appropriate response to your brother.

Gratitude is due him for both his loving thoughts and his appeals for help, for both are capable of bringing love into your awareness if you perceive them truly. And all your sense of strain comes from your attempts not to do just this. How simple, then, is God's plan for salvation. There is but one response to reality, for reality evokes no conflict at all. There is but one Teacher of reality, Who understands what it is. He does not change His Mind about reality because reality does not change. Although your interpretations of reality are meaningless in your divided state, His remain consistently true. He gives them to you because they are for you. Do not attempt to "help" a brother in your way, for you cannot help yourself [Ur: yourselves]. But hear his call for the Help of God, and you will recognize your own need for the Father.

The beauty of accepting the Holy Spirit's interpretation of our brothers' motivations is that we can be grateful for our brothers either way. If they offer love, we can respond gratefully with love. If they offer a call for help (even in the form of an attack), we can respond equally gratefully with loving help. How simple! Instead of straining to figure out just what is "really" behind our brothers' actions, we can let our Teacher tell us whether a brother is expressing love or calling for love. Then we can then offer a single, unconflicted response: love. Our own attempts to "help" our brothers by pointing out the error of their ways and trying to drag them up from their state of sinfulness will inevitably backfire. But being truly helpful under the Holy Spirit's tutelage will open us to our need for the Help of God.

Application: Bring to mind the same person you used in the last application, or a different person if you wish. Say to this person, *"Only appreciation is an appropriate response to you, [name]. I am grateful to you for both your loving thoughts and your appeals for help, for both are capable of bringing love into my awareness if I perceive them truly."*

7.   Your interpretations of your brother's needs are your interpretation of <u>yours</u>. By giving help you are <u>asking for it</u>, and if you perceive but one need in yourself you <u>will</u> be healed. For you will recognize God's Answer as you want It to be, and if you want It in truth, It will be truly yours. Every appeal you answer in the Name of Christ brings the remembrance of your Father closer to <u>your</u> awareness. For the sake

of <u>your</u> need, then, hear every call for help as what it is, so God can answer *you.*

Again, it comes down to *wanting.* Do we really want God's Answer? We can honestly answer yes only if we recognize that our brothers want It just as much and if we are willing to help them find It. The way we ask for help truly is by *giving* it. Every time we give it, we bring the memory of God closer to our awareness. How much more helpful would you be to the people in your life if you really believed this?

> 8.   By applying the Holy Spirit's interpretation of the reactions of others more and more consistently, you will gain an increasing awareness that <u>His</u> criteria are equally applicable to <u>you.</u> For to <u>recognize</u> fear is not enough to escape <u>from</u> it, although the recognition <u>is</u> necessary to demonstrate the <u>need</u> for escape. The Holy Spirit must still <u>translate</u> the fear into truth. If you were <u>left</u> with the fear, once you had <u>recognized</u> it, you would have taken a step <u>away</u> from reality, not <u>towards</u> it. Yet we have repeatedly emphasized the need to recognize fear and face it <u>without disguise</u> as a crucial step in the undoing of the ego. Consider how well the Holy Spirit's interpretation of the motives of others will serve you then. Having taught you to accept [as real] only loving thoughts in others and to regard everything else as an appeal for help, He has taught you that <u>fear</u> itself is an appeal for help. This is what <u>recognizing</u> fear really means. If you do <u>not protect</u> it, <u>He</u> will reinterpret it. That is the ultimate value [Ur: *to you*] in learning to perceive attack as a call for love. We have already learned [Ur: surely] that fear and attack are inevitably associated. If <u>only</u> attack produces fear, and if you see attack as the call for help that it <u>is</u>, the unreality [Ur: *reality*] of fear <u>must</u> dawn on you. For fear <u>is</u> a call for love [this is the "reality" of fear, the real nature of fear], in unconscious recognition of what has been denied.

These last few paragraphs shift into a discussion of fear. The Course has emphasized that we must recognize our fear and face it without blinders if we want our egos to be undone by the Holy Spirit. Here, we are told that the Holy Spirit's interpretation of the motives of others will help us do this. How?

I find the explanation here a bit difficult to follow, but here's what I think Jesus is saying. By seeing everything that comes from our brothers as either an expression of love or a call for help, we will see that their attacks on us are a call for help. When we see this, we will see that our fear—which stems from our attacks on them, the attacks we "justify" by seeing dark motives in them—is *also* a call for help. We will recognize that the true nature of fear is a call for love. With this recognition, we can then call upon the Holy Spirit to undo our fear, to translate our fear into truth.

> 9.   Fear is a symptom of your own deep sense of loss. If when you perceive it in others you learn to <u>supply</u> the loss, the basic <u>cause</u> of fear is removed. Thereby you teach yourself that fear does not exist <u>in you</u> [Ur: for you have in *yourself*, the means for removing it]. The means for removing it is in yourself, and you have <u>demonstrated</u> this by <u>giving</u> it. Fear and love are the only emotions of which you are capable. One is false, for it was made out of denial; and denial <u>depends</u> on the belief in what is denied for its <u>own</u> existence. By interpreting fear correctly as a <u>positive affirmation of the underlying belief it masks</u>, you are undermining its perceived usefulness by rendering it useless. Defenses that do not work <u>at all</u> are <u>automatically</u> discarded. If you raise what fear conceals to <u>clear-cut unequivocal predominance</u>, fear becomes meaningless. You have denied its power to conceal love, which was its only purpose. The veil [Ur: mask] that <u>you</u> have drawn across the face of love has disappeared.

What is the purpose of fear? According to this paragraph, it is to "conceal love." It is a defense against love. But the Holy Spirit's interpretation of others' motivations has the power to render this defense against love useless. How? The presence of fear in us seems to prove to us that we have truly lost love. But if we see other people's fears and attacks as calls for love and then actually *give* them love in response, we prove to ourselves that we haven't lost love. We demonstrate that love—the means of removing fear—truly exists in us, and therefore fear can *not* truly exist in us. Fear is just a false belief designed to deny love. Even the apparent existence of fear indirectly proves we have love in us, because if we didn't, why would we have to work so hard to deny it?

Therefore, though the ego has used fear to deny love, the Holy Spirit's reinterpretation of fear turns the tables and raises love "to clear-cut unequivocal predominance." Fear as a defense against love has proven to be utterly futile. What's the point of using a defense if it doesn't work?

10. If you would look upon love, which *is* the world's reality, how could you do better than to recognize, in every defense <u>against</u> it, the underlying appeal *for* it? And how could you better learn of its reality than by answering the appeal for it by <u>giving</u> it? The Holy Spirit's interpretation of fear <u>does</u> dispel it, for the <u>awareness</u> of truth cannot <u>be</u> denied. Thus does the Holy Spirit replace fear with love and translate error into truth. And thus will <u>you</u> learn of Him how to replace your dream of separation with the fact of unity. For the separation is only the <u>denial</u> of union, and correctly interpreted, attests to your eternal knowledge that union is true.

What an amazing plan the Holy Spirit has given us to enable us to see the real world, the world that consists of nothing but loving thoughts. When we see defenses against love (like fear) in others or ourselves, He can reinterpret them as affirmations of the love being defended against. When we analyze motives and tell ourselves that our brothers are bent on attacking or deserting or enslaving us, He can reinterpret their motives as calls for love and guide us to recognize the reality of love in ourselves by answering that call *with* love. In this way, all the ego's defenses are turned on their ear. All the ego's lemons are turned into lemonade. Fear is translated into love, error is translated into truth, and separation is translated into union.

Application: For me, the idea of interpreting everything as an expression of love or a call for help is a profoundly beautiful idea with staggering implications for the world. I also think there's great power in imagining how things might look if our highest ideals were realized—a power we see in the enduring appeal of the John Lennon song "Imagine." So, dare to dream. Try to imagine what your life would be like if you saw every single attack—from your spouse's dirty look to the horror of 9/11—as a call for help. Try to imagine how the world would be transformed if everyone perceived attack this way. What might such a life and such a world look like? I'm not looking for any particular answer here. This is simply an invitation to stretch your mind and let yourself speculate. Enjoy!

II. The Way to Remember God
Commentary by Robert Perry

This section is really two different discussions. The first three paragraphs are a discussion of the function of the miracle worker, whose role is to deny his patient's denial of his inherent perfection. The final seven paragraphs are a powerful discussion of our need to look at our hateful perceptions and let the Holy Spirit show us that they are just groundless illusions, so that we can be led past their frightening images to our goal—the memory of our perfectly loving nature.

> 1.   Miracles are merely the translation of denial into truth. If to love oneself is to <u>heal</u> oneself, those who are sick do <u>not</u> love themselves. Therefore, they are asking for the love that would heal them, but which they are <u>denying to themselves</u>. If they knew the truth about themselves they could not be sick. The task of the miracle worker thus becomes *to deny the denial of truth*. The sick must heal <u>themselves</u>, for the truth is <u>in</u> them. Yet having <u>obscured</u> it, the light in <u>another</u> mind must shine into theirs because that light *is* theirs.

A person is only ill because she is denying the truth of who she is, which makes her unable to love herself, and thus unable to *heal* herself. Can someone else heal her? Yes—that is, after all, the whole role of the miracle worker. The light in his mind shines into her mind. This light is not really from the outside, for the light in the miracle worker's mind is the same light that lies buried within the sick person's mind. It's like receiving a blood transfusion from your identical twin. Is it really someone else's blood?

Application: How do we heal another? We deny his denial of truth. Let's try applying this. Think of someone you know who is sick. Then imagine yourself looking deep within that person's mind, far below the conscious level. There, you see a dark cloud, the content of which is this belief: "I am not God's Son, and therefore I'm not lovable, and therefore I don't deserve to be healed." This is his denial of the truth about himself.

This is the root of the illness. Now speak to this part of the person's mind, and deny the truth of this dark belief. Say happily,

My brother, what you think is not the truth (W-pI.134.7:5)

2.   The light in them shines as brightly <u>regardless</u> of the density of the fog that obscures it. If you give no power to the fog to obscure the light, it <u>has</u> none. For it has power <u>only</u> if the Son of God gives power <u>to</u> it. He must <u>himself</u> withdraw that power, remembering that all power is of God [see 11.V.3:6]. <u>You can remember this for all the Sonship.</u> Do not allow your brother not to remember, for his forgetfulness is <u>yours</u>. But <u>your</u> remembering is <u>his</u>, for God cannot be remembered alone. *This is what you have forgotten.* To perceive the healing of your brother as the healing of yourself is thus the way to remember God. For you forgot your brothers <u>with</u> Him, and God's Answer to your forgetting is but the way to remember.

I love this image of seeing our brothers' bodies and personalities as nothing but fog that obscures the light in them. It's not that the light in people comes in different strengths. The light in your worst enemy is the exact same strength as the light that shone in Jesus. The *only* thing that differs is "the density of the fog that obscures it." Each person has given power to his or her personal fog—which is why it seems to be there. Yet healing occurs when that power is withdrawn, when that person remembers that *all* power is of God. It is our job to remember this for everyone, for by remembering this *for* them we remember God *with* them.

Application: Again think of someone you know who is sick. Visualize their sickness and the dark beliefs that give rise to it as nothing but a thick layer of fog. Then look beneath the fog to the light in this person, which shines just as brightly as it has shone in any of history's great saints and masters. Then say,

I give no power to this fog
For all power is of God.
*If I remember this **for** you,*

*I will remember God **with** you.*
Only the light in you is real.

3.   Perceive in sickness but another call for love, and offer your brother what he believes he cannot offer himself. Whatever the sickness, there is but one remedy. You will be made whole as you make whole, for to perceive in sickness the appeal for health is to recognize in hatred the call for love. And to give a brother what he really wants is to offer it unto yourself, for your Father wills you to know your brother as yourself. Answer his call for love, and yours is answered. Healing is the Love of Christ for His Father and for Himself.

In every instance of hate, no matter how vehement, our job is to see the hidden desire for love. In every sickness, our job is to see the desire for wholeness. In our brother's darkest manifestations, we must see only his wish for light, and then we must grant him this wish. We must give our brother what he wants but believes he can't have. And when we do, we have given it to ourselves. For by treating his call as if it were our own, we will discover that his call *is* our own, because his *being* is our own. We will come to know our brother *as* ourselves. We will have done our Father's Will.

4.   Remember what was said about the frightening perceptions of little children [11.VIII.13-14], which terrify them because they do not understand them. If they ask for enlightenment and accept it, their fears vanish. But if they hide their nightmares they will keep them. It is easy to help an uncertain child, for he recognizes that he does not understand what his perceptions mean. Yet you believe that you do understand yours [Ur: that you *do* know]. Little child, you are hiding your head under the cover [Ur: covers] of the heavy blankets you have laid upon yourself. You are hiding your nightmares in the darkness of your own false certainty, and refusing to open your eyes and look at them.

In "The Problem and the Answer" (11.VIII.13-14), Jesus spoke of little children who in the dark of their bedrooms think that a curtain is really a ghost, that a shadow is really a monster, and that their dream of a dragon was actually real. Now the metaphor continues, as the children are so certain of what they see that their only option is to hide under their covers, shut their eyes, and refuse to look. If they would only really look, and if they would only ask an adult who knows, their fears would vanish.

We, of course, are those children. And the ghosts, monsters, and dragons are what we perceive as our brothers and our Father. Are we willing to really look at those perceptions and see that they are not bad or mean, but simply false? Are we willing to ask the real Adult in this situation—the Holy Spirit—for the truth? Or would we rather stay in the smug—and terrifying—darkness of our own false certainty?

> 5.   Let us not save nightmares, for they are not fitting offerings for Christ, and so they are not fit gifts for <u>you</u>. Take off the covers and look at what you are afraid of. Only the anticipation will frighten you, for the reality of nothingness cannot be frightening. Let us not delay this, for your dream of hatred will not leave you without help, and Help is here. Learn to be quiet in the midst of turmoil, for quietness is the <u>end</u> of strife and this [the journey we are on] is the journey to peace [the journey to the end of strife]. Look straight at every image that rises to delay you, for the goal is inevitable because it is eternal. The goal of love is but your right, and it belongs to you <u>despite</u> your dreams [Ur: your preference].

Application: Think of someone who seems to you to be a monster, or a ghost, or a dragon. Then say silently to this person,

> *I see you as a [monster, ghost, dragon, etc.]*

Now look at your image of that person (as a monster, ghost, dragon, or whatever). Be willing to look at the hate in that image—*your* hate, not the other person's hate. See how the image is literally a picture of your hate, a caricature whose shape has been contorted by the force of your hate. As such, it is commentary on *your* mind, not on the other person. Now say to yourself,

> *I need not be frightened by this image.*
> *For my hate is really nothing dressed up as something.*

Then try to get a sense of looking past the image to the light of love behind it. Say to the Holy Spirit,

Holy Spirit, help me look past this image of hate.
Help me realize it is just an image, nothing more.
Help me see past it to my goal, the goal of love.

6.   You still want what God wills, and no nightmare can defeat a child of God in his purpose. For your purpose was given you by God, and you must accomplish it because it is His Will. Awake and remember your purpose, for it is your will to do so. What has been accomplished for you must be yours. Do not let your hatred stand in the way of love, for nothing can withstand the Love of Christ for His Father, or His Father's Love for Him.

This paragraph explains why we will succeed in our attempts to look past the images of hate that we have made up. We will succeed because love is what we really want. Love is our purpose. It is our true goal. It is God's Will that we reach it and it is *our* will. Given this, nothing can stand in our way. No hateful image, flimsy and insubstantial, will stand before our will to find and rest in eternal love.

7.   A little while and you will see me, for I am not hidden because *you* are hiding. I will awaken you as surely as I awakened myself, for I awoke for you. In my resurrection is your release. Our mission is to escape from crucifixion, not from redemption. Trust in my help, for I did not walk alone, and I will walk with you as our Father walked with me. Do you not know that I walked with Him in peace? And does not that mean that peace goes with *us* on the journey?

While we refuse to look at our hateful images, we will not see the real brothers behind them. Yet they are there, in all their glorious reality. Jesus is one of them. The only reason we cannot see him is that we are sure that he is the monster we have made of him, and so we are hiding under our covers, refusing to look. Yet the whole reason he is here is to wake us up from our crazy nightmares. He woke up from all nightmares, and not for himself alone; he awoke for us. He, therefore, holds the key to our awakening. He is not a monster in the dream; he is the guide *out* of the dream. He is the one who can show us that all the monsters and dragons and ghosts and witches and ogres we see around us are actually beautiful divine brothers. Why not, then, trust in his help? Why not invite him to walk with us as our guide in perception? If we do, we will surely walk in peace.

> 8.   There is no fear in perfect love. We will but be making perfect to you what is already perfect in you [i.e., love]. You do not fear the unknown but the known [the love in you]. You will not fail in your mission because I did not fail in mine. Give me but a little trust in the name of the complete trust I have in you, and we will easily accomplish the goal of perfection together. For perfection *is*, and cannot be denied. To deny the denial of perfection is not so difficult as to deny truth, and what we can accomplish together will [Ur: *must*] be believed when you see it as accomplished.

To understand this paragraph, you need to realize that Jesus is taking us on a journey to the goal of attaining perfect love within us. Have we ever thought about this as our goal? Do we hold as our goal the idea of being perfectly loving? Whether we do or not, that *is* our goal.

We cannot fail to reach this goal because we have a guide—Jesus—who has made this journey before. He knows the way there. We drag our feet along the way simply because we fear the destination. We fear our buried knowledge of perfect love. Yet we have no reason to fear it, for fear cannot exist in perfect love. Moreover, this is not a journey *up* the mountain, going *against* gravity. We already did that when we denied the perfect love in us. That was an incredibly difficult feat. Now, Jesus is leading us back down the mountain. This is the easy way. We are simply going back to our nature, to what we already are: perfect love.

> 9.   You who have tried to banish love have not succeeded, but you who choose to banish fear must [Ur: *will*] succeed. The Lord is with you, but you know it not. Yet your Redeemer liveth, and abideth in you in the peace out of which He was created. Would you not exchange this awareness for the awareness of fear? When we have overcome fear—not by hiding it, not by minimizing it, and not by denying its full import in any way—this is what you will really see [that your Redeemer abides in you]. You cannot lay aside the obstacles [Ur: obstacle] to real vision without looking upon them [Ur: it], for to lay aside means to judge

against. If <u>you</u> will look, the Holy Spirit will judge, <u>and</u> He <u>will judge truly</u>. Yet He cannot shine away what <u>you</u> keep hidden, for you have not offered it <u>to</u> Him and He <u>cannot</u> take it <u>from</u> you.

We have tried to banish our knowledge of perfect love and replace it with a state of chronic fear. However much it appears we have succeeded at this, we will never succeed. Yet we must succeed when we try to reverse this condition, when we choose to banish fear. How could we fail when the Holy Spirit abides in us? If only we could see His presence there, we would be filled with certain hope. And we will see it, when we have overcome our fear.

How do we overcome our fear? Our typical answer is that we find ways to stuff it down. We hide it, minimize it, and deny its full import. Yet that is the way to *keep* it. Instead, we have to look our fears straight in the face. That's all we need to do—just look. If *we* will look, *He* will judge them truly. He will show us that our fears are groundless.

> 10. We are therefore embarking on an organized, well-structured and carefully planned program aimed at learning how to offer to the Holy Spirit everything you do <u>not</u> want. <u>He</u> knows what to <u>do</u> with it. You do <u>not</u> understand how to use what He knows. Whatever is given [Ur: revealed to] Him that is not of God is gone. Yet you must look at it [Ur: must reveal it to] <u>yourself</u> in perfect willingness, for otherwise His knowledge remains useless <u>to</u> you. Surely He will not fail to help you, since help is His <u>only</u> purpose. Do you not have greater reason for fearing the world as you perceive it, than for looking at the cause of fear and letting it go forever?

This paragraph needs to be seen as the conclusion to the discussion that began in paragraph 4. In other words, *because* we need to look at our nightmares—so that the Holy Spirit can show us that they are just illusions—we have this course. It is "an organized, well-structured and carefully planned program aimed at learning how to offer to the Holy Spirit" all of our nightmarish perceptions, so that He can undo them. If we simply reveal to Him what is not of God in our mind, it will be gone. But to do this, we must reveal it to ourselves in *perfect willingness*— perfect willingness to see it for what it really is. This may sound fearful, but we will be looking at what is really nothing and letting it go. Can that be as fearful as the world we see around us every day?

III. The Investment in Reality
Commentary by Robert Perry

This is a truly amazing section. It is the well-known section where Jesus tells us, "If your brothers ask you for something 'outrageous,' do it *because* it does not matter." This line has frustrated and puzzled Course students since day one. Yet it is the encapsulation of an absolutely brilliant discussion that leads up to it. Because of the importance of this discussion, I will allow myself more space to discuss the first four paragraphs of this section, after which my comments will return to their usual length. Yet don't take that to mean that the latter paragraphs are not important. If we can really understand them, they have the power to rock our world. You'll see what I mean.

> 1.   I once asked you to [Ur: asked if you were willing to] sell all you have and give to the poor and follow me. This is what I meant: If you [Ur: had] have no investment in anything in this world, you can [Ur: could] teach the poor where <u>their</u> treasure is. The poor are merely those who have invested wrongly, and they are poor indeed! Because they are in need it is given you to help them, since you are among them. Consider how perfectly your lesson would be learned <u>if you were unwilling to share their poverty</u>. For poverty is lack, and there is but one lack since there is but one need.

Jesus here claims to reveal what he really meant when he told us to sell all we have and give to the poor and follow him. Before going further, let's turn to the place where he says this. It is often called the story of the rich young ruler:

> And behold, one came up to him, saying, "Teacher, what good deed must I do, to have eternal life?" And he said to him, "...If you would enter life, keep the commandments"....The young man said to him, "All these I have observed; what do I still lack?" Jesus said to him, "If you would be perfect, go, sell what you possess and give to the poor, and you will have treasure in heaven; and come, follow me." When the young man heard this he went away sorrowful; for he had great

possessions. (Matthew 19:16-22 RSV)

This counsel, though directed at the life of one person, significantly shaped Christianity's view of what it meant to really follow Jesus. Drawing upon the authority of these words, the vow of poverty became one of the three basic vows (along with obedience and chastity) of monastics. The message became clear: If you really want to follow Jesus all the way—"if you would be perfect"—you must go beyond mere observance of a righteous life, you must renounce all worldly possessions. You must remove yourself from normal society.

Jesus here wants to set the record straight. He wants to clarify what he was really driving at. "This is what I meant," he says. "If you have no investment in anything in this world, you can teach the poor where their treasure is." The important thing was not the physical act of selling your possessions, but what that act symbolized: the inner act of relinquishing your investment in this world. Likewise, the real gift to the poor was not the money from selling your possessions. It was *showing* the poor your lack of investment in the world. This is what teaches them "where their treasure is." The word "treasure" refers to the biblical passage's mention of "treasure in heaven." It also refers to that famous saying from the gospels: "Store up for yourselves treasures in heaven…for where your treasure is, there will your heart be also." In summary, if you let go of all your investment in the world, your example can show the poor that their treasure is not on earth but in Heaven.

But what does that mean? We need clarification on the clarification! Let us, then, turn to the next lines in this section.

The third sentence radically redefines the class of the poor: "The poor are merely those who have invested wrongly." In financial terms, of course, if you invest all your money in a bad business venture, you lose your shirt. But Jesus here is referring not to financial investment in a certain business venture. The poor are those who are *emotionally* invested in the *world*. They thought that investing their minds and hearts in the world would make them wealthy inside. Instead, they lost it all. They lost the one thing truly worth having: the peace of God. This is the "one lack" and "one need" mentioned in the passage above.

By this definition, nearly everyone in the world is poor, including those we would call the super-rich, and including ourselves. We too are deeply invested in this world, and as a result we feel empty and impoverished inside. Though we may have nice clothes and fancy houses, we are poor in the truest sense of the word. We lack our heart's desire. We lack the awareness of God. Our mission, as the above passage says, is to leave our own condition of poverty behind, and to help the rest of the poor do likewise. But how? The answer to this becomes startlingly clear as the section continues.

> 2.   Suppose a brother insists on having you do something you think you do not want to do. His very insistence should tell you that <u>he believes salvation lies in it</u>. If you insist on refusing and experience a quick response of opposition, <u>you</u> are believing that <u>your</u> salvation lies in *not* doing it. You, then, are making the same mistake <u>he</u> is, and are making his error real to both of you. Insistence means <u>investment</u>, and what you invest in is <u>always</u> related to your notion of salvation. The question is always two-fold; first, *what* is to be saved? And second, *how* can it <u>be</u> saved?

Jesus here gives an example of investment in the world. What specifically are we invested in here in this passage? The answer: external happenings. When we think of investment in the world, we probably think of investment in material possessions and money. But the investment he's talking about here goes much deeper. It's investment in what happens, in how things go.

This paragraph shows poverty in action. It portrays in everyday terms exactly what Jesus means by being poor. A brother insists that you do something. His insistence means he is *invested* in your doing this because he thinks his *salvation* lies in it. He has invested in the world—in the *happenings* of the world. He has done so believing that he will obtain salvation from this investment. That is why he is poor. The happenings of the world will never make him genuinely happy, never give him real inner wealth. He has invested everything he's got in a worthless company.

But so have you. For you too insist. You insist on refusing his request. This means that you also are invested in the happenings of the world, thinking that salvation lies in them. "You, then, are making the same mistake he is."

How many times have we found ourselves in such a situation? Someone insists that we do something, and we refuse. Our wife insists that we take out the trash. Our husband insists that we stop nagging him. Our child insists that we fix her a certain kind of food. And we refuse, and not just because we don't want to do it. We refuse on principle, as a way of salvaging our self-esteem, and as a way of closing the door on all those future demands we will surely invite if we give in. It is as if we are a sand castle, and refusing is our way of holding back the waves from washing us into oblivion.

I know this feeling very well. By refusing I feel like I am standing my ground and keeping myself intact. How ironic it is that what I am really doing, says the Course, is impoverishing myself. I am investing my heart and mind in a bunch of meaningless forms outside myself. How can they ever make me happy? Even if they are arranged exactly as I want, how complete will I really feel? As he insists and I refuse, my brother and I are like two homeless guys fighting over a crumb, not realizing that the only thing our fight accomplishes is to reinforce in our minds just how destitute we are.

> 3.   Whenever you become angry with a brother, for <u>whatever</u> reason, you are believing that the <u>ego</u> is to be saved, <u>and to be saved by attack</u>. If <u>he</u> attacks, you are agreeing with this belief; and if <u>you</u> attack, you are reinforcing it. *Remember that those who attack are poor.* Their poverty asks for gifts, <u>not</u> for further impoverishment. You who could help them are surely acting destructively if you accept their poverty <u>as yours</u>. If you had not invested <u>as they had</u>, it would never occur to you to overlook their need.

The last paragraph ended by saying that our notion of salvation is our answer to two questions: "First, *what* is to be saved? And second, *how* can it be saved?" This paragraph says that whenever we become angry, we are "believing that the ego is to be saved, and to be saved by attack." This puts a new perspective on our refusal. We thought that refusing was a justified defense needed to save our self-respect. But what we call our cherished self-respect is what the Course calls our *ego*. And what we call defense is what the Course calls *attack*. What we were really doing, then, was attacking in order to save our ego. The ego is just an image we hold in our mind, an image of ourselves as separate, miserable, and vicious. Using attack to save the face of this image is our notion of salvation. Yet no matter how much we save *it*, we never truly respect ourselves, nor feel like *we* have really been saved.

While we are busy making ourselves poor, we have also blinded ourselves to what our brother is really asking for. He is asking for relief from poverty. His attack demonstrates that he is poor, and in his lack he is grasping at whatever scrap he can get. The solution is not to try to further impoverish him, and deepen our own poverty in the process. The solution is to give him gifts, to help lift him out of poverty altogether.

Application: Think of a time when you insisted on refusing a request. In what way were you trying to save your ego? Perhaps you were trying to save face or save your dignity. Or perhaps you were trying to keep control. Whatever it was, can you see that this amounted to an attempt to save your image, to save your ego?

Now think of the person you saw as attacking you. See this person not as rich with what he or she was taking from you, but as poor, and therefore in need. You thought you were the one in need, but actually, it was the other person, the aggressor, who was in need. How does that change the picture?

> 4.   *Recognize what does not matter*, and if your brothers ask you for something "outrageous," do it *because* it does not matter. Refuse, and your <u>opposition</u> establishes that it <u>does</u> matter to you. It is only you, therefore, who have <u>made</u> the request outrageous, [Ur: for nothing can *be* asked *of* you,] and <u>every</u> request of a brother is <u>for</u> you. Why would you insist in <u>denying</u> him? For to do so is to deny yourself and impoverish both. He is asking for salvation, as <u>you</u> are. Poverty is of the ego, and never of God. No "outrageous" requests <u>can</u> be made of one who recognizes what is valuable and wants to accept nothing else.

We come at last to that difficult line! Yet now we have all the context we need to understand it. When someone asks something "outrageous" of us, we go ahead and do it. Why? As a relinquishment of our investment in the world. We let go of the idea that our salvation lies in external happenings. We let go of the notion that happiness comes from controlling situations (i.e., attacking) in order to save our ego. We realize it simply doesn't matter if things go the way our ego prefers. Now our bodies will still ride the roller coaster of outer events, but our minds will remain at peace, resting safely in their real treasure house beyond this world.

The reason that "outrageous" is in quotes is because we now see that our brother's request was not outrageous at all. We see that he was really asking for salvation. He was making a holy request. He may have been asking in a strange form, but, as we now realize, the form is precisely what doesn't matter. What matters is that he is poor and needs our help. How do we help him? By showing him our freedom from investment in outer circumstances. By showing him it just doesn't matter. Our gift to him takes the *form* of doing what he asks, but the gift itself is the demonstration of our lack of investment.

Further, *we* need the help we can give him: "and every request of a brother is for you." If we deny his request, we deny ourselves. We impoverish ourselves. As you can see above, the original dictation of this part went like this: "It is only you, therefore, who have *made* the request outrageous, for nothing can *be* asked *of* you, and *every* request of a brother is *for* you." It changes everything when I think of this request as being not *of* me, but *for* me.

Think of some of the tug-of-wars you have been in: which channel to watch on the TV, which restaurant to go to, which vacation to take, which color to paint the house. Is it possible that the real pain in these situations was not the threat of not getting your way, but your investment in *any* way? Is it possible that caring so intensely about meaningless forms is a symptom of inner poverty—and a cause as well? Could it be that what was most needed in those situations was for you to demonstrate a whole other way of being, free of the stifling investment in external events?

> 5.   Salvation is for the mind, and it is attained through peace. This is the only thing that <u>can</u> be saved and the <u>only</u> way to save it. Any response <u>other</u> than love arises from a confusion about the "what" and the "how" of salvation, and this is the <u>only</u> answer. Never lose sight of this, and never allow yourself to believe, even for an instant, that there is another answer. For you will surely place yourself among the poor, who do not understand that they dwell in abundance and that salvation is come.

While we're trying to save our image (ego) through defending our boundaries (through attack), we ought to be trying to save our *mind* through acquiring *peace*. And how can we obtain this peace of mind?

We'll never get it by defending the image. That only leaves us feeling petty, hollow, and guilty—in short, *poor*. The only way to gain peace is to reach out to our poverty-stricken brothers with love. This is so central to the entire way home that Jesus urges us to never forget it: "Never lost sight of this, and never allow yourself to believe, even for an instant, that there is another way."

> 6.   To identify with the ego is to attack yourself and make yourself poor. That is why everyone who identifies with the ego feels deprived. What he experiences then is depression or anger, because [Ur: but] what he did was to exchange Self-love for self-hate, making him afraid of himself. He does not realize this. Even if he is fully aware of anxiety he does not perceive its source as his own ego identification, and he always tries to handle it by making some sort of insane "arrangement" with the world. He always perceives this world as outside himself, for this is crucial to his adjustment. He does not realize that he makes this world, for there is no world outside of him.

Let's approach these ideas in reverse order. We think there is a world outside of us, one that is clearly independent of us. We know it is, because it keeps acting against our wishes and making us terribly anxious. To calm our anxiety, we seek an "arrangement" with the world. If the arrangement is sufficiently to our liking, we assume that the anxiety will abate. To see the relevance of this, you might ask yourself, "What arrangement am I seeking with the world?"

What we don't realize is that we are making the world we see. We are dreaming up the overall structure; we are inviting certain forms into our experience; and we are interpreting those forms as we wish. The world, then, is our effect; it cannot be the cause of our anxiety.

Why, then, are we all so anxious? If it's not because the world won't agree to the arrangement we want, why is it? It's because we are identifying with the ego. It's because the image we are trying so desperately to save is fundamentally unlovable. To adapt a saying from the Course, you can take a skeleton, paint rosy lips on it, and put it in a gorgeous dress, but can you really love it? Let's be honest: On some level, thinking we are this image results in feeling poor and deprived. It results in hating ourselves. Can you feel that within you?

7.   If only the loving thoughts of God's Son <u>are</u> the world's reality, the real world <u>must</u> be <u>in his mind</u>. His insane thoughts, too, must be in his mind, but an <u>internal</u> conflict of this magnitude he cannot tolerate. A split mind <u>is</u> endangered, and the recognition that it encompasses <u>completely</u> opposed thoughts within itself <u>is</u> intolerable. Therefore the mind projects the split, <u>not</u> the reality. <u>Everything</u> you perceive as the outside world is merely your attempt to maintain your ego identification, for everyone believes that identification is salvation. Yet consider what has happened, for thoughts do have consequences to the thinker. You have become <u>at odds</u> with the world as you perceive it, because you think <u>it</u> is antagonistic to you. <u>This is a necessary consequence of what you have done.</u> You have projected outward what <u>is</u> antagonistic to what is inward, and therefore you would <u>have</u> to perceive it this way. That is why you <u>must</u> realize that your hatred <u>is</u> in your mind and <u>not outside it</u> before you can get rid of it; and why you <u>must</u> get rid of it <u>before</u> you can perceive the world as it really is.

This is a very important account of projection and very similar to the one in "The Unbelievable Belief" (7.VIII.3). Our minds contain two classes of thoughts. There is what is natural to us: loving thoughts. But then there is also what is antagonistic to our nature: hateful thoughts. These hateful thoughts are not so much *related* to the ego as they *are* the ego. The ego *is* hate. The presence of such hate within us is intolerable. It is so contradictory to our loving nature that we can't stand the inner conflict. It produces incredible anxiety.

The solution? Project the hate onto the world. Now we look within and see loads of loving thoughts. We seem so good, so spiritual, so well-intentioned. And now we look without and see wave upon wave of hate breaking upon our shores, causing us never-ending anxiety. Why does the world keep treating us like this, we wonder? Yet the hate that is coming at us from the world, the hate that so conflicts with our pure, loving nature, the hate that causes us so much anxiety, is our *own*. We are just seeing it *as if it were outside*. A very spooky thought, is it not?

You'd think we were projecting the hate to escape it, but the real reason we project it is to *keep* it, "to maintain...ego identification." Because now we are convinced that the hate within (the ego) is not the problem—what, me hate? No, it's the hate out there. That's the problem. Of that we are all certain.

8.   I said before [Ur: Long ago we said] that God so loved the world that He gave it <u>to</u> His only-begotten Son [Ur: (that whosoever believeth on him should never see death)] [see 2.VII.5:14]. God <u>does</u> love the real world, and those who perceive its reality <u>cannot</u> see the world of death. For death is not <u>of</u> the real world, in which everything reflects the eternal. God gave you the real world in exchange for the one you made out of your split mind, and which <u>is</u> the symbol of death. For if you could <u>really</u> separate yourself from the Mind of God you <u>would</u> die. [Ur: And the world you perceive *is* a world of separation {from the Mind of God}.]

Thank God that He gave us the real world. For the world we see now is one in which we are separate from God (after all, when I look around this world, I don't see any God). Yet if we could really separate ourselves from God, we would cease to be. We would die. This world, therefore, is just one long exercise in death. The good news is: We don't have to see this world.

What is not said here but implied is that, just as our hateful thoughts show us the world, so our loving thoughts show us the real world. And if we let go of our hate, the real world is the only thing that we will see.

9.   The world you perceive is a world of separation. Perhaps you are [Ur: You were] willing to accept even death to deny your Father. Yet He would not have it so, and so it is <u>not</u> so. You still cannot will against Him, and that is why you have no control over the world you made. It is <u>not</u> a world of will because it is governed by the desire to be unlike God, and this desire <u>is not will</u>. The world you made is therefore totally chaotic, governed by arbitrary and senseless "laws," and without meaning of <u>any</u> kind. For it is made out of what you do <u>not</u> want, projected <u>from</u> your mind because you are <u>afraid</u> of it. Yet this world is <u>only</u> in the mind of its maker, along with his <u>real</u> salvation. Do not believe it is outside of yourself, for only by recognizing <u>where</u> it is will you gain control over it. For you <u>do</u> have control over your mind, since the mind is the mechanism of decision.

In paragraph 7, we saw that there were two classes of thoughts: loving and hateful. We keep the former and project the latter. Now this paragraph adds a new twist. The loving thoughts represent our real will, and God's Will, too. They are what we really want. The hateful thoughts are not our true will. We can never be truly wholehearted about them. We can never put all of ourselves behind them. We don't *really* want them.

Yet they are what the world is made of. This means that it is a world devoid of real will, which means devoid of control, order, lawfulness, and meaning. Yes, there are physical laws. And yes, all the clocks run at the same speed (more or less). But on the level that *matters*, the level of fairness, sanity, reason, and interpersonal harmony, it's nuts out there. Nothing makes any sense. Things are out of control.

I'm struggling for an analogy, and what comes to mind is a garbage dump. Is a garbage dump an organized affair or is it chaos? Do the discarded records of someone's personal finances get carefully placed next to the discarded records of other people's finances? No, because all of that stuff is what we don't want anymore, and you don't carefully organize what you no longer want. That is why this world is so full of chaos. It's the garbage dump of the mind.

> 10. If you will recognize that <u>all</u> the [Ur: that *all*] attack you perceive is in your own mind and <u>nowhere else</u>, you will at last have placed its source, and where it begins it must end. For in this same place also lies salvation. The altar of God where Christ abideth is there. You have defiled the altar, but <u>not</u> the world. Yet Christ has placed the Atonement on the altar <u>for</u> you. Bring your perceptions of the world to this altar, for it is the altar to truth. There you will see your vision changed, and there you will learn to see truly. From this place, where God and His Son dwell in peace and where you are welcome, you will look out in peace and behold the world truly [behold the real world]. Yet to find the place, you must relinquish your investment in the world as <u>you</u> project [Ur: have projected] it, allowing the Holy Spirit to extend [Ur: project] the real world <u>to</u> you from the altar of God.

The latter paragraphs of this section provide a deeper context for the earlier discussion of our investment in the happenings of the world. When we are insisting that external events treat us right, what is really going on is that we have projected the inner cause of our anxiety—our hate—outward, and now appear to see anxiety-causing hate coming at us from without. The only solution seems to be to make an arrangement with the world, to get it to agree to treat us as we want it to. Sometimes we seek this arrangement gently. Sometimes we *insist*—which brings us back to the first four paragraphs.

Yet in this paragraph, we have the real solution: Withdraw your investment in the world by pulling your projections back into your mind. Realize that all attack you see in the world "is in your mind and nowhere else." Not some attack, *all* attack. It is your own hate, projected outward. It has never really left your mind. See it on the altar within, where it has been sitting all along, defiling the altar.

Then realize that sitting right next to it is the Atonement, the correction for all of our errors, including the original error of separation from God. There, on this altar, the Atonement will shine away your hate. When you finally see them side by side, only one will be left. Only the love will remain. And from that love, you will look out on the real world, the world composed of only the Son's loving thoughts.

Final exercise

How do we carry out the radical guidance of the first four paragraphs? Perhaps our first step is to decide that we *want* to learn this way. Something in us genuinely wants to learn how to respond to hatred with love. Something in us wants to go beyond the usual tit-for-tat and find a higher way. Something in us knows that Jesus is holding out a way that leads beyond the prison walls of our ego, and that is where we want to go.

A next step might be to start with the small things. Household issues are a hotbed of the kinds of situations we have been discussing. No matter how dedicated we are to our spiritual path, most of us are still quite invested in how the refrigerator is organized, how the dishes are done, where the thermostat is set, whether the top of the toothpaste tube is replaced. Consequently, we still do a lot of insisting. We are still among the poor. I will never forget walking in on some spiritual seekers who were sharing a hotel room and were in the midst of a heated argument about whether or not to peel the organic carrots. Who of us is completely free of this kind of investment?

We can start, therefore, by identifying one situation in which someone else is insisting and we are resisting, either recent or ongoing. If we don't share a household with anyone, perhaps we can find a situation at work.

For the time being, we might want to pick a situation in which the stakes are not particularly high in our perception. Pick a situation where no one is going to really be hurt, whatever you do. Let's write the situation down here:

Having identified a situation, let's apply to it the teachings we have examined. Look at your investment in this situation. What are you defending? What outer thing do you want to make sure isn't taken away from you? Please write your answer:

Ask yourself: How much has this thing you are defending given you? Has it given you the gift of everything, or in hanging onto it have you been like the person "who stored a heap of snow that shone like silver" (T-28.III.7:2)? Has your attachment to it made you poor? Again, write your answer.

Now look more deeply at your investment. Is it not true that you are trying in some way to save your ego? In what way are you trying to save your ego? Again, write.

Now consider that saving your ego, identifying with your ego, is what really impoverishes you, for it deprives you of God, and it makes you "exchange Self-love for self-hate" (paragraph 6). It is a hateful image, and so it makes you hate yourself. How does hanging onto this petty external thing, this worthless heap of snow, make you feel about yourself? Again, write.

Try to realize that you don't want this investment; you are better off without it. Say to yourself:

> *I release this investment.*
> *I will to be free of its chains.*
> *I want to love myself.*

Now turn your attention to your brother, the one making this outrageous request. You see him as having a kind of wealth, since he has taken something from you. What do you see him as having? Again, write your answer.

Try to realize that he, too, feels impoverished inside. That is why he is clutching at such tiny crumbs. Say to yourself,

> *Those who attack are poor.*
> *[Name's] poverty asks for gifts, not for further impoverishment.*

Realize that this brother's request is really for you, that if you respond with love, you give to yourself. Say,

> *Nothing can be asked **of** me.*
> *This request is **for** me.*
> *It is only I who have made it outrageous.*

Now imagine yourself giving what this person asks for. Make sure, however, that you see yourself doing it for the right reasons. Don't do it as an admission that your brother was right about the situation. Remember, the external outcome doesn't matter. Don't do it to be the martyr and restore the peace. Don't do it as a way of showing your moral superiority. Don't do it out of a grudging sense of obligation. Do it *because* it does not matter. Do it as a way of expressing your recognition of this. Do it to show your brother the way out of prison—the prison of investing in the world. Do it because what matters is freedom for your brother and yourself. You might even say to him in the silence of your mind:

> *OK, I'll do it.*
> *But my real gift to you is showing you a better way,*
> *Which is freedom from investment in this world.*
> *I hereby free both of us from poverty.*

IV. Seeking and Finding
Commentary by Robert Perry

This section contains a foreshadowing of the later discussions of the special relationship. In the process, it challenges our whole search for love.

> 1.   The ego is certain that love is dangerous, and this is <u>always</u> its central teaching. It never <u>puts</u> it this way; on the contrary, everyone who believes that the ego is salvation seems to be intensely engaged in the <u>search</u> for love. Yet the ego, though encouraging the search for love very actively, makes one proviso; do not <u>find</u> it. Its dictates, then, can be summed up simply as: "Seek and do *not* find." This is the <u>one</u> promise the ego holds out to you, and the one promise <u>it will keep</u>. For the ego pursues its goal with fanatic insistence, and its judgment [Ur: reality-testing], though severely impaired, is completely consistent.

The ego is all about false promises. Under its system we seek and seek and seek, yet never find. The excitement in life is almost always associated with the promise, with looking forward to something slightly distant that promises to be wonderful, isn't it? It is hardly ever brought on by the actual fulfillment of the promise. Nowhere is this truer than in our search for love. The ego very actively sends us on this search, yet as we charge off, it mutters under its breath one very slight condition: "You will never find it." The ego breaks all its promises to us except this one. It has to make sure we stay away from love, for its central teaching is that "love is dangerous." Keeping promises is about being faithful. Isn't it ironic, then, that the *one* way in which the ego is faithful to us is in making sure we never find what we want?

> 2.   The search the ego undertakes is therefore bound to be defeated. And since it also teaches that <u>it</u> is your identification, its guidance leads you to a journey which <u>must</u> end in perceived <u>self</u>-defeat. For the ego <u>cannot</u> love, and in its frantic search <u>for</u> love it is seeking <u>what it is afraid to find</u>. The <u>search</u> is inevitable because the ego is part of your mind, and because of its source the ego is not wholly split off, or it

143

could not be believed at all. For it is your mind that <u>believes</u> in it and gives existence <u>to</u> it. Yet it is <u>also</u> your mind that has the power to <u>deny</u> the ego's existence, and you will surely do so when you realize exactly what the journey <u>is</u> on which the ego sets you.

When our search for love fails, we assume that either fate screwed us over, by giving us unattractive genes or, more likely, the wrong partner, or we assume that *we* messed up by not being intriguing or bold or lovable enough. Either way, we feel defeated, don't we? What we don't realize is that the search didn't fail because of bad conditions or poor execution. Rather, it was designed to fail from the very beginning.

The ego is playing a tricky game. It is trying to accommodate the mind's innate need for love—for otherwise the mind would disown it—while serving its own primal need to *avoid* love. It accommodates these two opposing needs by allowing for the *seeking* but not the *finding* of love. Yet this is not really accommodating our needs at all. It is an illusion of concession to our needs. If we truly realized this, we would relinquish the ego.

> 3.　It is surely obvious that no one <u>wants</u> to find <u>what would utterly defeat him</u>. Being <u>unable</u> to love, the ego would be totally inadequate in love's presence, for it could not respond at all. Then, <u>you</u> would <u>have</u> to abandon the ego's guidance, for it would be quite apparent that it had <u>not</u> taught you the response [Ur: response pattern] you <u>need</u>. The ego will therefore <u>distort</u> love, and teach you that <u>love</u> really calls forth the responses the ego *can* teach. Follow its teaching, then, and you will search for love, <u>but will not recognize it</u>.

This is a poignant picture of us finding ourselves in the presence of real love while still having an ego. Love is pouring at us and we want to respond, but we feel cold, empty, unable to reciprocate. We are emotionally frigid. We have at last found the love we've been seeking and we can't return it. In a moment of insight, we finally understand that the ego, our teacher in the ways of love, has left us totally unequipped to love, and so we look at the ego and say, "You're fired." And we dive into love's presence.

This is the ego's nightmare scenario. It wakes up in cold sweats fearing this exact situation. Yet the ego has a great solution. It distorts the idea of love in our mind, turning love into an ego enterprise (which the Course will later call special love). This has two crucial results. First, it makes love into something that we *can* respond to from our ego. Second, it makes us blind to real love, so that we never notice that we are in its presence. This allows the ego to avoid that devastating situation we saw above.

4.   [Ur: But] <u>Do</u> you realize that the ego <u>must</u> set you on a journey which cannot <u>but</u> lead to a sense of futility and depression? To seek and <u>not</u> to find is hardly joyous. Is this the promise <u>you</u> would keep? The Holy Spirit offers you another promise, and one that will lead to joy. For His promise is always, "Seek and you *will* find," and under <u>His</u> guidance you cannot <u>be</u> defeated. His is the journey to <u>accomplishment</u>, and the goal <u>He</u> sets before you <u>He will give you</u>. For He will never deceive God's Son whom He loves with the Love of the Father.

It seems to us that with the Holy Spirit's plan, we can seek and seek but never find, whereas with the ego's plan, we at least have some hope. If we can just find the right person, and give him a little training, we can find the love we've always wanted. Yet we have it all backwards. With the ego's plan, we always end up with "a sense of futility and depression," for in it we make a hidden promise to ourselves: "I will seek and never find." Only the Holy Spirit is on our side. Only He will keep all His promises. Only He will make sure we really find the love we seek. Therefore, if we haven't found love by following His plan, perhaps we haven't *really* been following it.

5.   You *will* undertake a journey because you are not at home in this world. And you *will* search for your home whether you realize where it is or not. If you believe it is <u>outside</u> you the search will be futile, for you will be seeking it where it is <u>not</u>. You do not remember how to look within for you <u>do not believe your home is there</u>. Yet the Holy Spirit remembers it <u>for</u> you, and He will guide you <u>to</u> your home because that is His mission. As He fulfills <u>His</u> mission He will teach you <u>yours</u>, for your mission is the same as His. By guiding your <u>brothers</u> home [which is your mission] you are but following <u>Him</u>.

This paragraph further clarifies things. The search for love is really a search for home, a search we *will* undertake because in this world we don't feel at home. The ego, as we all know, tells us to search for both love and home *outside* of us. Yet that is quite simply not where love and home are. The Holy Spirit, however, remembers what we have forgotten, that love and home are within. He will teach us how to find the love we have always sought, as well as the home we have always yearned for, deep within ourselves. We may not think love and home are in there, but that is because we've forgotten how to look truly, deeply within. Yet the Holy Spirit will teach us. He will guide us to our home within, for that is His mission. And as He fulfills His mission of guiding us to the home within us, we will learn our own mission in life, which is guiding our brothers to the home within *them*.

> 6. Behold the Guide your Father gave you, that you might learn you have eternal life. For death is not your Father's Will nor yours, and whatever is true <u>is</u> the Will of the Father. You pay no price for life for that was given you, but you <u>do</u> pay a price for death, and a very heavy one. If death is your treasure, you will sell everything else to purchase it. And you will believe that you <u>have</u> purchased it, <u>because</u> you have sold everything else. Yet [Ur: *But*] <u>you cannot sell the Kingdom of Heaven</u>. Your inheritance can neither be bought <u>nor</u> sold [an apparent reference to the biblical story of Esau selling his inheritance for a mess of pottage]. There can <u>be</u> no disinherited parts of the Sonship, for God is whole and all His extensions are like Him.

The last two paragraphs puzzle me. They seem like such an abrupt transition. Yet it helps if we see their discussion of *investment* and *death* in light of the previous section, where investment referred to our investment in external events, and death referred to the worldly experience of being apart from God. Here, we can see death as the experience of being apart from home.

We have sold everything to buy the treasure of an external home and external love. We have even tried to sell our inheritance. We've sold the true home within in order to afford the dream house without. What we didn't realize, though, is that the external home is a false promise that delivers only death. It's like a real estate scam in which the scammers are also murderers. To fall prey to this scam is to lose everything. Yet we cannot sell our true home, we cannot get rid of our inheritance, and we cannot really die. All of this would violate our wholeness, which cannot be violated, for we share in the Wholeness of God.

7.   The Atonement is [Ur: was] not the price of your wholeness, but it *is* [Ur: *was*] the price of your <u>awareness</u> of your wholeness. For what you chose to "sell" had to be kept <u>for</u> you, since you <u>could</u> not "buy" it back. Yet <u>you</u> must invest in it, not with money but <u>with</u> [Ur: *your*] <u>spirit</u>. For spirit is will, and will <u>is</u> the "price" of the Kingdom. Your inheritance awaits only the recognition that you have <u>been</u> redeemed. The Holy Spirit guides you into life eternal, but <u>you</u> must relinquish your investment in death, or you will not see life though it is all around you.

Christianity teaches that the Atonement—meaning, the crucifixion—bought back ("ransomed") our wholeness. This paragraph, however, teaches that the Atonement—meaning, the *resurrection*—merely took the wholeness we threw away and put it in safekeeping for us, until the day we wanted it again. Our job now is to mentally and emotionally invest in it, to put the power of our will into it. Very simply, our job is simply to *want* it. To do that, we must withdraw the investment we have poured into finding a home out there in the world of death, and transfer that investment to finding our true home within. How serious are we about doing that?

Exercise

Please ponder the following questions. You may want to write out your answers—it will help them have more impact on you.

1.   Have you been intensely engaged in the search for love?
2.   Where are the main places in which you have looked for it? From which people in your life?
3.   To what extent do you feel like you found it?
4.   How defeated do you feel in your search?
5.   What reasons have you given yourself to explain why you didn't find the love you wanted?
6.   Is it possible that you sought love through a system that encouraged the search but was designed to keep you from *ever*

finding the love you sought?

7. Deep down, how much do you doubt your adequacy to love?
8. Are you afraid that you are unable to really and truly love?
9. Are you afraid that, in the presence of real love, you would be simply unable to *respond*, and so would feel totally inadequate and defeated?
10. Could it be that, to avoid this feeling, you have made sure you never found yourself in the presence of real love?
11. Could it also be that you have distorted your definition of love, defining it in terms of responses that you *did* feel capable of making?
12. What if your ego is totally unable to love, but *you* are not?
13. What if real, egoless love is the natural response of who you really are, more natural to you than breathing?
14. How would you feel if the Holy Spirit promises that He can awaken that natural response in you, and show you how to give and receive real love?
15. How would you feel if He could show you a way in which your seeking of love was matched by finding, so that all of the love you sought you *found*?
16. Would you be willing to give up your way for His?

V. The Sane Curriculum
Commentary by Robert Perry

1. Only love is strong because it is <u>undivided</u>. The strong do not attack because they see no need to do so. <u>Before</u> the idea of attack can enter your mind, <u>you must have perceived yourself as weak</u>. Because you attacked yourself and <u>believed that the attack was effective</u>, you behold yourself as weakened. No longer perceiving yourself and your brothers as equal, and <u>regarding yourself as weaker</u>, you attempt to "equalize" the situation <u>you</u> <u>made</u>. You use attack to do so because you believe that <u>attack was successful in weakening you</u>.

Normally, we see attack in the following way: We were attacked by our brothers. This weakened us and strengthened them, and so, in order to regain our strength and reverse our degraded status, we must stand up for ourselves and attack back. This paragraph offers a similar story after the first step, but the first step is very different. Rather than our brothers attacking us, the Course said that we attacked ourselves. This is what weakened us. This is what made us feel lower than our brothers. With this different first step, the whole story becomes a deeply ironic one. First, we attacked and damaged ourselves, and then, to set things right, we turned and attacked our brothers. It's as if you threw a rock through the window of your own house and then, noticing that your house now looked worse than the neighbors' place, threw another rock through their window to equalize things!

2. That is why the recognition of your <u>own</u> invulnerability is so important to the restoration of your sanity. For if you accept your invulnerability, you are recognizing that <u>attack has no effect</u>. Although you have attacked yourself, [Ur: and very brutally] you will be demonstrating that <u>nothing</u> really <u>happened</u>. Therefore, by attacking you have <u>not done anything</u>. Once you realize this you will no longer see any <u>sense</u> in attack, for it manifestly <u>does not work</u> and cannot <u>protect</u> you. Yet the recognition of your invulnerability has more than negative value. If your attacks on yourself have <u>failed</u> to weaken you, <u>you are still strong</u>. You therefore <u>have</u> no need to "equalize" the

149

situation to <u>establish</u> your strength.

The key is to erase that first step. We need to realize that our attack on ourselves had no effect. I see this as boldly affirming to myself, that the whole saga of changing myself from a limitless Son of God into a petty, selfish, vulnerable body resulted in nothing. I'm still the limitless Son of God. Nothing has changed.

Erasing this first step undoes the whole scenario. It means that since my attack on myself had no effect, there is no use in attacking my brothers, for that too will have no effect. It also means that since my attack didn't actually weaken me, I have no need to equalize things.

The punch line: If you realize that you're invulnerable to your attack on yourself, you will never attack another living soul.

> 3.   [Ur: But] You will never realize the utter uselessness of attack <u>except</u> by recognizing that your attack on <u>yourself</u> has no effects. For others <u>do</u> react to attack if they perceive it, and if you <u>are</u> trying to attack them you will be unable to avoid interpreting this as reinforcement. The <u>only</u> place you can cancel out <u>all</u> reinforcement is <u>in yourself</u>. For <u>you</u> are always the first point of your attack, and if this has never been, it <u>has</u> no consequences.

This paragraph makes an important point: You will only realize that attack has no power if you realize your attack on *yourself* had no power. In contrast, when you attack others, they *will* react as if they have been damaged, thus providing apparent evidence that attack has power.

Application: Think of a situation in which you felt weaker, less than, and wanted to attack another to equalize things. Then say,

> *I feel weak because I have attacked myself.*
> *But my attack on myself had no effect.*
> *Therefore, attacking my brother is useless because attack does not work.*
> *Further, I have no need to attack—I am still strong.*
> *I am still the holy Son of God Himself.*

4.   The Holy Spirit's Love is your strength, for yours is divided and therefore not real. You cannot [Ur: could not] trust your own love when you attack [Ur: you have *attacked*] it. You cannot learn of perfect love with a split mind, because a split mind has made itself a poor learner. You tried to make the separation eternal, because you wanted to retain the characteristics of creation, but with your own content [see 11.VII.3:7]. Yet creation is not of you, and poor learners do need special teaching.

What is truly strong is love, not attack. Yet our love is not strong right now, for it is divided. When we attacked ourselves, we attacked the love within us. Now our minds are split between love and hate. This means that we can't rely on our love (which I'm sure we all realize by now), and that we can't teach ourselves real, undivided love. For the time being, then, we need to rely on a greater Love, the Holy Spirit's Love. We need to consider His Love to be our strength.

5.   You have learning handicaps in a very literal sense. There are areas in your learning skills that are so impaired that you can progress only under constant, clear-cut direction, provided by a Teacher Who can transcend your limited resources. He becomes your Resource because of yourself you cannot learn. The learning situation in which you placed yourself is impossible, and in this situation you clearly require a special Teacher and a special curriculum. Poor learners are not good choices as teachers, either for themselves or for anyone else. You would hardly turn to them to establish the curriculum by which they can escape from their limitations. If they understood what is beyond them, they would not be handicapped.

Nowadays we say "learning disabilities." But back when the Course was dictated they used the term Jesus uses here: "learning handicaps," which of course meant mentally retarded. Jesus is calling us retarded! And let's face it: When it comes to learning egolessness, we *are* retarded. "Poor learner" is putting it mildly. Slow learner is more like it; or even better, just plain slow.

Now imagine turning to a bunch of learning disabled kids and saying, "OK, you're the teachers now. Design your own curriculum. Make up lesson plans. From now on, you're going to teach yourselves." This, of course, is insane. Think of all the resources that the developmentally disabled need. They need highly trained teachers, with carefully planned curriculums, and lots of learning aids.

The point is: When it comes to the journey home, this is what we are like. We are retarded. We should not be charting our own journey. We need to rely on the Holy Spirit, on His resources, and on His curriculum.

> 6.   You do not know the meaning of love, and that is your handicap. Do not attempt to teach yourself [Ur: *yourselves*] what you do not understand, and do not try to set up curriculum goals where yours have clearly failed. [Ur: For] Your learning goal has been *not* to learn, and this cannot lead to successful learning. You cannot transfer what you have not learned, and the impairment of the ability to generalize is a crucial learning failure. Would you ask those who have failed to learn what learning aids are for? They do not know. If they could interpret the aids correctly, they would have learned from them.

Perhaps you've been trying to teach yourself to be a more loving person for a long time. How far have you gotten? Have you learned the kind of love the Course is talking about? A love without favorites, without degree, and without change—a love that is undivided? The reason you haven't is because, quite frankly, you are retarded when it comes to love. You are "love disabled"; not because you are brain-damaged, but because, unconsciously, you are dead-set against love. Your goal, therefore, has been to *not* learn it, which has led to learning failure, inability to generalize your learning, and not realizing what the various learning aids (such as the body and time) in your classroom are for. The developmentally disabled child is trying to play the teacher, with perfectly predictable results.

> 7.   I have said that the ego's rule is, "Seek and do not find." Translated into curricular terms this means [Ur: this is the same as saying], "Try to learn but do not succeed." The result of this curriculum goal is obvious. Every legitimate teaching aid, every real instruction, and every sensible guide to learning will be misinterpreted, since they are all for facilitating the learning this strange curriculum is against [Ur: they are all for learning *facilitation*, which this strange curriculum goal is *against*]. If you are trying to learn how not to learn, and the aim of your teaching is [Ur: and are using the *aim* of teaching] to defeat itself, what can you expect but confusion? Such a curriculum does not make

[Ur: any] sense.

Realize that when Jesus is asking Helen to accept the Holy Spirit's teaching and the Holy Spirit's curriculum, he is really talking about her accepting *his* teaching and *his* curriculum. This section is therefore a powerful argument about why we need the Course, why we need to follow its curriculum, rather than try to set up our own. I used to be passionately eclectic when it came to spirituality. I believed that the wisest, healthiest thing to do was have many teachings at my disposal, and then, inspired by all of them, set up my own curriculum. Yet I can tell you that the things I am doing now, under the Course's instruction, are things I would never have done on my own. They are just too challenging to my love affair with lovelessness.

I see tremendous resistance among Course students to treating the Course in the way this section implies. We conveniently misinterpret its teachings. We conveniently brush over its practice instructions, or conveniently decide that they are an unreasonable burden that is not in our best interests. Could it be that this teacher (Jesus) knows exactly what he is doing, yet we are neutralizing him because we are secretly against learning the love he is trying to teach us?

> This attempt at "learning" [Ur: This kind of learning] has so weakened your mind that you <u>cannot</u> love, for the curriculum you have chosen is <u>against</u> love, and amounts to a course in <u>how to attack yourself</u>. A supplementary goal in this curriculum [Ur: A necessary minor, supplementing this major curriculum goal,] is learning how *not* to overcome the split that makes its primary aim [Ur: which made this goal] believable. And <u>you</u> will <u>not</u> overcome the split in this curriculum, for all <u>your</u> learning will be on its <u>behalf</u>. Yet your mind [Ur: will] speaks against your learning as your learning speaks against your mind [Ur: will], and so you fight <u>against</u> all learning [Ur: *against* learning] and <u>succeed</u>, for that is what you want [Ur: that is your will]. But perhaps you do <u>not</u> realize, even yet, that there <u>is</u> something you want [Ur: will] to learn, and that you <u>can</u> learn it because it *is* your choice [Ur: will] to do so.

The early paragraphs said that we started out filled with pure, undivided love, and that this was our strength. Then we decided to attack ourselves, to attack the love in us. This split our mind into a love camp and a hate camp. Being divided inside between these camps, we were now weak, not strong. What is divided against itself is not strong.

Now this paragraph makes clear that all of the subsequent talk about learning and curriculums is a continuation of this same picture. The love camp wanted us to return to love, and so we have been trying to learn how to love again. Yet the hate camp wanted to make sure that, however much we tried to learn love, we never succeeded. Unfortunately, the hate camp has had the upper hand. Under its influence, we have *majored* in repeating the original attack on ourselves, and have *minored* in keeping intact the split that allows that attack to continue. After all, you don't attack yourself unless you are split, unless the attacking part of you (the hate camp) looks upon the other part (the love camp) as something other than you, as not-you, and thus something to be attacked.

Unfortunately, trying to learn something we cannot really want to learn (how to continually attack ourselves) has soured us on learning itself. What we need to realize is that there *is* something we truly want to learn, something that every legitimate impulse in us yearns to take hold of.

> 8.   You who have tried to learn what you do <u>not</u> want [Ur: will] should take heart, for although the curriculum you set yourself is depressing indeed, it is merely ridiculous <u>if you look</u> at it. Is it <u>possible</u> that the way to achieve a goal is <u>not to attain it</u>? Resign <u>now</u> as your own teacher. <u>This</u> resignation will <u>not</u> lead to depression. It is merely the result of an honest appraisal of what you have taught yourself, and of the learning outcomes that have resulted. Under the proper learning conditions, which you can neither provide nor understand, you will become an excellent learner <u>and</u> an excellent teacher. But it is not so yet, and will not <u>be</u> so until the whole learning situation as <u>you</u> have set it up is reversed.

Application: Ask yourself the following questions as sincerely as you can:

• Have I treated Jesus' teaching in the Course as a developmentally disabled student ought to treat his teacher? Have I embraced his instruction, taken to heart his injunctions, and done what he told me to do?

- Or with each bit of his instruction, have I reserved the right to set it aside or modify it, as if I know what's better for me?
- Have I lived my life as if *he* is my teacher or as if I am my *own* teacher?
- [Assuming the latter…] How have I done as my own teacher? Have I learned the love I really want to learn?
- Could it be that the curriculum I set myself is all about *trying* to learn love but never *succeeding*?
- [Assuming a "yes"…] I admit that my curriculum has been ridiculous.
- I therefore resign as my own teacher.
- I accept Jesus as my teacher instead.
- But I do not resign in depression.
- I resign in the happy faith that I will become an excellent learner and even an excellent teacher,
- Once I am willing to act like a real student of my real teacher.

9.   Your learning <u>potential</u>, properly understood, is limitless <u>because it will lead you to God</u>. You can <u>teach</u> the way to Him <u>and</u> learn it, if you follow the Teacher Who knows the way to Him and understands His curriculum for learning it [Ur: if you follow the Teacher Who knows it, and the curriculum for learning it]. The curriculum is totally unambiguous, because the goal is <u>not</u> divided and the means and the end are in <u>complete</u> accord. <u>You</u> need offer only <u>undivided attention</u> [recognize this line from your school days?]. Everything else will be <u>given</u> you. For you really want to learn aright [Ur: For it is *your* will to learn aright], and <u>nothing</u> can oppose the decision [Ur: will] of God's Son. His learning is as unlimited as <u>he</u> is.

Application: On the heels of your decision to follow Jesus' teaching, not your own, repeat the following to yourself with as much genuine conviction as you can:

> *My teacher will provide all that I need.*
> *I need offer only undivided attention.*

Everything else will be given me.
For it is my will to learn aright,
And nothing can oppose the will of God's Son.
My learning potential is limitless, because it will lead me to the
  Limitless.

VI. The Vision of Christ
Commentary by Robert Perry

1. The ego is trying to teach you how to gain the whole world and lose your own soul. The Holy Spirit teaches that you <u>cannot</u> lose your soul and there <u>is</u> no gain in the world, for <u>of itself</u> it profits nothing. To invest [Ur: in something] <u>without</u> profit is surely to impoverish yourself, and the overhead [the ongoing costs of this business] is high. Not only is there no profit in the investment, but the cost <u>to you</u> is enormous. For this investment costs you the world's reality by <u>denying yours,</u> and gives you nothing in return. You <u>cannot</u> sell your soul, but you <u>can</u> sell your <u>awareness</u> of it. You cannot perceive your soul, but you will not <u>know</u> it while you perceive something [Ur: anything] <u>else</u> as more valuable.

This section opens with the biblical saying about gaining the world and losing your soul. That saying conjures up images of gaining something real but corrupt, while losing what should be far more precious to you. You gain, but your gain is evil, and this causes you to lose the spiritual element in you. This paragraph, however, has a whole different take on this saying. It's not that you gain evil; you gain nothing at all, for the world in itself contains no profit. And it's not that you lose your soul; you simply lose your *awareness* of it. You try to sell your soul in order to gain the world. Indeed, you invest everything you have in the world's stock, and in addition you are even required to pay operating costs each month, yet you never see a dime in return. Instead, you lose everything: awareness of your own reality and awareness of the world's reality (the real world). Does this capture our experience of seeking happiness from the world?

The underlying message is that we shouldn't be thinking in religious terms of guilt and holiness before God, but instead in business terms of profit and loss. Does it really make good business sense to throw everything away on worthless investment? Yet that's what we are doing.

2. The Holy Spirit is your strength because He knows nothing <u>but</u> the spirit <u>as you</u> [Ur: nothing *but* your Soul *as you*]. He is perfectly aware

that you do <u>not</u> know yourself, and perfectly aware of how to teach you to remember what you are. <u>Because</u> He loves you, He will gladly teach you what He loves, for He wills to share it. Remembering you always, He cannot let you forget your worth. For the Father never ceases to remind Him of His Son, and He never ceases to remind His Son of the Father. God is in your memory <u>because</u> of Him. You <u>chose</u> to forget your Father but you do <u>not</u> really want [Ur: but you did *not* will] to do so, and <u>therefore</u> you <u>can</u> decide otherwise. As it was <u>my</u> decision, so is it <u>yours</u>.

Imagine that you have met someone whom you see as the most amazing person in the world. This person is filled with such remarkable qualities that you immediately gain a deep love for her. Yet you observe that she does not value herself. She does not see her remarkable qualities. In fact, she is depressed about herself. Wouldn't you be dying to share with her how truly wonderful she is?

This is how the Holy Spirit sees us. He sees something in us that evokes such deep love in Him that all He wants to do is show us what we are, help us see our incomparable worth. He reminds us of this 24 hours a day, and He will never stop until we see in ourselves what He sees. He also reminds us of God 24 hours a day. We may have chosen to forget God, but our heart wasn't in it. Hence, we will inevitably decide to undo our forgetting, just as Jesus decided to undo his.

> 3.   <u>You do not want the world</u>. The only thing of value in it is whatever part of it <u>you</u> look upon with love. This <u>gives</u> it the only reality it will ever have. <u>Its</u> value is <u>not</u> in itself, but yours <u>is</u> in you. As self-value comes from self-<u>extension</u> [in Heaven], so does the <u>perception</u> of self-value come from the extension of loving thoughts outward [on earth]. Make the world real unto <u>yourself</u>, for the real world is the gift of the Holy Spirit, and so it <u>belongs</u> to you.

If something has no value in itself, can you really want it? That is the case with this world. However, when you extend loving thoughts to some part of the world, you are seeing beyond the valueless outer form. You are seeing the real world. This extension of love also reveals to you your own value. If all you see come out of you, day-in and day-out, are petty, judgmental thoughts, how much can you value yourself? Only your loving thoughts will reveal to you the unlimited worth that the Holy Spirit sees in you always.

> 4.   Correction is for all who cannot see. To open the eyes of the blind is the Holy Spirit's mission, for He knows that they have not <u>lost</u> their vision, but merely sleep. He would awaken them from the sleep of forgetting to the remembering of God. Christ's eyes are open, and He will look upon whatever you see with love if you accept His vision as yours. The Holy Spirit keeps the vision of Christ for every Son of God who sleeps. In His sight the Son of God is perfect, and He longs to share His vision <u>with</u> you. He will <u>show</u> you the real world because God <u>gave</u> you Heaven. Through Him your Father calls His Son to remember. The awakening of His Son begins with his investment in the <u>real</u> world, and <u>by</u> this he will learn to <u>re</u>-invest in <u>himself</u>. For reality is one with the Father <u>and</u> the Son, and the Holy Spirit blesses the real world in Their Name.

We do not see the real world. All we see is form, and this means that we are blind in the most important sense of the word. The Course says, "Nothing so blinding as perception of form. For sight of form means understanding has been obscured" (22.III.6:7-8). First, therefore, we need to recognize that we are blind.

We need to *recognize* it, but not *accept* it, for we haven't really lost our sight. We are just asleep. We have just closed our eyes. We could see if we would only open them, and this is what the Holy Spirit is here to help us do. As He teaches us to open our eyes, Christ will look through us with love upon whatever we see. Even if we see murder, He will see a meaning past the form that is worthy of His unchanging love.

We will be looking on the real world, and the loveliness we see will cause us to increasingly invest in the real world. Through this, we will begin, tentatively at first, to invest in ourselves. For what we see behind the forms of the world will be the glory of God's Son, and we will slowly realize that that glory is our own, that we are God's Son.

> 5.   When you have seen this real world, as you will surely do, you <u>will</u> remember Us. Yet you must learn the cost of sleeping, <u>and refuse to pay it</u>. Only then will you decide to awaken. And then the real world will spring to your sight, for Christ has never slept. He is waiting to be seen, for He has never lost sight of <u>you</u>. He looks quietly on the

real world, which He would <u>share</u> with you because He knows of the Father's Love for Him. And knowing this, He would give you what is yours. In perfect peace He waits for you at His Father's altar, holding out the Father's Love to you in the quiet light of the Holy Spirit's blessing. For the Holy Spirit will lead everyone home to his Father, where Christ waits as His Self.

Our first task is to recognize that we are asleep. We are in a groggy, reason-impaired, unaware state in which our eyes are shut to what is real. Our second task is to recognize the cost of being in this state. Our third task is to refuse to pay this cost. This leads to our fourth task: to decide to awaken. How deeply have we made this decision? When we do, Christ will look through us, and the real world will spring to our sight. And when we open our eyes all the way and fully see the real world, we will be led to our Father's altar, where we will at last awaken as the Christ.

Application: Visualize the following:

Imagine that you have been allowing Christ to look through you for some time now.
And thus everywhere you look, you look with love.
You are deeply invested in this real world you've been seeing.
Its beauty never ceases to enchant you.
As a result, you have learned to re-invest in yourself.
Now, as you look upon yourself, you see the endless worth the Holy Spirit sees.
Yet this is all a waking dream, and you are ready at last for total awakening.
See yourself walking towards God's altar, where your awakening will occur.
There, Christ stands at the altar, waiting for you with joy.
Visualize Him however you like, as Jesus, as an androgynous figure, as a light, whatever works for you.
As He stands there, the Holy Spirit's blessing shines down on Him as a soft light from above.
See Christ holding out God's Love to you, wanting only to give you what is yours.
Take this priceless gift from His hands.

Feel God's Love for you dawn upon your mind as an unspeakable
   revelation.
Spend a moment in that revelation.
And now, look up at Christ's face, and realize this is *your* face.
Christ is you. He is your true Self.
This is the secret you have tried to keep hidden for eons.
Feel the scene vanish as you merge with Him, as you awaken at last
   as your Self.

6.   Every child of God is one in Christ, for his being is in Christ as
Christ's is in God. Christ's Love for you is His Love for His Father,
which He knows because He knows His Father's Love for Him. When
the Holy Spirit has at last led you to Christ at the altar to His Father,
perception fuses into knowledge because perception has become so
holy that its transfer to holiness is merely its natural extension. Love
transfers to love without <u>any</u> interference, for the two are one [Ur: for
the situations are identical. Only the *ability* to make this transfer is
the product of learning.]. As you perceive more and more common
elements in <u>all</u> situations, the transfer of [Ur: your] training under the
Holy Spirit's guidance increases and becomes generalized. Gradually
you learn to apply it to everyone and everything, for its applicability <u>is</u>
universal. When this has been accomplished, perception and knowledge
have become so similar that they share the unification of the laws of
God.

How do we get to the altar of awakening? Our perception becomes so
pure, so holy, that it becomes like knowledge, like holiness itself. This
doesn't happen all at once. We are in the process of reaching that place
now. It starts with isolated shifts in perception. Yet as we see one thing
differently, that shift transfers to other things (for a lengthy discussion
of transfer of training, see the introduction to the Workbook, paragraphs
4-6). This transfer is at first quite limited, yet eventually we will realize
that all situations have common elements, that all situations are really
just different forms of one situation. And then we will apply our learning
to everything, without exception. We will always see nothing but love.

It is hard to imagine perception becoming so perfect that its natural
extension is to fuse into knowledge. The Course talks about knowledge

in such exalted terms. It is a state in which there is only love, only joy, without the tiniest change, without the slightest trace of disturbance or the barest hint of separate interests. Can you imagine your perception on earth becoming a perfect reflection of this state, a spotless mirror of Heaven? According to the Course, whether you can imagine it or not, that is where you are headed.

> 7.   What is one [knowledge and perfected perception] cannot be perceived as separate, and the denial of the separation is the reinstatement of knowledge. At the altar of God, the holy perception of God's Son becomes so enlightened that light streams into it, and the spirit of God's Son shines in the Mind of the Father and becomes one with it. Very gently does God shine upon Himself, loving the extension of Himself that is His Son. The world has no purpose as it blends into the Purpose of God. For the real world has slipped quietly into Heaven, where everything eternal in it has always been. There the Redeemer and the redeemed join in perfect love of God and of each other. Heaven is your home, and being in God it must also be in you.

This paragraph is such a beautiful account of our homecoming, of what will happen when our perception is at last perfect. It is such poetry that I hesitate to explain it. Therefore, I would simply encourage you to read it again, very slowly, as I have laid it out below (which is minus the first sentence). As you do, savor each line. Visualize the images. And remember that what this speaks of will one day really happen when you reach the end of the road.

At the altar of God, the holy perception of God's Son becomes so
    enlightened that light streams into it, and the spirit of God's Son
    shines in the Mind of the Father and becomes one with it.
Very gently does God shine upon Himself [His Son], loving the
    extension of Himself that is His Son.
The world has no purpose as it blends into the Purpose of God.
For the real world has slipped quietly into Heaven, where everything
    eternal in it [the real world] has always been.
There the Redeemer [the Holy Spirit] and the redeemed join in perfect
    love of God and of each other.
Heaven is your home [name], and being in God it must *also* be in you.

162

VII. Looking Within
Commentary by Robert Perry

This is a very important series of paragraphs. They lay out a way to become aware of the Holy Spirit in us, a way which is counter-intuitive, yet which *is* the Course's way.

> 1.   Miracles demonstrate that learning has occurred under the right guidance, for learning is invisible and what has been learned can be recognized <u>only</u> by its <u>results</u>. Its <u>generalization</u> is demonstrated as you use it in more and more situations. You will recognize that you have learned there is no order of difficulty in miracles when you apply them to <u>all</u> situations. [Ur: For] There <u>is</u> no situation to which miracles do not apply, and by applying them <u>to</u> all situations you will gain the <u>real</u> world. For in this holy perception you will be made whole, and the Atonement will radiate from your acceptance of it <u>for yourself</u> to everyone the Holy Spirit sends you for your blessing. In every child of God His blessing lies, and in your blessing of the children of God is His blessing to <u>you</u>.

How do we know when we have learned—when we have made spiritual progress? We know it by seeing miracles go forth from us. We know it when we extend healed perception to others and see the impact on them. I see three stages in this paragraph.

1.   We know that we have learned something when miracles extend from us, at least in *some* situations (first sentence).
2.   We know that our learning has generalized when we perform miracles in *more and more* situations (second sentence).
3.   We know that we have learned there is no order of difficulty in miracles when we apply them to *all* situations (third sentence).

At stage 3, we will gain the real world. We will have truly accepted the Atonement. In this state, we will radiate blessings to everyone the Holy Spirit sends to us, and blessing them will make us aware of God's eternal blessing on us.

> 2. Everyone in the world must play his part in its redemption, in order to recognize that the world <u>has been</u> redeemed. You cannot see the invisible. Yet if you see its effects <u>you know it must be there</u>. By perceiving what it <u>does</u>, you recognize its being. And by <u>what</u> it does, you learn what it <u>is</u>. You cannot <u>see</u> your strengths, but you gain confidence in their <u>existence</u> as they enable you to <u>act</u>. And the results of your actions you *can* see.

This paragraph announces the general principle that this section applies in many ways: You become aware of the invisible only as it produces visible results. By seeing what it does, you become aware of its *existence* ("its being") and its *nature* ("what it is"). More specifically, this means: You become aware of something *in* you only as you see it produce effects *through* you.

Here, this principle is applied to our strengths: We will only gain confidence in our strengths as we see them produce effects through us, through our actions.

The principle is also applied to the redemption of the world: We will only see that the world has been redeemed when we see redemption manifesting through our actions right now. This happens as we play our special part in the world's redemption. In other words, when we see redemptive power acting through us, this will prove to us that redemption is already a fact, already accomplished. The world's redemption, then, is one of those invisible things that will only become real to us as it produces effects through us.

> 3. The Holy Spirit is invisible, but you <u>can</u> see the results of His Presence, and through them you will learn that He is there. What He enables you to do is clearly <u>not</u> of this world, for miracles violate every law of reality as this world judges it. Every law of time and space, of magnitude and mass [Ur: of prediction and control,] is transcended, for what the Holy Spirit enables you to do is clearly beyond <u>all</u> of them. Perceiving His <u>results</u>, you will understand where He <u>must</u> be, and finally <u>know</u> what He is.

Now this principle is applied to the Holy Spirit. He is invisible, and so He will only become real to us as He produces effects through us. And those effects are, of course, miracles. Not all miracles heal bodies, but those that do prove to us that there is a Presence in us that is not of this world. Otherwise, how could we do something that overturns the most basic laws of this world?

Therefore, if you want to be aware of the Holy Spirit *in* you, let Him do miracles *through* you. This is the exact same message we were given back in Chapter 9:

> How can you become increasingly aware of the Holy Spirit in you except by His effects? You cannot see Him with your eyes nor hear Him with your ears. How, then, can you perceive Him at all? If you inspire joy and others react to you with joy, even though you are not experiencing joy yourself there must be something in you that is capable of producing it. (9.VI.1:1-4)

4.   You cannot see the Holy Spirit, but you <u>can</u> see His <u>manifestations</u>. And <u>unless you do</u>, you will not realize He is there. Miracles are His witnesses, and speak for His Presence. What you cannot see becomes real to you only through the witnesses that speak <u>for</u> It. For you can be <u>aware</u> of what you cannot see, and It can become compellingly real to you as Its Presence becomes manifest <u>through</u> you. Do the Holy Spirit's work, for you <u>share</u> in His function. As your function in Heaven is creation, so your function on earth is healing. God shares His function with you in Heaven, and the Holy Spirit shares <u>His</u> with you on earth. As long as you believe you have other functions, so long will you need correction. For this belief is the <u>destruction</u> of peace, a goal in direct opposition to the Holy Spirit's purpose.

Now we can see that all the applications of this principle are really the same thing. Let's look at each one:

- We become aware that we have learned when our learning manifests as miracles that we do in the situations we encounter.
- We become aware that the world has been redeemed when world-redeeming power manifests through us in the performing of our function (our part in the world's redemption).
- We become aware of our strengths as they manifest through us in our

actions (presumably as we perform our function, which the Course says is designed to be the ideal use of our strengths).

• We become aware of the Holy Spirit in us as He manifests through the miracles we do.

• They are all different ways of talking about the same thing: "Do the Holy Spirit's work." Clearly, "do" and "work" mean just as they sound. The whole idea is that you act in ways that are *visible* on the outside to prove to yourself the presence of something *invisible* on the inside.

Application: Think of a time when you felt that the Holy Spirit moved through you to help another. Say to yourself,

> *This is the proof that the Holy Spirit is in me.*
> *This is the proof that holiness resides at the core of my being.*

5.   You see what you expect, and you expect what you invite. Your perception is the result of your invitation, coming to you as you sent for it. Whose manifestations would you see? Of whose presence would you be convinced? For you will believe in what you <u>manifest</u>, and as you look out so will you see in. Two ways of looking at the world are in your mind, and your perception will reflect the guidance you have chosen.

The focus now shifts from manifestations you produce via your behavior to manifestations you perceive due to an internal process of desiring and expecting. A four-step process is outlined:

1. You *invite*—you desire to see either the ego or the Holy Spirit manifest outside of you.
2. You *expect*—you expect to see the manifestation you invited.
3. You *perceive*—you see the manifestation you invited and expected.
4. You *believe*—based on whose manifestation you saw, you believe in the presence of either the ego or the Holy Spirit in you.

This principle works. For example, when you see only the faults in others, whose presence do you become convinced of in yourself—the ego or the Holy Spirit?

> 6.   I am the manifestation of the Holy Spirit, and when you see me it will be because you have invited Him. For He will send you His witnesses if you will but look upon them. Remember always that you see what you seek, for what you seek you <u>will</u> find. The ego finds what it seeks, and <u>only</u> that. It does not find love, for that is <u>not</u> what it is seeking. Yet seeking and <u>finding</u> are the same, and if you seek for two goals you will <u>find</u> them, but you will <u>recognize neither</u>. [Ur: For] You will think they are the same <u>because you want</u> [Ur. *them both*] both of them. The mind always strives for integration, and if it is split and <u>wants to keep the split</u>, it will still believe it has <u>one</u> goal by <u>making it</u> seem to be <u>one</u>.

Now Jesus applies this four-step process to seeing him. When you desire to see the manifestation of the Holy Spirit (step 1: invite), you will see Jesus (step 3: perceive), because Jesus *is* the manifestation of the Holy Spirit. What does Jesus mean by seeing him? I frankly don't know. Maybe he is talking about an inner vision of him or inner sensing of him.

The essence of that four-step process is that you will see what you want to see. You will find what you seek. Jesus then applies this principle to seeking love. Our conventional search for love is actually composed of *two* searches: Our *mind* is seeking love, while our *ego* is seeking the opposite of love. We have no idea how opposed these two searches are, because we have melded them into one search, in order to manufacture an illusion of inner unity. What does this search find? It finds relationships in which what we call love is really hate in disguise, and in which there are elements of real, egoless love, but we tend to overlook them. In other words, we find both goals—love and not-love—but we "recognize neither."

> 7.   I said before that <u>what</u> you project or extend is up to you, but you must do one or the other, for that is a law of mind, [Ur: Perception *is* projection,] and you must look in <u>before</u> you look out. As you look <u>in</u>, you choose the guide for seeing [the ego or the Holy Spirit]. And <u>then</u> you look out and behold his witnesses. This is why you find what you seek. What you want <u>in yourself</u> you will make manifest [Ur:

by *projection* {or extension}], and you will accept it <u>from</u> the world because you put it there <u>by</u> wanting it.

What Jesus makes clear here is that the whole process of perception is aimed at step 4: believing in either the ego or the Holy Spirit in you. Every step along the way is aimed at convincing you that one or the other exists in you. The implications of this are quite startling.

Application: Think of an instance in which you saw the ego manifest in someone recently. Then say,

> *The whole reason I saw the ego manifest in [name] is that I wanted to convince myself of the presence of the ego in me.*

Now think of an instance in which you saw the Holy Spirit manifest in someone. Then say,

> *The whole reason I saw the Holy Spirit manifest in [name] is that I wanted to convince myself of the Presence of the Holy Spirit in me.*

When you think you are projecting what you do <u>not</u> want, it is still because you *do* want it. This leads <u>directly</u> to dissociation, for it represents the acceptance of two goals, each perceived <u>in a different place</u>; separated from each other <u>because you made them different</u>. The mind then sees a divided world <u>outside itself</u>, but <u>not</u> within. This gives it an illusion of integrity, and enables it to believe that <u>it</u> is pursuing one goal. Yet as long as you perceive the world as split, <u>you</u> are not healed. For to be healed is to pursue one goal, because you have <u>accepted</u> only one and <u>want</u> but one.

When we see the ego within, we project it out in horror, hoping that if we can see it in others, we won't see it in ourselves. What we don't realize is that seeing the ego in others *proves* to us that it is within. What we especially don't realize is that, on some level, we are *seeking* this proof.

The result is that we see a world filled with the hateful manifestations of the ego, while, when we look within, we see a sincere person who just wants love. We see a world split between evil (outside) and good (within). We are clearly unified inside behind the search for love (or so we think), yet the world is constantly thwarting our search by throwing all those unloving people our way. Be honest: Isn't that the situation as we see it? We have colossally fooled ourselves. Yes, we want love, but we also want hate. We are split inside. What we see as a split between us and the world is really a split between two sides of our own mind.

To keep our split from dawning on us, we have taken one half of it—the evil half—and projected it onto the world. We have thrown the evil out there, because we still want it, but just don't want to see it *within*. We want to believe that on the inside we are united behind a single benign goal. Yet as we have learned from the previous paragraphs, by seeing ego manifest all around us, we are constantly convincing ourselves of its presence within us. This leaves us in a strange contradiction. On the surface, we view ourselves as unified behind a sincere and constructive goal, yet deep-down we are full of self-loathing, convinced that at our core looms the dark and brooding presence of the ego.

> 8.   When you want only love you will see nothing else. The contradictory nature of the witnesses you perceive is merely the reflection of your conflicting invitations. You have looked upon your mind and accepted opposition there, having sought it there. But do not then believe that the witnesses for opposition are true, for they attest only to your decision about reality, returning to you the messages you gave them. Love, too, is [Ur: Love is] recognized by its messengers. If you make love manifest, its messengers will come to you because you invited them.

We look out at the world and think that we see the world as it really is. The world we see, of course, is a very mixed bag, blanketed with hate and dotted with sparks of love. What we do not realize is that we are seeing these witnesses not because they are true, but because *we* called them forth. Our mind is split between love and hate. Each side calls forth witnesses to back it up, and so we see a world that mirrors our mind, a world split between love and hate.

The good news is that we are not chained to our current perception. If what we see is what we invited, we can write a new invitation. We can invite only love, and when we do, that is all we will see.

> 9.   The power of decision is your one remaining freedom as a prisoner of this world. <u>You can decide to see it right</u>. What you <u>made</u> of it is <u>not</u> its reality, for its reality is only what you give [Ur: *gave*] it. You cannot <u>really</u> give anything <u>but</u> love to anyone or anything, nor can you really receive anything but love <u>from</u> them. If you think you have received anything <u>else</u>, it is because you have looked within and thought you saw the power to <u>give</u> something else <u>within yourself</u>. It was only <u>this</u> decision that determined what you found, for it was the decision for <u>what you sought</u>.

It may seem too hard to decide to see the world differently, yet the power to do so is the only freedom we have in this world. It is the last remaining reflection of the unlimited freedom of Heaven.

Application: Repeat with conviction,

> *I think I am not free to see a different world.*
> *Yet that is my one remaining freedom here.*
> *I **can** decide to see it right.*

When you look out now, you are not seeing the world's reality. Its reality (referring to the real world) is only the love you gave it, for in truth, only love *can* be given or received. We think, of course, that we receive something else—namely, attack—all the time. Yet that is merely an example of that four-step process of perception. First, we look within and see an attacking ego, possessing the apparent power to give something besides love. Then we invite the witnesses to the ego; we desire to see those witnesses in the world. And then we see them, and of course they are attacking us.

> 10.   You are afraid of me because you looked within and are afraid of what you saw. Yet you <u>could</u> not have seen reality, for the reality of your mind is the loveliest of God's creations. Coming only from God, its power and grandeur could only bring you peace *if you really looked upon it*. If you are afraid, it is because you saw something <u>that is not there</u>. Yet in that same place you could have looked upon me and all

your brothers, in the perfect safety of the Mind which created us. For we are there in the peace of the Father, Who wills to extend His peace through <u>you</u>.

We look within and see this awful power to give something besides love. We look within and see a monster. Now, because of how perception works, we will now expect others to wield this same destructive power *against* us. Near the top of this list will be Jesus, who will now appear to be the fearful messenger of divine retribution.

Yet he is challenging the beginning premise of our fear. He is saying that when we look within, we don't *really* look. If we really looked, we would see not a monster, breathing heavily and with claws unsheathed; instead, we would see "the loveliest of God's creations." Take a moment to let that in. There also, we would see Jesus and all our brothers. We would see the paradise of our true home. And rather than fear, we would feel nothing but peace.

11. When you have accepted your mission to extend peace you will <u>find</u> peace, for by <u>making it manifest</u> you will <u>see</u> it. Its holy witnesses will surround you because you <u>called upon them</u>, and they will come to you. I <u>have</u> heard your call and I have answered it, but you will not look upon me nor hear the answer that you sought. That is because you do not yet want *only* that. Yet as I become more real to you, you will learn that you <u>do</u> want only that. And you will see me as you look within, and we will look upon the real world together. Through the eyes of Christ, <u>only</u> the real world exists and only the real world can <u>be</u> seen. As you decide so will you see. And all that you see but witnesses to your decision.

"Your mission to extend peace" is composed of the two kinds of extension we have seen in this section—extending peace through our actions and extending peace through our perceptions. Both are ways of making peace manifest through us and *to* us. Thus, by taking on our mission, we will see only peace. As the paragraph says, "its holy witnesses will surround" us. What a beautiful image. It brings to mind this biblical passage about angels: "Since we are surrounded by so great a cloud of witnesses, let us also lay aside every weight" (Hebrews 12:1).

Yet for now, we are still divided inside. This means that our loving side has called to Jesus, and he has heard our call and answered it. But we are at best only dimly aware of this, because we are so divided, and this blinds us to his presence. We don't yet want *only* what he has to offer.

However, as he becomes more and more real to us, we will slowly learn that we "do want only that." And then we will see him. We will look inside ourselves and feel his presence, as distinctly as we feel the presence of a loved one beside us (this answers my question in the first half of this section of what was meant by "when you see me"—paragraph 6). And together we and Jesus will look upon the real world. For we will have lost all desire to see anything else.

> 12. When you look within and see me, it will be because you have decided to manifest truth. And as you manifest it you will see it both without <u>and</u> within. You will see it without *because* you saw it first within. Everything you behold without is a <u>judgment</u> of what you beheld within. If it is <u>your</u> judgment it will be wrong, for judgment is not your function. If it is the judgment of the Holy Spirit it will be right, for judgment *is* His function. You share His function only by judging <u>as He does</u>, reserving no judgment at all for yourself. You will judge against yourself, but He will judge *for* you.

When you look within and see/feel Jesus' presence, this will be the sign that you have decided to use that four-step process of perception (invite/expect/perceive/believe—see paragraph 5) to manifest *only* *truth*. Then you will look within and see only your holiness, and you will look without and see only the manifestations of holiness. You will stop judging anything on your own. You will no longer judge yourself or the world. You will throw away your judge's robes and your gavel, and merely receive the Holy Spirit's judgments, which, unlike yours, are on everyone's side, including yours.

> 13. Remember, then, that whenever you look without and react unfavorably to what you see, you have judged yourself unworthy and have condemned yourself to death. The death penalty is the ego's ultimate goal, for it fully believes that you are a criminal, as deserving of death as God knows you are deserving of life. The death penalty never leaves the ego's mind, for that is what it always reserves for you in the end. Wanting to kill you as the final expression of its feeling for you, it lets you live but to await death. It will torment you while you

live, but its hatred is not satisfied until you die. For your destruction is the one end toward which it works, and the only end with which it will be satisfied.

The first line sounds harsh, but it is merely what the four-step process predicts. What you see in the world is the witness to the presence that you see within. Thus, if you see a witness outside that you don't like, that is because you first looked within and saw something horrible—the power to attack and the inevitable self-condemnation that results.

Application: Think of someone you reacted to unfavorably recently, and say,

> *When I looked without and reacted unfavorably to [name]*
> *that was because I have judged myself unworthy and condemned*
> *myself to death.*

That self-condemnation is really the ego's condemnation of us. The ego has condemned us to death. That is hard to take on board, yet it is essential that we do so. The ego is mainly what we identify with as ourselves. Its prescriptions for how to think and behave are what we mainly follow in life. By buying into the ego, we have placed a program on our hard drive that is running our lives for us, yet we don't realize that this program is really a virus with one aim: to fry our hard drive, to kill us.

14. The ego is not a traitor to God, to Whom treachery is impossible. But it is a traitor to you who believe that you have been treacherous to your Father. That is why the undoing of guilt is an essential part of the Holy Spirit's teaching. For as long as you feel guilty you are listening to the voice of the ego, which tells you that you have been treacherous to God and therefore deserve death. You will think that death comes from God and not from the ego because, by confusing yourself with the ego, you believe that you want death. And from what you want God does not save you.

The ego constantly whispers to us, "You are a traitor to God." This, however, is a lie. The ego is betraying us by telling us this lie, and we are betraying ourselves by believing it. The outcome of believing this is that we feel guilty, assume that we deserve death, and even desire death (by identifying with the ego's desire for our death). Then, because God won't stop our desire's natural results from flowing out of it, we assume that God is responsible for our death, that He is giving us our just punishment.

It is hard to identify with all of this, and for good reason: It is primarily buried deep in our unconscious. Yet these beliefs are so foundational that they actually built this world, a world that constantly punishes us until it finally carries out the death penalty. These are not beliefs that some of us have and some of us don't, or that we acquired some time in the last few decades. These are beliefs that came before the atom and determined the architecture of the physical world.

> 15. When you are tempted to yield to the desire for death, *remember that I did not die*. You will realize that this is true when you look within and *see* me. Would I have overcome death for myself alone? And would eternal life have been given me of the Father <u>unless</u> He had also given it to <u>you</u>? When you learn to make <u>me</u> manifest, <u>you</u> will never see death. For you will have looked upon the deathless <u>in yourself</u>, and you will see only the eternal as you look out upon a world that cannot die.

When you are tempted to believe that you are hopeless, that your lack of love has placed you beyond redemption, remember the example of Jesus. He was given the death penalty, and yet he could not be killed. The evidence that he could not be killed is that he is alive in you, and you can directly see him there if you truly want to.

The fact that he could not be killed has huge implications for us. How could deathlessness be true only of him? How could it not be true of us as well? Thus, if we will look inside and see him, we will also be looking on the deathless in ourselves, and will look out with him upon a new world, "A world that cannot die."

VIII. The Attraction of Love for Love
Commentary by Robert Perry

1.   Do you <u>really</u> believe that you can kill the Son of God? The Father has hidden His Son safely within Himself, and kept him far away from your destructive thoughts, but <u>you</u> know neither the Father nor the Son because of them. You <u>attack</u> the real world every day and every hour and every minute, and yet you are surprised that you cannot <u>see</u> it. If you seek love in order to attack it, <u>you will never find it</u>. For if love is <u>sharing</u>, how can you find it except through <u>itself</u>? Offer it and it will come to you, because it is drawn to itself. But offer attack and love will remain hidden, for it can live only in peace.

This paragraph picks up with the theme that ended the last section: We cannot kill ourselves, even if our ego wants to do so. A single principle runs throughout this paragraph: When you attack something that is true, *it* is not damaged; rather, *you* lose sight of it. Thus, when you attack your Self, the Son of God within you, he is not injured; you simply lose sight of him. When you attack the real world, you cannot see it. When you attack love (which seems to serve as a synonym for the real world here), you will never find it. Love can only be approached through its own qualities of sharing and peace. Since "love is sharing," you have to share it, offer it, in order to have it.

Can you accept the idea that you are attacking "the real world every day and every hour and every minute"? What makes this easier for me to accept is the realization that if I wasn't attacking it, I would be seeing it right now.

2.   God's Son is as safe as his Father, for the Son knows his Father's protection and <u>cannot</u> fear. His Father's Love holds him in perfect peace, and needing nothing, he asks for nothing. Yet he is far from you whose Self he is, for you chose to attack him and he disappeared from your sight into his Father. <u>He</u> did not change, but <u>you</u> did. For a split mind and all its works were not created by the Father, and could not live in the knowledge <u>of</u> Him.

175

It may seem as if we have already killed the pure Son of God in us, as if we extinguished that light a very long time ago. The following analogy, however, captures what really happened: Let's say you believe that your mind is so powerful that with it you can make something shrink until it doesn't exist. So you sit in front of a giant sun and focus your psychic destructiveness on it. And sure enough, you see it shrink and shrink before your eyes, until it is simply not there. What you don't realize is that the sun hasn't changed one bit. You simply withdrew yourself further and further away from it, until it looked like it was gone. That's what happened with the Son of God within us.

> 3.   When you made visible what is <u>not</u> true, what *is* true became <u>invisible</u> to you. Yet it cannot be invisible in <u>itself</u>, for the Holy Spirit sees it with perfect clarity. It <u>is</u> invisible to you because you are looking at <u>something else</u>. Yet it is no more up to you to decide what is visible and what is invisible, than it is up to you to decide what reality is. What can be seen is <u>what the Holy Spirit sees</u>. The definition of reality is God's, not yours. <u>He</u> created it, and He knows what it is. You who knew have forgotten, and unless He had given you a way to remember you would have condemned yourself to oblivion.

Here is another slant on the sun analogy. You sit there concentrating on the sun vanishing, and suddenly it is gone. In its place, you see an earthly landscape, full of grass and trees and people. What you don't realize is that the sun is still there, but you have tuned it out. In its place you are seeing your own hallucinations. The landscape you see is actually invisible—it's not there to see. But you see it, simply because you have poured so much belief into it.

This is our story. We are sitting in the midst of the light of the real world right now. It is all around us. It is the only thing there is to see here. Yet we have tuned it out. In its place we are seeing our own hallucination. Think about this: All that you see before you is actually invisible—an hallucination (albeit a collective one). Yet it blinds you to what is really here. The Urtext, in speaking of sex, says, "How can man 'come close' to others thru the parts of him [body parts] which are really invisible?"

> 4.   Because of your Father's Love you can <u>never</u> forget Him, for no one can forget what God Himself placed in his memory. You can <u>deny</u>

it, but you <u>cannot lose it</u>. A Voice will answer every question you ask, and a vision will correct the perception of everything you see. For what you have made invisible is the only truth, and what you have not heard is the only Answer. God would reunite you with yourself, and did not abandon you in your [Ur: seeming] distress. You are waiting only for Him, and do not know it. Yet His memory shines in your mind and cannot <u>be</u> obliterated. It is no more past than future, being forever always.

We have so tuned out God's infinite sun that He became to us a tiny star, and then became invisible completely in the bright daylight of our hallucination. We seem to have forgotten the eternal Love Who once meant everything to us. Yet we are literally incapable of doing that. He loves us too much to let us forget Him. His memory shines in our mind. His Voice will answer our every question. His true perception will correct everything we see. We can *try* to leave a Love like this, but we cannot succeed.

Application: Think of some of the things you think you are waiting for, and realize that the actual list is far longer than these few things. Then say,

> *Father, I am waiting only for you, and do not know it.*
> *Your memory shines in my mind.*
> *It is neither past nor to come; it is forever always.*

5.   You have but to ask for this memory, and you <u>will</u> remember. Yet the memory of God cannot shine in a mind that has obliterated it and <u>wants to keep it so</u>. For the memory of God can dawn only in a mind that chooses to remember, and that has relinquished the insane desire to control reality. You who cannot even control yourself should hardly aspire to control the universe. But look upon what you have made of it, and rejoice that it is not so.

The remembering of God is the final reawakening to Heaven, to knowledge. To have it, all we need to do is ask. Yet the whole spiritual journey is one of reaching the place where our asking is truly *sincere*.

And to sincerely want to remember God, we need to have relinquished the desire to play god ourselves.

Application: Say the following to God as sincerely as you can:

> *Let me remember You.*
> *I relinquish my insane desire to control the universe,*
> *for I cannot even control myself.*
> *I look upon the chaos that my "control" has made,*
> *and I rejoice that it never really happened.*
> *Thank God this world is not true.*
> *I am ready now.*
> *Father, let me remember You.*

6. Son of God, be not content with nothing! What is not real [the visible world] cannot <u>be</u> seen and has <u>no</u> value. God could not offer His Son what has no value, nor could His Son receive it. You were redeemed the instant you thought you had deserted Him. Everything you made [the visible world] has never been, and is invisible because the Holy Spirit does not see it. Yet what He <u>does</u> see is yours to behold, and through <u>His</u> vision <u>your</u> perception is healed. You have made <u>in</u>visible [Ur: *in*visible] the only truth that this world holds. Valuing nothing, you have sought nothing [Ur: you have sought it and found it]. By making nothing real to you, you have <u>seen</u> it. *But it is not there.* And Christ is invisible to you <u>because of what you have made visible to [Ur: yourselves]</u> yourself.

To understand this paragraph, you need to see it in light of the previous ones. This means that "what is not real" and "everything you made" refer to what we call the visible world. That is the "nothing." That is what "cannot be seen and has no value." The message, then, is this: We are the Son of God. How can *we* be content with the nothingness of the visible world? How can we let our eyes be dazzled by what is not there to see? How can we let such nothingness blind us to the glory of Christ? We left home on a journey that was mad indeed, yet God redeemed us the very instant we deserted Him. He made sure that the world we made was never real. And He gave us the sure correction for our errors of perception. Through the Holy Spirit's vision our perception is healed, once and for all.

> 7.   Yet it does not matter how much distance you have tried to interpose between your awareness and truth. God's Son <u>can</u> be seen because his vision is shared. The Holy Spirit looks upon him, and sees nothing else in you. What is invisible to you is perfect in His sight, and encompasses <u>all</u> of it. He has remembered <u>you</u> because He forgot not the Father. You looked upon the unreal and found despair. Yet by <u>seeking</u> the unreal, what else <u>could</u> you find? The <u>un</u>real world *is* a thing of despair, for it can never be. And you who share God's Being with Him could never be content <u>without</u> reality. What God did not give you has no power over you, and the attraction of love for love remains irresistible. For it is the function of love to unite all things unto itself, and to hold all things together by extending its wholeness.

Application: Sometimes these paragraphs can seem so dry, until I slow down, insert my name, and savor each line. Let's go ahead and *slowly* read the paragraph again, just slightly reworded, with asterisks added for inserting your name, and with emphasis added from the Urtext:

Yet it does not matter* how much distance you have tried to interpose
  between your awareness and truth [thank God!].
[No matter what the distance,] God's Son *can* be seen....
The Holy Spirit looks upon him, and sees nothing else in you*.
What is invisible to you* [the Son] is perfect in His sight, and
  encompasses *all* of it.
He has remembered *you** because He forgot not [your] Father.
You looked upon the unreal [world] and found despair.
Yet by *seeking* the unreal*, what else *could* you find?
[How ironic that what I *found* was despair of ever *really* finding.]
The *un*real world *is* a thing of despair, for it can never be [real].
And you who share God's Being with Him* could never be content
  without reality.
[Yet the world that] God did not give you* has no power over you,
  and the attraction of love for [you]* remains irresistible.
For it is the function of love to [draw] all things [together into] itself,
  [including you,]*

and to hold all things together by extending its wholeness.

> 8.   The real world was given you by God in loving exchange for the world <u>you</u> made and the world you <u>see</u>. Only take it from the hand of Christ and look upon it. <u>Its</u> reality will make everything <u>else</u> invisible, for beholding it is <u>total</u> perception. And as you look upon it you will remember that it [the real world] was always so. Nothingness will become invisible, for you will at last have seen truly. Redeemed perception is easily translated into knowledge, for <u>only</u> perception is capable of error and perception has never been. Being corrected it gives place to knowledge, which is forever the <u>only</u> reality. The Atonement is but the way back to what was never lost. [It was never lost because] Your Father could not cease to love His Son.

This whole section has been about the emptiness of the visible world. Since it's not really there, there's nothing real to obtain from it. Seeking happiness from it, then, can only lead to despair. Looking on its painful sights can only make our eyes tired. Shouldn't we be glad, then, that God gave us another world to look on? When we at last see it, we will realize that it has always been there to see. And then the "visible" world will become invisible to us, not to our eyes, but to our *mind*. For the real world is not a *component* of what can be seen; it is *all* there is to see. And then our perception will be perfect, and will be translated into the knowledge of Heaven, the knowledge of God. This knowledge is forever the only reality. Therefore, we could not lose it. Our Father loves us too much to let us lose it.

Commentaries on Chapter 13

THE GUILTLESS WORLD

Introduction
Commentary by Robert Perry

1. If you did not feel guilty you could not attack, for condemnation is the root of attack. It [condemnation] is the judgment of one mind by another as <u>unworthy</u> of love and <u>deserving</u> of punishment. But herein lies the split. For the mind that judges [condemns] perceives itself as <u>separate</u> from the mind being judged, believing that by punishing <u>another,</u> <u>it</u> will escape punishment. All this is but the delusional attempt of the mind to deny itself [deny its true nature by condemning itself], and <u>escape the penalty of denial</u> [by putting the penalty on someone else]. It is <u>not</u> an attempt to <u>relinquish</u> denial, but to <u>hold on to it</u>. For it is guilt that has obscured the Father to you, and it is guilt that has driven you insane.

This is a hard paragraph to follow. Here is what I understand it as saying. We feel guilty; we condemn ourselves as being unworthy of love and deserving of punishment. Through this, we deny our true innocence and obscure our Father, all of which carries tremendous pain, so much so that it has driven us insane. We then try to solve this pain by attacking a brother, by condemning a brother, by punishing a brother. We transfer our sense of guilt to him, and this seems to relieve our sense of guilt. Now it's his, not ours. We have escaped punishment because the sentence has fallen on his head.

Yet we don't realize two crucial things. First, that this "other" that we are transferring our guilt to is no other at all, but a part of our very Self. In a very real sense, then, the guilt hasn't gone anywhere. Second, that we are not actually trying to escape our denial of our innocence. We are simply trying to get rid of the pain of it so that we can "hold onto it." It's like taking a pill to get rid of the hangovers so that you can keep on getting drunk.

2. The acceptance of guilt into the mind of God's Son was the beginning of the separation, as the acceptance of the Atonement is its end. The world you see is the delusional system of those made mad by guilt. Look carefully at this world, and you will realize that this is so.

> For this world is the symbol of punishment, and all the laws that seem to govern it are the laws of death. Children are born into it through pain and in pain. Their growth is attended by suffering, and they learn of sorrow and separation and death. Their minds seem to be trapped in their brain, and its powers to decline if their bodies are hurt. They seem to love, yet they desert and are deserted. They appear to lose what they love, perhaps the most insane belief of all. And their bodies wither and gasp and are laid in the ground, and are no more. Not one of them but has thought that God is cruel.

This is an extremely important paragraph, one whose meaning is very easy to overlook. Jesus first tells us that this world is a *delusional system*. This means that the world is not a real, solid place, but a mere belief system, one that is spun around a core *delusion* (like the belief system an insane person might weave around the core delusion that he is the messiah). What is the core delusion in this system? Guilt. Guilt has driven us all insane, and as an expression of this insanity, we made the world.

Then he says a rather remarkable thing: "Look carefully at this world, and you will realize that this is so." If we just carefully look around, he says, we will realize that the world was made by those driven insane by guilt. What a claim!

And then, in typical Course fashion, he carries out this observation exercise for us. When you look carefully at the world, what do you see? You see the human life cycle, which is filled with pain. You see pain at birth, pain in growing up, pain in aging, and pain at death.

Who can deny this? What he describes here are the facts of life. Yet how does this translate into proof that the world was made by those driven mad by guilt? The answer is in the fourth sentence: "For this world is the symbol of punishment, and all the laws that seem to govern it are the laws of death." What the pain-filled human life cycle shows us is that this world punishes us from the moment we are born until the moment we die, when it carries out capital punishment on us. The world is designed to do this, from the bottom up. Even its physical laws are the laws of death. All of this implies a foundational assumption—that we are guilty. Just as the Nazi death camps were built on the presumption of Jewish guilt so this entire world was built on the presumption of *our* guilt.

The last line—"Not one of them but has thought that God is cruel"— is significant. It shows that we already carried out Jesus' observation exercise, and concluded something similar. We looked at the painful human life cycle and concluded that whoever the world's designer was, he is obviously obsessed with punishing us. He clearly believes in our profound guilt. The only difference is that we assumed the designer was God, whereas in truth it was *us*. *We* designed this crazy world based on a single core delusion: that we are guilty and deserve to be punished until we expire.

> 3. If this were the real world, God *would* be cruel. For no Father could subject His children to this as the price of salvation and *be* loving. *Love does not kill to save.* If it did, attack <u>would</u> be salvation, and this is the ego's interpretation, not God's. Only the world of guilt could demand this, for only the guilty could <u>conceive</u> of it. Adam's "sin" could have touched no one, had he [Ur: you] not believed it was the <u>Father</u> Who drove him out of paradise. For in <u>that</u> belief the knowledge of the Father was lost, since only those who do not understand Him <u>could</u> believe it.

If God was the one who set this system up, He would be cruel, no doubt about it. What would His idea be? That if we get punished enough, then we can pay off all our guilt, so that, having paid our debt, we can come back home? A pretty sick idea, one that clearly smacks of the ego, not God. However, when we believe it is *God's* idea, we give validity to the notion of guilt and the punishment of guilt. This is precisely how "the knowledge of the Father was lost."

> 4. This world *is* a picture of the crucifixion of God's Son. And until you realize that God's Son <u>cannot</u> be crucified, this is the world you will see. Yet you will <u>not</u> realize this [that God's Son cannot be crucified] until you accept the eternal fact that <u>God's Son is not guilty</u>. He <u>deserves</u> only love because he has <u>given</u> only love. He cannot be condemned because he has never condemned. The Atonement is the final lesson he need learn, for it teaches him that, never having sinned, <u>he has no need of salvation</u>.

"This world *is* a picture of the crucifixion of God's Son." *It is.* The crosses are set up all over—in every home, in every workplace, on every street—and we are all getting nailed up all the time. And one only gets crucified as punishment for guilt.

We therefore need to realize two things. First, that God's Son *cannot* be guilty. Whatever dark dreams we may have had, our nature is eternally pure. And therefore, second, we cannot be crucified. We *cannot* die because we don't *deserve* to die. When we realize these two things, the physical world and all its crosses will become invisible to us. Our eyes will still see it, but our mind will look right past it as we gaze in rapture upon the real world.

I. Guiltlessness and Invulnerability
Commentary by Robert Perry

1.   Earlier, I [Ur: Long ago we] said that the Holy Spirit shares the goal of all good teachers, whose ultimate aim is to make themselves unnecessary by teaching their pupils all they know. The Holy Spirit wants <u>only</u> [Ur: wills *only*] this, for sharing the Father's Love for His Son, He seeks [Ur: wills] to remove all guilt from his mind that he may remember his Father in peace. Peace and guilt are antithetical, and the Father can <u>be</u> remembered <u>only</u> in peace. Love and guilt cannot coexist, and to accept one is to <u>deny</u> the other. Guilt hides Christ from your sight, for it is the denial of the blamelessness of God's Son.

It is quite amazing to think that the Holy Spirit wants to render Himself unnecessary by teaching us to know all that He knows. And what does He know? The Father. The Holy Spirit loves us so deeply that His only aim is to bring us to the point where we know God again, to the same degree that He does. Think about something you felt you received from the Holy Spirit, and realize that He gave it to you for the sake of this single aim.

How does He bring us to this knowledge? By removing all guilt from our minds. Guilt is the big block. It is what blocks us from peace, from love, and from the sight of Christ. To really have these things, we need to be willing to shed every last trace of guilt.

2.   In the strange world that you have made the Son of God *has* sinned. How could you see him, then? By making <u>him</u> invisible, the world of retribution rose in the black cloud of guilt that you accepted, and you hold it dear. For the blamelessness of Christ is the proof that the ego never was, and can never be. Without guilt the ego <u>has</u> no life, and God's Son *is* without guilt.

The image in the third sentence is an important one. We started out gazing on the shining innocence of our true Self, the Christ. But then we accepted instead the reality of guilt, which mushroomed in our mind into a vast black cloud, blocking out the light of Christ's innocence. As we gazed at this cloud, we saw it shape itself into a world, full of figures acting and being acted on. And since the cloud was made of guilt, the action was all about punishment. We saw figure after figure nailed to shadowy crosses as punishment for their sins.

As insane as it sounds, we actually cherish the black cloud. Why? Because it conveniently blocks out the innocence of Christ, which is the definitive evidence that the ego never existed. And we'll do anything to keep from realizing the ego never existed.

> 3.   As you look upon yourself and judge what you do honestly, [Ur: as you have been asked to do,] you may be tempted to wonder how you can be guiltless. Yet consider this: You are <u>not</u> guiltless in time, but <u>in eternity</u>. You <u>have</u> "sinned" <u>in the past</u>, but there <u>is</u> no past. Always [all ways] has no direction. Time seems to go in one direction, but when you reach its end it will roll up like a long carpet spread along the past behind you, and will disappear. As long as you believe the Son of God is guilty you will walk along this carpet, believing that it leads to death. And the journey will seem long and cruel and senseless, for so it is.

What an important paragraph! We've been asked to look at ourselves and judge our actions honestly. And as we do, we are forced to admit one stark fact: If the world of time is real, then *we have sinned.*

Thank God, then, that time is not real. We only seem to be walking along this long carpet of time, doing selfish things, making ourselves guilty. Yet our guilt, as we'll see, is what *keeps* us on this carpet, what keeps us making this "long and cruel and senseless" journey, this journey to the grave.

When we at last learn our guiltlessness, we will have reached the end. Then, we will look back on this incredibly long carpet, and see all of our life experiences woven onto it, like a tapestry, one event after another. Then, to our astonishment, we will see the carpet begin to roll up behind us, gathering into a gigantic roll. When this roll finally reaches us, we will at last realize what time really was. Looking at the roll from the side, we will see all of our life experiences on top of each other, not one after another. We will realize that they all happened at once. We will see that time didn't really go in one direction. Like this spiral of carpet, it went all ways at once. Instead of a linear train of different moments, it was really a single unchanging "always." And when we realize this, the entire roll of carpet, along with all of our experiences, all of the attacking and being attacked, all of the sin and guilt, will vanish. Time will be gone. And then we will *know* that we never sinned.

> 4.   The journey the Son of God has set himself is useless [Ur: foolish] indeed, but the journey on which his Father sets him is one of release and joy. The Father is not cruel, and His Son cannot hurt himself. The retaliation that he fears and that he sees [Ur: *and which he sees*] will never touch him, for although he believes in it the Holy Spirit knows it is not true. The Holy Spirit stands at the end of time, where you must be because He is with you. He has already [Ur: has *always*] undone everything unworthy of the Son of God, for such was His mission, given Him by God. And what God gives has always been.

This paragraph speaks of three things.

1.   The foolish journey we have set ourselves on, in which we walk along the carpet, dishing it out and taking it, believing that at the end we will receive the death penalty for our sins.
2.   The journey that God sets us on, in which we step into ever-increasing release and joy.
3.   The truth that we stand at the end of the journey, where we have already stepped off the carpet, which has already rolled up and disappeared behind us.

> 5.   You will see me as you learn the Son of God is guiltless. He has always sought his guiltlessness, and he has found it. For everyone is seeking to escape from the prison he has made, and the way to find release is not denied him. Being in him, he has found it. *When* he finds it is only a matter of time, and time is but an illusion. For the Son of God is guiltless now, and the brightness of his purity shines untouched forever in God's Mind. God's Son will always be as he was created. Deny your world and judge him not, for his eternal guiltlessness is in the Mind of his Father, and protects him forever.

Here again I see three different states:

1. We are always seeking our guiltlessness—usually through

trying to pay off our sins—and we have found it. Yet, it is still buried deep within us, and so we don't *realize* we have found it.

2. One day, at the end of our personal timeline, after long journeying and great spiritual dedication, we will find our guiltlessness in full awareness.

3. Yet when we finally reach that place, we will realize that we were guiltless all along. We will discover that we are *eternally* guiltless.

Application: Think of someone you have recently judged or been irritated with, and repeat these lines:

I deny the world in which [name] did those things.
I judge him not, for as God's Son, he is guiltless now.
And the brightness of his purity shines untouched forever in the Mind of God.

6. When you have accepted the Atonement for yourself, you will realize <u>there is no guilt in God's Son</u>. And <u>only</u> as you look upon him as guiltless can you understand his oneness. For the <u>idea</u> of guilt brings a belief in condemnation of one by another, projecting separation in place of unity. You can condemn only yourself, and by so doing you cannot know that you are God's Son. You have denied the condition of his being, which is his perfect blamelessness. Out of love he was created, and in love he abides. Goodness and mercy have always followed him, for he has always extended the Love of his Father.

As long as we believe in guilt, we cannot truly believe in oneness. For guilt always entails a picture in which one person is condemning the guilt in another. One is the judge; the other, the defendant. How, then, can they be one? What we do not realize is that each judge is secretly a defendant, who hopes that as long he sits in the judge's chair no one will notice his crimes.

Yet what we further don't realize is that labeling ourselves the defendant is the biggest lie of all, for it represents the denial of our true blamelessness.

7.   As you perceive the holy companions who travel with you, you will realize that there <u>is</u> no journey, but only an awakening. The Son of God, who sleepeth not, has kept faith with his Father <u>for</u> you. There is no road to travel <u>on</u>, and no time to travel <u>through</u>. For God waits not for His Son in time, being forever unwilling to be without him. And so it has always been. Let the holiness of God's Son shine away the cloud of guilt that darkens your mind, and by accepting his purity <u>as</u> yours, learn of him that it *is* yours.

The people who travel with us seem not just to be *on* the carpet of time; they seem to be *of* the carpet of time. They are defined by the action on the carpet, by what they do and what is done to them. Or so it seems. If we really saw them, our perspective on everything would change. Imagine looking at someone who shares the journey with you and realizing that she genuinely is the Son of God. Imagine realizing that, as God's Son, she is eternally pure. Finally, imagine realizing that she only *seems* to be on the carpet, that in reality this person is beyond time, beyond the dream, forever changeless and eternally awake.

If you really saw this, you would instantly realize that, if she is God's holy Son, then you must be as well. And if she is not *really* on this journey, if she is not really going anywhere, then you are not, either. You would realize there is no journey, only an awakening from the sleep of guilt. And all you need do to have this joyous realization is to really *see* the person you journey with.

8.   You are invulnerable <u>because</u> you are guiltless. You can hold on to the past <u>only</u> through guilt. For guilt establishes that you <u>will be</u> punished for what you have done, and thus depends on one-dimensional time, proceeding from past to future. No one who believes this can understand what "<u>always</u>" means, and therefore guilt <u>must</u> deprive you of the appreciation of eternity. You are immortal <u>because</u> you are eternal, and "always" <u>must</u> be now. Guilt, then, is a way of holding past and future in your mind to ensure the ego's continuity. For if what <u>has been will be</u> punished, the ego's continuity is guaranteed. Yet the guarantee of your continuity is God's, not the ego's. And immortality is the opposite of time, for time passes away, while immortality is constant.

This paragraph makes a totally logical yet deeply original connection:

Guilt chains us to *time*. Guilt says that you sinned in the past, and thus are guilty in the present, and so will be punished in the future. As long as you carry guilt, then, you will think, "Time is where I belong." You will be like the abused wife who, for reasons no one else can understand, stays in the abusive household even though she could just get up and walk out. Somehow, her concept of herself chains her to that household. In the same way, our concept of ourselves chains us to the abusive world of time.

If we didn't have that concept, we would simply get up and walk into eternity. We would feel completely at home in "always." We would grasp that our continuity is not our continuing in time, but our being in the "always" of eternity. And we would understand that immortality does not mean lasting forever in time, but being in the "forever always" of timelessness.

> 9. Accepting the Atonement teaches you <u>what immortality is</u>, for by accepting your guiltlessness you learn that the past has never been, and so the future is needless and will not be. The future, <u>in time</u>, is <u>always</u> associated with expiation, and <u>only</u> guilt could induce a sense of a <u>need</u> for expiation. Accepting the guiltlessness of the Son of God <u>as yours</u> is therefore God's way of reminding you of His Son, and what he is in truth. For God has never condemned His Son, and being guiltless he <u>is</u> eternal.

"The future, in time, is always associated with expiation." What a profound insight! Isn't it true that somewhere inside you look at the future and think, "That's where I'll make up for all that I've done wrong"? Therefore, if the future is nothing but a projection of your mind, then your *guilt* is what is fueling that projection. It is the "light" that shines through the projector, without which the projector would project nothing.

Therefore, if you can accept your brother's guiltlessness, and then realize that his guiltlessness is yours, then the projector will stop, the future will disappear from the screen, and you will realize you are sitting in the theater of eternity.

> 10. You cannot dispel guilt by making it real, and <u>then</u> atoning for it. This is the ego's plan, which it offers <u>instead</u> of dispelling it. The ego believes in <u>atonement through attack</u> [on yourself], being fully

committed to the insane notion that attack is salvation. And you who cherish guilt must also believe it, for how else but by identifying with the ego could you hold dear what you do not want [guilt]?

11. The ego teaches you to attack yourself because you are guilty, and this must increase the guilt, for guilt is the result of attack. In the ego's teaching, then, there is no escape from guilt. For attack makes guilt real, and if it is real there is no way to overcome it. The Holy Spirit dispels it simply through the calm recognition that it has never been. As He looks upon the guiltless Son of God, He knows that this is true. And being true for you, you cannot attack yourself, for without guilt attack is impossible. You, then, are saved because God's Son is guiltless. And being wholly pure, you are invulnerable.

We need to look hard at our plan to use the future to atone for our sins, and realize the plan is bankrupt. We are constantly telling ourselves "I'll make up for it, I'll pay for it....And then I'll be clean." But we will never reach that goal, not this way.

Why won't we? Because making up for it amounts to paying for it, which equals attacking ourselves. In other words, we assume that if we attack ourselves enough, we will wipe our slate clean. Yet sins that are real enough to warrant self-punishment are genuinely real, and that means they are our reality and there is no way to wipe them clean.

No, the only way out is not to make up for it, to pay, to seek expiation. The way out is the Holy Spirit's calm recognition that our sins *have never been.* They took place on the carpet of time, and there is no carpet of time.

One caveat: In the early dictation, Jesus does speak of certain good deeds as acts of atoning for the past. This principle is also mentioned later in the Course, which says that each gift to a brother "allows a past mistake to go, and leave no shadow on the holy mind my Father loves" (W-pII.316.1:2). However, this same early dictation also criticized Bill for trying to "atone on his own," by self-selecting a "good" deed that was simultaneously designed to slight Helen. So we can distinguish between good deeds that are truly good because they extend a genuinely loving and caring perception of the other person (and thus contain a vision of that person's guiltlessness), and "good" deeds in which we are just trying to pay off our past sins—a kind of private transaction with our score sheet in which the other person doesn't really matter. We are just opening up a vein to pay for our sins.

II. The Guiltless Son of God
Commentary by Robert Perry

1.   The ultimate purpose of projection is <u>always</u> to get rid of guilt. Yet, characteristically, the ego attempts to get rid of guilt <u>from its viewpoint only</u>, for much as the ego wants to <u>retain</u> guilt *you* find it intolerable, since guilt stands in the way of your remembering God, Whose pull is so strong that <u>you</u> cannot resist it. On this issue, then, the deepest split of all occurs, for if you are to <u>retain</u> guilt, as the ego insists, *you cannot be you.* Only by persuading you that <u>it</u> is you could the ego possibly induce you to <u>project</u> guilt, and thereby keep it in your mind.

To capture the sense of this paragraph, we can imagine the following dialogue:

You: I feel so guilty. How can I get rid of this awful feeling?

Your ego: Well, that's simple. You should project it. See the other guy, not yourself, as the guilty party.

You: But when I blame my brother, I feel even guiltier in the end.

Ego: Is that really so bad?

You: Yes. I find guilt intolerable. It keeps me from awakening to God, and the pull of Him is so strong that I can't resist it.

Ego: I wouldn't take that "pull" too seriously. It's kind of like when you thought you really wanted that seafood dish the other night, but it didn't taste so good and you got sick afterwards.

You: So this is not a genuine pull? How do you know?

Ego: I know because I am you—the *real* you—and I don't feel any attraction to God whatsoever.

You: Oh, so you're me? I get it now. I guess I was just mistaken about that attraction to God.

Ego: Of course you were. Now go ahead and blame your brother. It will feel good, and you can live with a little guilt.

You: OK, this is gonna be good.

2.   Yet consider how strange a solution the ego's arrangement is. You project guilt to get rid of it, but you are actually merely concealing it. You do experience the guilt, but you have no idea why. On the contrary, you associate it with a weird assortment of "ego ideals," which the ego claims you have failed. Yet you have no idea that you are failing the Son of God by seeing him as guilty. Believing you are no longer you, you do not realize that you are failing yourself.

What a fascinating account of what happens when we project our guilt. We think that when we do this, we suddenly feel unburdened, guilt-free. Now it's the other guy's guilt. What we've really done, however, is simply conceal our guilt.

More ironic still, we do *experience* this guilt; we just don't know where it's coming from. We *think* it comes from violating our ego ideals. We could call this the "I'm so stupid" guilt. For example: "I'm so stupid for that driving error I just made." "I can't believe I forgot about that appointment (I'm so stupid)." "I can't believe I missed that business opportunity—I'm losing my edge (I'm so stupid)."

The guilt now seems to be about failing our personal code, our ideals of what it means to be a smart, considerate, effective, superior *ego*—which of course implies that our ego is what we are supposed to be faithful to. This is a profound distortion of the real nature of guilt, for our guilt is really over betraying not our ego, but our divine nature. And we betray this nature not just by attacking our brother; we betray it simply by *feeling guilty*. Feeling guilty is just as much a betrayal of our true nature as acting stupidly is a betrayal of our ego.

3.   The darkest of your hidden cornerstones holds your belief in guilt from your awareness. For in that dark and secret place is the realization that you have betrayed God's Son by condemning him to death. You do not even suspect this murderous but insane idea lies hidden there, for the ego's destructive urge is so intense that nothing short of the crucifixion of God's Son can ultimately satisfy it. It does not know who the Son of God is because it is blind. Yet let it perceive guiltlessness anywhere, and it will try to destroy it because it is afraid.

To appreciate the imagery here (which hearkens back to the introduction to Chapter 11), we need to think of ourselves as living on the top story of some tall building, the building of our life. Everything seems fine. Life is a struggle, but basically OK. What we don't even vaguely suspect is that many stories below lie the building's dark, hidden cornerstones. And inside one of these, the very darkest one, is the premise on which the whole building rests: "I have betrayed the holy Son of God in me by seeing him as so guilty that he deserves death. And I will carry out this death sentence if I possibly can." Deep-down, way below consciousness, each of us feels like a Judas in relation to our own divine nature. Can you feel at least a sliver of that sense in you?

> 4.   Much of the ego's strange behavior is directly attributable to its definition of guilt. To the ego, *the guiltless are guilty.* Those who do not attack are its "enemies" because, by not valuing its interpretation of salvation [see 12.III.3:1], they are in an excellent position to let it go. They have approached the darkest and deepest cornerstone in the ego's foundation, and while the ego can withstand your raising all else to question, it guards this one secret with its life, for its existence depends on keeping this secret. So it is this secret that we must look upon, for the ego cannot protect you against truth, and in its presence the ego is dispelled.

The ego *has* to keep this cornerstone hidden. It can't let us really look at it, because if we do, we will see that it's nonsense. It's a contradiction. Remember when we looked at another one of these cornerstones in Chapter 11? It said, "You made your own father"—a blatant contradiction. Now this one says, "The Son of God is guilty because he is so guiltless." His sin is that he is completely sinless—free of attack and free of guilt. He deserves death because he is purely good. This is the real issue the ego has with our true nature, and yet this is complete nonsense. And that is why the ego can never let us look on it.

> 5.   In the calm light of truth, let us recognize that you believe you have crucified God's Son. You have not admitted to this "terrible" secret because you would still wish to crucify him if you could find him. Yet the wish has hidden him from you because it is very fearful, and so you are afraid to find him. You have handled this wish to kill yourself by not knowing who you are, and identifying with something else. You have projected guilt blindly and indiscriminately, but you have not uncovered its source. For the ego does want to kill you, and if you identify with it you must believe its goal is yours.

Application: What does it mean to believe we have crucified God's Son? It means believing that we have killed our divine nature, that we have snuffed out the divine light in us. Try to recognize that you do believe this. Sit a minute with it, trying to locate this belief in you, because it *is* in there, or you wouldn't be here.

According to this paragraph, we have joined with the ego's goal of killing the Son of God in us and responded to this urge in two ways. The first is guilt—feeling guilty for killing our divine nature, which is the real source of all guilt. The second is avoidance—making sure we don't find the Son of God in us so that we *won't* kill him. We are thus like a hit man who is so ambivalent about his job that he "inadvertently" loses his target's address so that, being unable to find him, he can't kill him. Could this be why we find it so hard to locate the Son of God in us in our meditations?

> 6.   I have said that the crucifixion is the symbol of the ego. When it [the ego] was confronted with the <u>real</u> guiltlessness of God's Son [in the person of Jesus] it <u>did</u> attempt to kill him, and the reason it gave was that guiltlessness is blasphemous to God. To the ego, <u>the ego</u> is God, and guiltlessness <u>must</u> be interpreted <u>as the final guilt that fully justifies murder</u>. You do not yet understand that any fear you may experience in connection with [Ur: You do not yet understand that *all* your fear of] this course stems ultimately from this interpretation, but if you will consider your reactions <u>to</u> it you will become increasingly convinced that this is so.

This is all pretty hard to swallow. Due to our identification with our ego, we are trying to kill God's Son within us *because* he's pure? How true can that be? And if it's true, might it not be some unconscious pattern that's so buried it's not really a factor in our lives?

As if in answer to our doubts, Jesus then brings out two concrete examples. The first is his own crucifixion. According to Matthew and Mark, Caiaphas delivers Jesus to Pilate to be crucified because Jesus commits the blasphemy of claiming to be God's Son. The implication in this paragraph is that his blasphemy was not just claiming to be but actually *being* God's guiltless Son. The authorities' reaction to Jesus was thus a concrete manifestation of how we all react to the Son of God within.

The next example is much closer to home. It's not about how "they" reacted to Jesus 2,000 years ago, but how we react to the Course now. The next two paragraphs will explain.

> 7.   This course has explicitly stated that its goal <u>for you</u> is happiness and peace. Yet you are <u>afraid</u> of it. You have been told again and again that it will set you free, yet you sometimes react [Ur; yet you react] as if it is trying to <u>imprison</u> you. You often <u>dismiss</u> it more readily than you dismiss the ego's thought system. [Ur: Most of the time you *dismiss* it, *but you do not dismiss the ego s thought system.* You *have* seen its results and you *still* lack faith in it.] To some extent, then, you <u>must</u> believe [Ur: You *must* believe, then,] that by <u>not</u> learning the course <u>you are protecting yourself</u>. And you do <u>not</u> realize that it is only your guiltlessness that *can* protect you.

> 8.   The Atonement has always been interpreted as the release from guilt, and this is correct if it is understood. Yet even when I interpret [Ur: interpreted] it <u>for</u> you [in the Course], you may reject [Ur: have rejected] it and do <u>not</u> accept [Ur: have *not* accepted] it <u>for yourself</u>. You have perhaps [Ur: You have] recognized the futility of the ego and its offerings, but though you do not want them, you may not yet [Ur: you will not] look upon the alternative [that the Course offers] with gladness. In the extreme ["In the extreme" seems to have been added by the editors], <u>you are afraid of redemption</u> and <u>you believe it will kill you</u>. Make no mistake about the depth of this fear. For you believe that, in the presence of truth, you might [Ur: will] turn on yourself and <u>destroy</u> yourself.

When Jesus says at the end of paragraph 6, "if you will consider your reactions to it you will become increasingly convinced that this is so," that's the cue that he is going to consider our reactions for us, which is exactly what he does in paragraphs 7 and 8.

Application: Go through the following questions and put a check mark next to the ones that have at least some truth in them. Try to see that they do describe your reactions to the Course, at least to some degree:

_____Even though the Course says it wants happiness and peace for me, I am afraid of it.

_____Even though it says it will set me free, I react to it as if it is
trying to imprison me.

_____In most of the actual living of my life, I dismiss the
Course, though I don't dismiss the ego's thought system.

_____I have seen the Course's results, and I still lack faith in it.

_____I seem to believe that by not learning the Course I am
protecting myself.

_____I have not really accepted the Atonement for myself, even
though it's all about release from guilt and the Course
has interpreted it for me in a very benign way.

_____Even though I recognize the futility of the ego and its
offerings, I do not look upon the Course's alternative
with gladness.

These questions add up to the idea that we fear and dismiss the Course even though it comes as a pure messenger of our deliverance. The Course, then, is for us the modern-day manifestation of the Son of God. And our reaction to the Course is the manifestation of our unconscious urge to kill the Son of God, not because he is horrible, but *because* he is pure. When we attack the Course, actively or passively, we are attacking it because it holds open the doorway to our innocence. We are attacking it in order to attack our own guiltlessness, in order to kill the Son of God *in us*. Can we admit that to ourselves?

> 9.   Little child, this is not so. Your "guilty secret" is nothing, and if you will but bring it to the light, the Light <u>will</u> dispel it. And then no dark cloud will remain between you and the remembrance of your Father, for you will remember His guiltless Son, who did not die because he is immortal. And you will see that you were redeemed <u>with</u> him, and have never been separated <u>from</u> him. In <u>this</u> understanding lies your remembering, for it is the recognition of love <u>without</u> fear. There will be great joy in Heaven on your homecoming, and the joy will be <u>yours</u>. For the redeemed son of man <u>is</u> the guiltless Son of God, and to recognize <u>him</u> *is* your redemption.

Our guilty secret is "I have killed the Son of God within, or I would if I could find him." That's the secret that we are afraid to bring to the light.

Can you feel the fear of bringing this secret out of hiding? Yet if we will bring it to the light of awareness, the Light of God will dispel it for us. And then we will see the guiltless Son in us, the Son that was not affected in the least by our attacks. Seeing him, we will realize we *are* him, and have always been him. And with this realization, we will be home.

III. The Fear of Redemption
Commentary by Robert Perry

This section contains so many important ideas. Several discussions in it have proved foundational for my whole understanding of the Course. I think this is also true of Greg Mackie and Allen Watson. Allen, after all, wrote an extended commentary on this section, which he self-published (in 1991) as the booklet which brought him to my attention, and made me want to have him at the Circle, and which the Circle then republished in *Through Fear to Love*.

1. You may wonder why it is so crucial that you look upon your hatred and realize its full extent. You may also think that it would be easy enough for the Holy Spirit to show it to you, and to dispel it <u>without</u> the need for you to raise it to awareness yourself. Yet there is one more obstacle [Ur: complication] you have interposed between yourself and the Atonement [Ur: which you do not yet realize]. We have said that no one will countenance fear <u>if he recognizes it</u>. Yet in your disordered state of mind <u>you are not afraid of fear</u>. You do not <u>like</u> it, but it is <u>not</u> your desire to attack that really frightens you. You are not seriously disturbed by your hostility. You keep it hidden because you are <u>more</u> afraid of what it covers. You could look even upon the ego's darkest cornerstone <u>without</u> fear if you did not believe that, <u>without the ego</u>, you would find within yourself something you fear even more. <u>You are not</u> really <u>afraid of crucifixion</u>. Your real terror is of <u>redemption</u>.

The previous section was all about the need to look on the ego's darkest cornerstone, which contains the hateful statement, "I have killed the Son of God, or I would if I could find him." There, we said that this statement is directed at the Son of God in you, but, as this paragraph implies, it is directed at the Son of God in *everyone*. The ego is pure attack, pure hostility—towards ourselves and everyone else. Looking at the ego's darkest cornerstone, then, means looking on this raw, unbridled, murderous hatred within us, without minimizing it.

This doesn't sound very attractive, does it? In reading the previous section, we may have thought, "Do I really have to look at *that*? And why can't the Holy Spirit just show it to me briefly and then get rid of it for me? Why do *I* have to go inside and dredge it up?"

This paragraph answers those questions. Why is it so crucial that we look on our ego's hatred? Because unless we look at it, we will never see what lies beneath it. Why can't the Holy Spirit just show it to us, without our cooperation? Because we are too intent on hanging onto it as a cover for what lies beneath it.

The hatred, then, is purely a means. Its only purpose is to cover up something else. This means that our real fear is not of looking on the hatred, not of seeing this terrible hostility in us. Our real fear is of removing the cover and looking on what is beneath it. Our real fear is of liberation.

> 2. Under the ego's dark foundation is the memory of God, and it is of this that you are really afraid. For this memory would instantly restore you to your proper place, and it is this place that you have sought to leave. Your fear of attack is nothing compared to your fear of love. You would be willing to look even upon your savage wish to kill God's Son, if you did not believe that it saves you from love. For this wish caused the separation, and you have protected it because you do not want the separation healed. You realize that, by removing the dark cloud that obscures it, your love for your Father would impel you to answer His call and leap into Heaven. You believe that attack is salvation [Ur: to prevent you from this] because it would prevent you from this. For still deeper than the ego's foundation, and much stronger than it will ever be, is your intense and burning love of God, and His for you. This is what you really want to hide.

Imagine a woman who likes to think that she is very kind and civil to a certain man. She sees herself as being quite respectful toward him. Yet in reality, she carries a great deal of hostility toward him. Everyone around her can see it. She never misses an opportunity to badmouth him. Yet she doesn't see this, simply because she couldn't bear to look on this hatred in herself. It would shatter her self-concept too much.

Yet let's say that this is all really a ruse. In truth, underneath the hate is an incredibly deep and powerful love for this man. This love is so overpowering that it threatens to sweep her away from herself. She fears that she would lose control. So she does two things. First, she puts on this show of hate, which very effectively hides the love. Second, she puts on the show of civility to hide the *hate*. From the standpoint of her kind and decent persona, she is terrified to face how hateful she is toward the man. But this is not really because she fears to see this ugliness in her. It's because if she looks at the hate, she might find it so undesirable that she gives it up. And if she gave it up, her cover would be gone, and she would be swept out to sea by the undertow of this love.

We, of course, are this woman. We seem to be all nice and well-intentioned, yet we live lives that are largely motivated by hate. We are tremendously resistant to looking at this hate, apparently because it makes us look so bad. But this is not the real reason we fear to look. The real reason is that the hate covers over our "intense and burning love for God." And if we looked at the hate, we might just give it up, and then we would be caught up in this love, helpless in its presence, swept away from ourselves.

> 3.   In honesty, is it not harder for you to say "I love" than "I hate"? [Ur: For]You associate love with weakness and hatred with strength, and your own <u>real</u> power [love] seems to you as your real weakness. For you could <u>not</u> control your joyous response to the call of love if you heard it, and the whole world you thought you made <u>would</u> vanish [Ur: and the whole world you *think* you control *would* vanish]. The Holy Spirit, then, seems to be <u>attacking your fortress</u>, for you would <u>shut out God</u>, and He does not will to <u>be</u> excluded.

> 4.   You have built your whole insane belief system because you think you would be <u>helpless</u> in God's Presence, and you would <u>save</u> yourself from His Love because you think it would crush you into nothingness. You are afraid it would sweep you <u>away</u> from yourself <u>and make you little</u>, because you believe that magnitude lies in defiance, and that attack is grandeur. <u>You think you have made a world God would destroy</u>; and by loving Him, <u>which you do</u>, you would throw this world away, <u>which you</u> *would*. Therefore, you have used the world to <u>cover your love</u>, and the deeper you go into the blackness of the ego's foundation, the closer you come to the Love that is hidden there. *And it is this that frightens you.*

Why is it so much easier for most of us to say "I hate" than "I love"? It is because we think hatred is strength, while love makes us weak. Isn't that what we think? This is a reflection of our underlying attitude toward God, for in God's Presence we would simply leap into His Arms. Our love would render us out of control, helpless, swept away from ourselves—all of which we associate with weakness and littleness. Therefore, we would rather fill ourselves with hate, make our own world that we control, be defiant toward God, make sure that we are on the offensive—all of which we associate with strength.

Application: You might, then, want to think about the persona you have made. To what extent and in what ways do you value being in control, being defiant and rebellious, asserting your independence, being in possession of yourself, being opinionated, judgmental, even hateful? Could this be a massive defense against a hidden love for God, an intense and burning love for God, a pull that is so overpowering that you feel helpless in its presence? Could it be that you fear what you see as the humiliation of being out of control in this love, swept away from yourself? That you fear abandoning your strong, independent image and turning into a love-struck child of God?

> 5. You can accept insanity <u>because you made it</u>, but you cannot accept love <u>because you did not</u>. You would rather be a slave of the crucifixion than a Son of God in redemption. Your <u>individual</u> death seems more valuable [Ur: is more valued] than your living oneness, for [Ur: and] what is <u>given</u> you is not so dear as what you <u>made</u>. You are more afraid of God than of the ego, and love cannot enter where it is not welcome. But hatred <u>can</u>, for it enters of <u>its</u> own volition [Ur: of *its* will] and cares not for <u>yours</u>.

This paragraph puts its finger on a core sickness of ours. We are so attached to being the maker, the author, the one in charge. As long as we can say "I did it my way," we'll put up with almost any consequence. According to this paragraph, we will put up with insanity, slavery, crucifixion, death, and hatred. All of these things are seemingly made tolerable by the simple phrase "I did it my way." Yet are they really tolerable? How much sickness are we willing to justify in the name of "I did it my way"?

> 6. [Ur: The reason] You must look upon your illusions [Ur: *delusions*] and not keep them hidden, because [Ur: is that] <u>they do not rest on their own foundation</u>. In concealment they <u>appear</u> to do so, and thus they seem to be <u>self-sustained</u>. <u>This</u> is the fundamental illusion on which the others [Ur: on which they] rest. For <u>beneath</u> them, and concealed as long as <u>they</u> are hidden, is the loving mind that <u>thought</u> it made them in anger. And the pain in this mind is so apparent, when it is uncovered, that its need of healing cannot <u>be</u> denied. Not all the tricks and games you offer [Ur: have offered] it can heal it, for <u>here</u> is the <u>real</u> crucifixion of God's Son [see 13.In.4:1].

We have so far seen three levels in our mind:

1. Our nice, well-intentioned face of innocence
2. The ego's cornerstone of raw hatred toward the Son of God in self and others
3. Our overpowering and self-abandoning love for God

Yet now we see that there is something in between 2 and 3. There is the loving, innocent mind that made that dark, hateful cornerstone. This is the loving mind that thought it turned itself into a devil. This mind is in deepest sorrow—indeed, in agony—over this belief. It is the agony of guilt. While it weeps, we throw various toys at it, various "tricks and games," to stop its crying. We throw at it cars, money, sex, status—anything we can find. And each time, between sobs, it says, "Don't you get it? I started out as God's beloved Son and I turned myself into a *devil*."

This profound sense of guilt is the *real* crucifixion of God's Son. The Introduction told us that this world is a *picture* of the crucifixion of God's Son (In.4:1). The world, then, is just the picture; here is the real thing. It is not outer events that are crucifying us; it is our own inner sense that we have destroyed the infinitely precious innocence that God placed at the core of our being.

> 7. And yet he is <u>not</u> crucified. Here is both his pain <u>and</u> his healing, for the Holy Spirit's vision is merciful and His remedy is quick. Do not <u>hide</u> suffering from His sight, but bring it gladly <u>to</u> Him. Lay before His eternal sanity <u>all</u> your hurt, and let Him heal you. Do not leave any spot

of pain hidden from His Light, and search your mind carefully for any thoughts you may fear to uncover. For He will heal every little thought you have kept to hurt you and cleanse it of its littleness, restoring it to the magnitude of God.

Here, in the tortured loving mind, is the key. The loving mind feels crucified by its own sins, yet bringing this mind to light is the way *out* of crucifixion. We must bring it to the Holy Spirit's light, and let Him show us that none of it is true. We are told to bring two classes of things: our pain/hurt/suffering and our petty, mean thoughts (the thoughts we are afraid to uncover). I think this means *any* pain and *any* meanness. Yet to uncover the true pain in the loving mind, we need to uncover the pain as it really is. We need to realize that all our pain is the hurt that comes from our own spiteful thoughts.

Application: Think of some recent hurt in your life. Bring this to the Holy Spirit, saying, "I feel hurt by_____." Then take it a step deeper. Acknowledge that you really feel hurt not by the lack of love displayed *toward* you, but displayed *by* you. Your hurt comes from your own failure in this situation to love more truly. Try to avoid making excuses for your lovelessness. Instead, hold in mind the hurt it has caused and bring it to Him and say,

Heal me of my lovelessness.
I trust that Your vision is merciful and Your remedy quick.
Holy Spirit, heal me.

8.   Beneath all the grandiosity you hold so dear is your real call for help. For you call for love to your Father as your Father calls you to Himself. In that place which you have hidden, you will only to unite with the Father, in loving remembrance of Him. You will find this place of truth as you see it in your brothers, for though they may deceive themselves, like you they long for the grandeur that is in them. And perceiving it you will <u>welcome</u> it, and it will be yours. For grandeur is the <u>right</u> of God's Son, and no illusions can satisfy him or save him from what he <u>is</u>. Only his love is real, and he will be content <u>only</u> with his reality.

Now we have the complete picture of the loving mind. It lies between what I called levels 2 and 3, and is in touch with both. It is in touch with the ego's hateful, grandiose cornerstone (for it made this cornerstone), which lies above it. Yet it is also in touch with what lies *below* it—our overpowering love for God. As a result of being in touch with both, it feels unredeemably sinful *and* it still yearns for God. And out of this poignant combination comes an inevitable result: It calls to God for help. It lets out a constant cry, "Father, deliver me from the awful thing I have done. I only want to be with You again." And God lovingly replies, "You never did what you thought you did. And you have never left Me."

This is why it is so essential that we uncover this loving mind, which I usually term "the call for help." For when we hear its cry, that cry becomes our own. And only then will we truly hear God's answer.

How do we uncover this loving mind? We see it in our brothers. Behind their attacks we see the loving mind that thought it made them in anger, the loving mind that constantly calls to God for deliverance from its sins and for return to the grandeur of God.

> 9.　Save him from his illusions that you may accept the magnitude of your Father in peace and joy. But exempt no one from your love, or you will be hiding a dark place in your mind where the Holy Spirit is not welcome. And thus you will exempt <u>yourself</u> from His healing power, for by not offering total love <u>you</u> will not be healed completely. Healing must be as complete as fear, for love cannot enter where there is one spot of fear to mar its welcome.

Application: Think of someone whose attacks were so blatant that you have decided to exempt this person from your love. Then try to imagine a secret, buried place in this person's mind, beneath their hate. Imagine a hidden place inside them where they are saying the following:

> *I hurt so deeply over my inability to love.*
> *I am mired in self-loathing.*
> *I feel that I have turned myself into a devil.*
> *I long to be clean, to be whole again.*
> *I long to be with God again.*
> *God, deliver me from the awful thing I have done.*

III. The Fear of Redemption

I only want to be with You again.

Now say silently to the secret place in this person's mind:

You never did what you thought you did.
And you never really left God.
Awake and be glad, for all your sins have been forgiven you.

10.   You who prefer separation [Ur: specialness] to sanity cannot obtain it in your right mind. You were at peace until you asked for special favor. And God did not give it for the request was alien to Him, and you could not ask this of a Father Who truly loved His Son. Therefore you made of Him an <u>un</u>loving father, demanding of Him what only such a father <u>could</u> give. And the peace of God's Son was shattered, for he no longer understood his Father. He feared what he had made, but still more did he fear his <u>real</u> Father, having attacked his own glorious equality <u>with</u> Him.

Here we have one of the most important accounts in the Course of the separation and what motivated it. The motivation? We asked for special favor from God. We asked to be His favorite Son (which only makes sense if already—*before* the separation—there were multiple Sons). God could not grant this request, yet the request itself implied its own view of reality. In this view, God became a God of unequal love, a God of domineering love, Whose so-called love would make us little and crush us into nothingness. This view remains to this day, for this (as we saw in paragraphs 3-4) is why we fear God's Love now.

11.   In peace he needed nothing and asked for nothing. In war he <u>demanded</u> everything and <u>found</u> nothing. For how could the gentleness of love respond to his demands, <u>except</u> by departing in peace and returning to the Father? If the Son did not wish to <u>remain</u> in peace, he could not remain at all. For a darkened mind cannot live in the light, and it must seek a place of darkness where it can believe it is where it is <u>not</u>. God did not <u>allow</u> this to happen. Yet you <u>demanded</u> that it happen, and therefore believed that it was so.

In Heaven, we had no needs and thus made no demands. These last two paragraphs speak of our very first demand: to be special in God's eyes. Yet instead of changing reality, all our demand did was remove us from being awake to reality. We withdrew into a dark place in our minds, where we believed that we were in a world where our demand could come true, a world where we could be special, both in the world's eyes and even in God's eyes.

The world of specialness that we seem to live in, then, is like one of those dreams in which some longstanding wish comes true, in which the person you've yearned to be with is finally in your arms. You could say that this world is one big wish-fulfillment dream, or better yet, one big *demand*-fulfillment dream.

> 12. To "single out" is to "make alone," and thus make lonely. God did not do this to you. Could He set you apart, knowing that your peace lies in His Oneness? He denied you only your request for pain, for suffering is not of His creation. Having given you creation, He could not take it from you. He could but answer your insane request with a sane answer that would abide with you in your insanity. And this He did. No one who hears His answer but will give up insanity. For His answer is the reference point beyond illusions [Ur: delusions], from which you can look back on them and see them as insane [see 9.VII.6:1-3]. But seek this place and you will find it, for Love is in you and will lead you there.

Here is why God couldn't grant our request—because we were asking to be His favorite, to be singled out. And "To 'single out' is to 'make alone,' and thus make lonely"—make *separate*. Our demand, then, was like one of those wishes people make with genies, which always turn out to be self-destructive. Yet God is not like a genie; He wouldn't grant a self-destructive wish. All He could do was respond to our insane demand with a sane answer. The answer is not specified here—it may be the Holy Spirit, or it may just be the idea that we never really left home. Either way, this answer is the reference point we need to find, so that we can look back from it onto our delusions of specialness, and see how truly insane they are.

IV. The Function of Time
Commentary by Robert Perry

1.   And now the reason why you are afraid of this course should be apparent. For this is a course on love, because it is about you. You have been told [see 12.VII.4:7] that your function in this world is healing, and your function in Heaven is creating. The ego teaches that your function on earth is destruction, and you have no function at all in Heaven. It would thus destroy you here and bury you here, leaving you no inheritance except the dust out of which it thinks you were made. As long as it is reasonably satisfied with you, as its reasoning goes, it offers you oblivion. When it becomes overtly savage, it offers you hell.

The first two sentences continue a theme from "The Guiltless Son of God" (Section II): We are afraid of the Course because it brings to us the realization of our true nature as guiltless and as loving. We fear the Course because it represents the nature we have been trying to kill.

Because our nature is love, our function is the extension of love—extending healing to our brothers on earth and extending being-ness to our creations in Heaven. The ego's notion of our function is as debased as our true function is lofty. The ego says that our function is to attack and destroy here on earth, and that we shouldn't even think of getting to Heaven. If we are always faithful to it, it says that upon our death, we can be released from the pain of existence. We can cease to be. But if we really piss the ego off, it threatens us with an eternity in hell.

2.   Yet neither oblivion nor hell is as unacceptable to you as Heaven. Your definition of Heaven is hell and oblivion, and the real Heaven is the greatest threat you think you could experience. For hell and oblivion are ideas that you made up, and you are bent on demonstrating their reality to establish yours. If their reality is questioned, you believe that yours is. For you believe that attack is [Ur: established] your reality, and that your destruction is the final proof that you were right.

We may consciously want Heaven, but why aren't we there? It's because we see Heaven as a fundamental threat. It is the final triumph of

211

the God-given over the self-made. We saw in the previous section that we are totally committed to being the author, the maker, being in control, being on the attack. This, we are told now, is what we think establishes our very reality.

Further, the attacking don't deserve Heaven. Thus, for us to end up in Heaven would establish the total *impotence* of our attack. On the other hand, if we end up being destroyed, that's good because that is what the attacking deserve. That would prove that our attack really *did* establish our reality. Somewhere inside, then, we actually desire death as the ultimate confirmation that "I did it my way."

> 3. Under the circumstances, would it not be <u>more desirable</u> to have been wrong, even apart from the fact that you <u>were</u> wrong? [Ur: For] While it could perhaps be argued that death suggests there *was* life, no one would claim that it proves there *is* life. Even the <u>past</u> life that death might indicate, could only have been futile if it must come to this, and <u>needs</u> this to prove that it <u>was</u> at all [Ur: that it *was*]. You question Heaven, but you do <u>not</u> question this. Yet you could heal and be healed if you <u>did</u> question it. And even though you know not Heaven, might it not be more desirable than death? You have been as selective in your questioning as in your perception. An open mind is more honest than this.

As an analogy, we can imagine a son who was always given everything by his saintly father. But he wants to be his own man, establish his own identity. So he embarks on a life of crime. Every crime becomes a secret statement "I am my own man." He finally is sentenced to death, yet this becomes dramatic confirmation that his crimes really did define him. And so he goes to the electric chair with a grim serenity, thinking, "This is the ultimate proof that I really was my own man"—the word "was" underscoring the utter insanity of the whole enterprise.

The Course is saying that somewhere deep inside us is this same sick, twisted impulse. That is why we are in this world. That is why we have an inexplicable resistance to giving in to God's joy. That is why we are all journeying toward our death. As we die, there is this sick place in us that says, "Take *that*, God. I did it *my* way."

We may not be conscious of this impulse, but we need to try to make it conscious. For until we do, it remains intact, governing our lives. We must make it conscious and *question it*. If we do, everything will change.

4.   The ego has a strange notion of time, and it is with this notion that your questioning might well begin. The ego invests heavily in the past, and in the end believes that the past is the <u>only</u> aspect of time that is meaningful. Remember that [Ur: You will remember that we said] its emphasis on guilt enables it to ensure its continuity by <u>making the future like the past</u>, and thus <u>avoiding</u> the present. By the notion of <u>paying for</u> the past in the future, the past becomes the <u>determiner</u> of the future, making <u>them</u> continuous <u>without</u> an intervening present. For the ego regards the present <u>only</u> as a brief transition <u>to</u> the future, in which it brings the past <u>to</u> the future <u>by interpreting the present in past terms</u>.

We can begin to question our dedication to death by questioning the ego's notion of time. As we saw in "Guiltlessness and Invulnerability" (I.8:3), guilt produces a view of time in which the future is all about paying for past sins. If you think about it, this means that all of time is determined by the past. The important stuff has already happened. Now, the only thing left is to pay for it. This makes the present truly insignificant. In this view of the present, we are merely on our way to a future of paying for our sins. In the present, we are "dead man walking," shuffling from our cell to the electric chair.

Application: How do you look at the present? Do you ever get the sense in the present you are merely hurrying to the future? Do you ever have the feeling that the past laid down such solid patterns that there is no hope of real change in the present?

5.   "<u>Now</u>" has no meaning to the ego. The present merely reminds it of <u>past</u> hurts, and it reacts to the present <u>as if</u> it *were* the past. The ego cannot tolerate <u>release</u> from the past, and although the past is over, the ego tries to preserve its <u>image</u> by responding as if it were present. It dictates your reactions to those you meet in the present from a <u>past</u> reference point, obscuring their <u>present</u> reality. In effect, if you <u>follow</u> the ego's dictates you will react to your brother as though he were <u>someone else</u>, and this will surely prevent you from recognizing him as he is. And you will receive messages from him out of your <u>own</u> past because, by making it real in the present, you are forbidding yourself

to <u>let it go</u>. You thus <u>deny</u> yourself the message of release that every brother offers you *now*.

Now we see a second way in which the ego holds onto the past. It sees the past as taking place all over again in the *present*. It leads you to interpret everything in the present from a past reference point, so that you respond to the present *as if* it were the past. Do you ever catch yourself doing that?

This is a very important paragraph. It introduces the concept of shadow figures, a little-known but important Course concept. Let's look at the fourth, fifth, and sixth sentences again:

It dictates your reactions to those you meet in the present from a past reference point, obscuring their present reality.	The ego makes sure that you react to people in the present based on a past reference point, based on things that happened in the past.
In effect, if you follow the ego's dictates you will react to your brother as though he were someone else, and this will surely prevent you from recognizing him as he is.	By interpreting the present in light of the past, you will react to your brother as if he were someone else, as if he were a person from your past.
And you will receive messages from him out of your own past because, by making it real in the present, you are forbidding yourself to let it go.	Seeing him as if he were someone from your past, you will think you hear him giving you messages that are actually messages from this other person.

6.   The shadowy figures from the past are precisely what you must <u>escape</u>. They are not real, and have no hold over you unless <u>you</u> bring them <u>with</u> you. They carry the spots of pain in your mind, directing you to attack in the present in retaliation for a past that is no more. <u>And this decision is one of future pain.</u> Unless you learn that <u>past</u> pain is an illusion [Ur: is delusional], you are choosing a future of illusions [Ur:

delusions] and losing the many opportunities you <u>could</u> find for release in the present. The ego would <u>preserve</u> your nightmares, and prevent you from awakening and understanding <u>they</u> are past.

Now we see how the shadow figures work. Let's say that your father was always (in your perception) giving you the message, "You're not wanted." Now you are with your husband, yet you are not *really* with him. Instead, you are projecting onto him the mask of your father. Your eyes see your husband, but your *mind* sees your father. And as your ears hear your husband say, "We had a great collaboration at the office today," you mind hears him saying, "You're not wanted." Your husband, then, appears to be delivering to you the hurt from the past all over again. And this gives you the right to retaliate now for a past that is over. By saying, "You're not wanted," he sends the covert message, "Go ahead and attack me. You have every right to. I'm doing it to you all over again." The shadow figures, then, are walking justifications for using the present to retaliate for past hurts.

This, of course, keeps you stuck in the past. But it is a far more brilliant strategy than that. Remember, the ego sees your past sins as determining the future, a future in which all you do is pay for those sins. Now, it sees the past sins of *others* as determining the *present*, a present in which all you do is pay them back for the past, i.e., attack them. Rather sneakily, this tricks you into constantly stacking up new sins to pay for in your future. The cycle never ends.

Application: Think of an important relationship in your life. What is the main message you receive from this person which you resent receiving?

Have you received that message from others in your past?

If so, do you think you could be projecting those past people onto the current person, and thereby hearing their messages "channeled" through the current person?

If so, do you think this might be distorting the message you are hearing now, by making you hear something this person is not saying, or at least by adding a meaning and significance onto what he or she is saying that is not there?

Do you find yourself attacking this person because of this message that you hear?

Is it possible that your ego has tricked you into seeing the past and attacking it, so that you can stack up new sins to punish yourself for in the future?

> Would you <u>recognize</u> a holy encounter if you are merely perceiving it as a meeting with your <u>own</u> past? For you would be meeting no one, and the <u>sharing</u> of salvation, <u>which makes the encounter holy</u>, would be excluded from your sight. The Holy Spirit teaches that you always meet <u>yourself</u>, and the encounter is holy because <u>you</u> are. The ego teaches that you always encounter your <u>past</u>, and because your dreams <u>were</u> not holy, the future <u>cannot</u> be, and the present is without meaning.

Again and again these paragraphs say that by seeing the shadow figure, you are not really seeing the person in front of you. Now we are told that this deprives us of the ability to truly encounter this person. You can't have a real encounter with someone when you think he is someone else.

Application: Think of the same person you were using in the previous application, and say to this person:

> *I don't want to see my past in you.*
> *For then I encounter no one.*
> *I want to encounter the real you, and share salvation with you.*
> *I want to have a holy encounter and realize that I am encountering*
>   *my Self.*

7.   It is evident that the Holy Spirit's perception of time is the exact opposite of the ego's. The reason is equally clear, for they perceive the <u>goal</u> of time as diametrically opposed. The Holy Spirit interprets time's <u>purpose</u> as rendering the need for time <u>unnecessary</u>. He regards the function of time as temporary, serving only His teaching function, which is temporary by definition. <u>His</u> emphasis is therefore on the <u>only</u> aspect of time <u>that</u> can extend to the infinite, for *now* is the closest approximation of eternity that this world offers. It is in the <u>reality</u> of "now," without past <u>or</u> future, that the beginning of the appreciation of eternity lies. For only "now" is <u>here</u>, and only "now" presents the

opportunities for the holy encounters in which salvation can be found.

Whereas the ego wants to keep time going forever, the Holy Spirit uses time purely as a means to regain eternity. Therefore, He has us focus on the one aspect of time that can be extended to eternity: the present. If we fully enter the present, we realize the present is not just a fleeting moment in between the previous moment and the coming one. We realize that it is not really part of a sequence at all; it is everything there is.

What does it mean to be in the present? Many traditions emphasize the importance of getting out of our head and being fully present to physical sensations. The final sentence, however, tells us how the Course sees entering the present: Rather than clearing our mind and entering into the pure experience of immediate sensation, we clear our mind of *past ghosts* and enter into a holy encounter with *another person*. For it is "holy encounters in which salvation can be found."

> 8.   The ego, on the other hand, regards the function of time as one of extending itself in place of eternity, for like the Holy Spirit, the ego interprets the goal of time as its own. The continuity of past and future, under its direction, is the only purpose the ego perceives in time, and it closes over the present so that no gap in its own continuity can occur. Its continuity, then, would keep you in time, while the Holy Spirit would release you from it. It is His interpretation of the means of salvation that you must learn to accept, if you would share His goal of salvation for you.

In the ego's use of time, we *repeat* past attacks in the present and *pay for* past attacks in the future. Both present and future simply repeat the past. There is no hope of change, and no hope of an end. It just goes on and on this way, forever. Is this the timeline we are on now? Is this the timeline we want to stay on? Do we not want to get on another track?

> 9.   You, too [like the ego and the Holy Spirit], will interpret the function of time as you interpret yours. If you accept your function in the world of time as one of healing, you will emphasize only the aspect of time in which healing can occur. Healing cannot be accomplished in the past. It must be accomplished in the present to release the future. This interpretation ties the future to the present, and extends the present rather than the past. But if you interpret your function as destruction,

217

you will lose sight of the present and hold on to the past <u>to ensure a destructive future</u>. And time <u>will</u> be as you interpret it, for <u>of itself</u> it <u>is</u> nothing.

If you see your function as healing, you will always be on the ready for those present moments in which the opportunity to heal arises. You will always be ready to set everything aside to have a holy encounter. In these acts of sharing salvation with another person, you leave the past and all its ghosts behind. Something new happens, something free of imprisoning memories. Out of these holy encounters, a new future arises. This future extends the new present, rather than repeating that old past.

This, of course, is what happened to Helen and Bill. When they had their holy encounter in June of 1965, in which they joined together to demonstrate a better way, they stepped out of past patterns. And from this encounter a new future opened up, a future that, as we read these sections, we are part of. Perhaps we have had similar experiences, in which in an unexpected moment we stumble into an out-of-pattern time interval, from which a new future unfolds.

Which, then, would we rather have—a present and future that merely repeat the painful past, or a present that steps out of the past and sets us onto a new track leading into a new future? We decide this by deciding for what we intend to use the present. Will we use it to heal or destroy?

And now we are finally in a position to truly question our idea (from paragraphs 1-3) that our being in charge, being the maker, being in control, being on the attack is supremely valuable. For this amounts to the idea that our function is destruction, which, as we have seen, leads to a present of retaliation and a future of punishment. Is that the existence we want?

V. The Two Emotions
Commentary by Robert Perry

This section explores the well-known Course teaching that there are only two emotions: love and fear. Yet it explores it in decidedly unexpected ways. One comment I want to make about this topic before we start is that this doesn't mean that fear is the real cause of all negative emotions. It means that fear is where all negative emotions *lead*. It is their inevitable *result*. All negative emotions end up dumping us into the same pool of fear.

> 1.   I have said you have but two emotions, love and fear. One is changeless but continually exchanged, being offered <u>by</u> the eternal <u>to</u> the eternal. In this exchange it is extended, for it <u>increases</u> as it is given. The other has many forms, for the content of <u>individual</u> illusions differs greatly. Yet they have one thing in common; they are all insane. They are made of sights that are <u>not</u> seen, and sounds that are <u>not</u> heard. They make up a <u>private</u> world that <u>cannot</u> be shared. For they are meaningful <u>only</u> to their maker, and so they have no meaning at all. In this world their maker moves alone, for only <u>he</u> perceives them.

This paragraph emphasizes that fear takes many forms, because individual illusions are so, well, individual. Think about the notion of an *individual illusion*. It suggests that the individual is caught inside his own private bubble. He lives in a reality all his own. He lives in his own private world. And isn't that the essence of insanity?

> 2.   Each one peoples his world with figures from his <u>individual</u> past, and it is because of this that private worlds <u>do</u> differ. Yet the figures that he sees were <u>never</u> real, for they are made up <u>only</u> of his <u>reactions</u> to his brothers, and do <u>not</u> include their reactions to <u>him</u>. Therefore, he does not see he <u>made</u> them, and that they <u>are not whole</u>. For these figures <u>have no witnesses</u>, being perceived in one <u>separate</u> mind only.

Why do our private worlds differ so much? Because each one is peopled with figures from our individual past—shadow figures. As

I explained yesterday, shadow figures are mental images of particular people from our past who didn't treat us the way we wanted. As we see and interact with our world, we are actually seeing, hearing, and interacting with these mental images.

These images are not the actual people from our past. They are one-side images made of our hate. They do not accurately capture those people as they were in relation to us, for the images only include how we felt impacted by them, and not how they felt impacted by us. What could be more unfair than that?

Application: Choose the parent you felt least loved by (or perhaps another significant childhood authority figure that you felt slighted by). Then ask yourself,

> *Is my image of this person made up only of how I felt he or she impacted me?*
> *Or does my image also and equally include how I impacted him or her?*

3.   It is <u>through</u> these strange and shadowy figures that the insane relate to their insane world. For they <u>see</u> only those who remind them of these images, and it is to <u>them</u> that they relate. Thus do they communicate with those who <u>are not there</u>, and it is <u>they</u> who answer them. And no one hears their answer save him who called upon them, and he <u>alone</u> believes they answered him. Projection <u>makes</u> perception, and you <u>cannot</u> see beyond it. Again and again have you [Ur: men] attacked your brother [Ur: each other], because you [Ur: they] saw <u>in</u> him [Ur: *them*] a shadow figure in your [Ur: their] private world. And thus it is you <u>must</u> attack yourself first, for what you attack is <u>not</u> in others. Its <u>only</u> reality is in your <u>own</u> mind, and by attacking others you are literally attacking <u>what is not there</u>.

This notion of us relating to others as if they were people from our past is not new. Many psychologists have taught that we choose romantic partners who remind us of the parent we felt least loved by. Yet the Course takes this to a chilling extreme. It says that we relate *only* to people who remind us of our shadow figures; we ignore everyone else. Once we zero in on these people, we then appear to be interacting with them, but in actuality we are having a private dialogue with the shadow figure(s) we project onto them.

To get a sense of this, imagine a homeless man at a local coffee shop. When the waitress delivers his food, he says, "Thank you, Amy Sue"— which was his sister's name. When the owner walks by, he says, "And how are you today, Mother?" When the other patrons speak to him, he addresses them by the names of other siblings or childhood friends. Further, when any of these people speak to him, he hears them saying what he would *expect* his sister or mother or childhood friends to say. Thus, when the owner says to him, "And how is your little dog today?" He hears, "Your dog isn't looking too good, son. Have you fed him today like I asked?" Then the homeless man lashes out, "Can't you ever cut me a little slack?!"

Sadly, we are this homeless man. We are carrying on conversations with the people around us, but are we really? We are attacking the people in front of us, but are we really? According to the Course, we are conversing only with the shadow figures in our mind. And we are attacking only those figures in our mind, which means we are attacking no one but ourselves.

> 4.   The delusional can be very destructive, for they do not recognize they have condemned <u>themselves</u>. They do not wish to die, <u>yet they will not let condemnation go</u>. And so they <u>separate</u> into their private worlds, where everything is disordered, and where what is within appears to be without. Yet what <u>is</u> within they do <u>not</u> see, for the <u>reality</u> of their brothers they <u>cannot</u> recognize.

What we see as another person—not his form, but his meaning—is really inside of us, not out there. As we look at him, we are seeing a shadow figure in our mind *as if* this figure was external. And thus when we condemn that person, we are actually condemning the figure in our mind, which means we are only condemning something inside of us. In other words, we are condemning ourselves, and do not realize it.

Yet as long as our self-condemnation remains externalized, we will remain in our private world, where we see our inner family of hated images as if it is the actual outside world. As long as we continue to see the inner as if it was the outer, we will not see the *true* inner—the light of

Christ. For that can only be shown to us by the true *outer*—the reality of our brothers, which we have obscured with the dark fog of our shadow figures.

> 5.   You have but two emotions, yet in your private world you react to each of them <u>as though it were the other</u>. For love cannot abide in a world apart, where when it comes [in the guise of your brothers] it is not recognized. If you see your own hatred <u>as</u> your brother, you are not seeing <u>him</u>. Everyone draws nigh unto what he loves, and recoils from what he fears. And you react with fear to love [the reality of your brothers], and draw <u>away</u> from it. Yet fear [in the form of the scary shadow figures] <u>attracts</u> you, and believing it is love, you call it to yourself. Your private world is [therefore] filled with [Ur: the] figures of fear you have invited into it, and all the love your brothers offer you, <u>you do not see</u>.

This is a subtle but profound paragraph. Let's break it down into simple ideas. First, the nature of love and fear: The nature of love is that you are attracted to what you love and draw close to it. Fear, however, works the opposite way. You recoil from what you fear and so draw back from it, trying to keep your distance.

What an odd reaction we have to our brothers, then. For their reality offers us nothing but love, yet we recoil from them. We cover over their reality with the fog of our shadow figures so that we cannot look upon their "frightening" gift of love. Instead, we are attracted to the fearful shadow figures, who send us constant messages of attack. We fill our private world with them because all we want is to draw close to them.

In other words, we have love and fear totally backwards. A person is attracted and draws nigh to what he loves, yet we recoil from the love our brothers offer. A person recoils and draws away from what he fears, yet we are attracted to and draw close to the fearful shadow figures. Are we crazy, or what?

> 6.   As you look with open eyes upon your world, it <u>must</u> occur to you that you have withdrawn into insanity. [Ur: For] You see what is not there, and you hear what makes no sound [Ur: what is soundless]. Your [Ur: behavioral] <u>manifestations</u> of emotions are the <u>opposite</u> of what the emotions <u>are</u>. You communicate with no one, and you are as isolated from reality as if you were <u>alone</u> in all the universe. In your

madness you <u>overlook reality completely</u>, and you see <u>only your</u> own <u>split mind</u> everywhere you look. God calls you and you do not hear, for you are preoccupied with your own voice. And the vision of Christ is not in your sight, for you look upon yourself <u>alone</u>.

Application: Here is the punch line. Can we try to let this in? Please read the following lines and, as much as you possibly can, silently acknowledge the truth in them:

When I see the people in my life, I am actually seeing the shadow figures who are not there.
When I hear people talk to me, I am hearing the shadow figures who make no sound.
I recoil from the love my brothers offer me, as if it were fearful.
I am attracted to the fearful shadow figures, as if they were objects of love.
Hence, I fear love, and love fear.
I communicate with no one but my shadow figures, and thus I communicate with no one.
In my private world, I am as isolated from reality as if I were alone in all the universe.
In my madness I overlook reality completely.
Everywhere I look, I see only the projection of my own inner split between love and hate.
God calls me and I do not hear, for I am preoccupied with my own voice.
Christ offers me His vision, yet I do not see, for I spend all my time looking at my own ego in the mirror.
As I review all this, it must occur to me that I have withdrawn into insanity.

7.   Little child, would you offer <u>this</u> to your Father? For if you offer it to yourself, you *are* offering it to Him. And He will <u>not</u> return it, for it is unworthy of you <u>because</u> it is unworthy of Him. Yet He <u>would</u> release you from it and set you free. His sane Answer tells you what you have offered <u>yourself</u> is <u>not</u> true, but <u>His</u> offering <u>to</u> you has never

changed. You who know not what you do <u>can</u> learn what insanity <u>is</u>, and look beyond it. It is <u>given</u> you to learn how to <u>deny</u> insanity, and come forth from your private world in peace. You will see all that you denied in your brothers <u>because</u> you denied it in yourself. For you will love them, and by drawing nigh unto them you will draw them to <u>yourself</u>, perceiving them as witnesses to the reality you share with <u>God</u>. [Ur: For] I am <u>with</u> them as I am with <u>you</u>, and we will draw them from their private worlds, for as we are united so would we unite with them. The Father welcomes all of us in gladness, and gladness is what <u>we</u> should offer Him. For every Son of God is given you to whom God gave <u>Himself</u>. And it is God Whom you must offer them, to recognize His gift to you.

Imagine that the homeless guy from the coffee shop finds himself before God and says to Him, "God, I have a gift for you. I want to give you my little world. My world is my life with my family at the diner. I cherish it so much. It is the most precious thing I can offer You."

And God replies, "You have already offered your little world to Me, for whatever you offer to yourself you *are* offering to Me. This world of yours, however, is not worthy of you because it is unworthy of Me. Yet I would release you from it and set you free, for *My* gift to *you* has never changed.

"Son, let Me teach you what insanity is, so that you can lay it down and emerge from your private world in peace. Then you will see what you have been blind to—your *real* brothers. They have so much love to offer you. Now you will draw nigh to them and draw them to yourself, and they will show you the beautiful light that is in you.

"I am with them as I am with you, and We will draw them from their private worlds. They have been as lost in their isolation as you have been in yours, but We will free them, so that all of Us are one. And when your little world has been thus transformed, think of the wonderful gift you will have to offer Me. And in return, I will offer you and all your beloved brothers the gift of Myself."

You may want to read this again, only imagining that these are God's words to you, about your little world.

8.   Vision depends on light. You <u>cannot</u> see in darkness. Yet in darkness, in the private world of sleep, you <u>see</u> in dreams although

your eyes are closed. And it is here that <u>what</u> you see <u>you made</u>. But let the <u>darkness</u> go and <u>all</u> you made <u>you will no longer see</u>, for sight of <u>it</u> depends upon <u>denying</u> vision [real sight]. Yet from denying vision <u>it does not follow you cannot see</u>. But this is what denial <u>does</u>, for <u>by</u> it you <u>accept</u> insanity, believing you can make a private world <u>and rule your own perception</u>. Yet <u>for</u> this, light <u>must</u> be excluded. Dreams disappear when light has come <u>and you can see</u>.

We have closed our eyes on what is really out there. But we don't know this, because we are still seeing things in front of us. Behind the closed eyes of our mind, we are seeing our dreams. We don't realize that the dream figures running around before us are just shadow figures running around in our mind. We also don't realize the deep attachment we have to a world that we are able to make up, a world that we rule with the "creative" power of fantasy.

Yet we have not lost the capacity to see. We still have the ability to open our eyes and see our brothers for who they really are. We will be looking on a world that has always been there, yet which we have never seen before.

9.   Do not seek vision through <u>your</u> eyes, for you <u>made</u> your way of seeing that you might see in darkness, and in this you <u>are</u> deceived. <u>Beyond</u> this darkness, and yet still <u>within</u> you, is the vision of Christ, Who looks on all in light. <u>Your</u> "vision" comes from fear, as His from love. And He sees <u>for</u> you, as your witness to the real world. He is the Holy Spirit's <u>manifestation</u>, looking always on the real world, and calling forth its witnesses [your brothers as they really are] and drawing them to <u>you</u>. He loves what He sees within you, and He would <u>extend</u> it. And He will not return unto the Father until He has extended your perception even unto Him. And there perception is no more, for He has <u>returned</u> you to the Father <u>with</u> Him.

We made these eyes to give us the illusion that we are seeing, when in fact our real eyes are closed. All our physical eyes see are *dream* figures, onto which we mentally project our *shadow* figures, so that we see a world of fear. This world is nothing but blindness dressed up like sight. All the sights we see before us, right now, today and every day, are nothing but blindness dressed up like sight.

Yet within us is Christ, Who sees through different eyes, through the

eyes of love. He looks always on the real world, the world peopled by
our brothers' reality, a world that will teach us of the love within us.

> 10. You have but two emotions, and one you made and one was <u>given</u>
> you [remember the recent discussions of the self-made vs. the God-
> given?]. Each is a <u>way of seeing</u>, and different worlds arise from their
> different sights. See through the vision that is <u>given</u> you, for through
> Christ's vision He beholds Himself. And seeing what <u>He</u> is, He knows
> His Father. Beyond your darkest dreams He sees God's guiltless Son
> within you, shining in perfect radiance that is undimmed by your
> dreams. And this *you* will see as you look with Him, for His vision is
> His gift of love to you, given Him of the Father <u>for</u> you.

Now we can appreciate the point in this section about love and fear.
We love fear because we made it. It is the proof that "I did it my way."
Loving this fear, we project a world that makes us afraid, a world filled
with frightening images, a world full of shadow figures, endlessly
repeating their scary messages to us ("You'll never amount to anything."
"I never wanted you in the first place." "How could anyone love *you?*").

We may fear love, because, being God's gift, it is the given. It makes
us the dependent, the created. Yet it can bring us Heaven on earth. Love
is not just an emotion; it is a way of seeing. With it, we can see a new
world. Quite naturally, we see this world through a vision that is *given*
us, given by the Christ within. This vision shows us God's guiltless Son
within us, shining in a perfect radiance that is undimmed by all our dark
and scary dreams. How could we not want to see that?

> 11. The Holy Spirit is the light in which Christ stands revealed. And
> all who would behold Him [Christ] can see Him, for they have <u>asked</u>
> for light. Nor will they see Him <u>alone</u>, for He is no more alone than
> <u>they</u> are [they will see the Father with Him]. Because they <u>saw</u> the Son,
> they have risen <u>in</u> Him to the Father. And all this will they understand,
> because they looked within and saw beyond the darkness the Christ
> in them, and <u>recognized</u> Him. In the sanity of His vision they looked
> upon themselves with love, seeing themselves as the Holy Spirit sees
> them. And <u>with</u> this vision of the truth in <u>them</u> came all the beauty of
> the world to shine upon them.

This is a lovely closing paragraph, which I almost hate to separate into its different ideas, but I'll do it anyway. We can see a whole process here:

We ask for light; we ask to see.

We see the Christ in us, and thus finally look upon ourselves with love.

With this vision of the Christ in us, we look out upon the radiance of the real world, and see our brothers as they really are. We see the Christ in them.

Having seen the Christ, we must also recognize the One Who is with Him: the Father. We therefore rise to the Father. Now that our perception is perfected, we return to the joy of knowledge.

VI. Finding the Present
Commentary by Robert Perry

1.   To perceive truly is to be aware of <u>all</u> reality through the awareness of your own. But for this [seeing all reality through the awareness of your own] <u>no</u> illusions can rise to meet your sight, for [Ur: *all*] reality leaves no room for <u>any</u> error. This means that you perceive a brother only <u>as you see him</u> *now*. His past has <u>no</u> reality in the present, so you <u>cannot</u> see it. Your past reactions <u>to</u> him are also <u>not there</u> [see V.2:2], and if it is to them that you react, you see but an image of him that you made and cherish <u>instead</u> of him. In your questioning of illusions [see IV.3:4], ask yourself if it is <u>really</u> sane to perceive <u>what was</u> as <u>now</u>. If you remember the <u>past</u> as you look upon your brother, you will be unable to perceive the reality that is <u>now</u>.

If our goal is true perception, what does it mean to perceive truly? It means to look out from our own reality onto all of reality, seeing only the real, having no perceptual errors of any kind. All right; that sounds good. But here is the crucial point: To do this, you cannot see a brother in light of his past. You cannot see him according to your past reactions to him, for this just means seeing the image you crafted of him, an image that you value more than you value him.

Back in "The Function of Time" (13.IV), we were asked to question our illusions more deeply. This is part of that. We need to question the sanity of seeing our brother in light of his past. Think about it. When someone is not in the present but instead lives in the past, so fully that she thinks the past is actually happening now, we see that person as being in the advanced stages of senility. Yet how are we any different when we act as if our brother's past is a current reality?

2.   You consider it "natural" to use your <u>past</u> experience as the reference point from which to <u>judge</u> the present. Yet this is *unnatural* because it is delusional. When you have learned to look on everyone with <u>no reference at all</u> to the past, either his <u>or</u> yours as you perceived it, you will be able to learn <u>from what you see</u> *now*. For the past can cast no shadow to darken the present, *unless you are afraid of light*.

228

And <u>only</u> if you are would you choose to bring darkness <u>with</u> you, and by holding it in your mind, see it as a dark cloud that shrouds your brothers and conceals their reality from your sight.

It does seem natural to use past experience as our reference point for interpreting the present. Yet Jesus tells us here that this is *delusional.* Why? Because it means believing that your brother is those things he did in the past, which means he *is* what *was.* How can the *was* be the *is*? How can the over and done with be the here and now? If someone said to you, "Isn't it great that someone invented the telephone today?" (meaning literally today, not today in a past year), would you think that person was sane? Might you not start to suspect that that person had a pathological fear of the present? And might that not be true of us when we see our brother as his past deeds?

Application: Think of someone you share a long past with, and say the following to him or her:

> *I look on you [name] with no reference at all to the past, either yours or mine.*
> *I am willing to learn what your reality is **now**.*

3.   *This darkness* [the shadows from the past] *is in you.* The Christ as revealed to you <u>now</u> [in your brother and in yourself] has no past, for He is changeless, <u>and in His changelessness lies your release.</u> For if He is as He was created, there <u>is</u> no guilt in Him. No cloud of guilt has risen to obscure Him, and He stands revealed in everyone you meet because you see Him through <u>Himself</u>. To be born again is to let the <u>past</u> go, and <u>look without condemnation upon the present.</u> The cloud that obscures God's Son to you *is* the past, and if you would have it past <u>and gone</u>, you must <u>not see it now.</u> If you see it now in your illusions [Ur: delusions], it has <u>not</u> gone from you, although it is not there.

We look out on a world and see darkness everywhere. It is the darkness of guilt. We see guilty politicians, guilty racists, guilty coworkers, and guilty spouses. Yet the guilt is not in them. We are carrying the hurtful past in our mind, and throwing its darkness over our brothers in the present, concealing them underneath its dark shroud. Yet underneath this shroud is the changeless Christ, forever guiltless.

If we could only let the past go, we could pull this dark shroud off of everyone. We could look out from the Christ in us and see the Christ in them. And how can the Christ fail to see Himself? This freedom from the past and glory in the present is what it means to be *born again*. Think of that term free of all negative associations. Who of us wouldn't want to be free of all past scars and all past wounds, to have the weight of decades fall off our shoulders, and feel truly born again, as if it all starts right now?

> 4. Time can release as well as imprison, depending on whose interpretation of it you use. Past, present and future are not continuous, unless you force continuity on them. You can perceive them as continuous, and make them so for you. But do not be deceived, and then believe that this is how it is. For to believe reality is what you would have it be according to your use for it *is* delusional. You would destroy time's continuity by breaking it into past, present and future for your own purposes. You would anticipate the future on the basis of your past experience, and plan for it accordingly. Yet by doing so you are aligning past and future, and not allowing the miracle, which could intervene between them, to free you to be born again.

The reason why being born again is so attractive is that time seems to imprison. The more time passes, the more imprisoned you feel. Why? Because we are misinterpreting time's continuity. We see its continuity as the flow from past to present to future. This continuity means that things have to go the way they've gone. That, of course, is how we can anticipate the future based on past experience. What could be more obvious?

Yet that is precisely what imprisons us. This flow of time in which things *will* go the way they *have* gone makes time into a narrow tunnel. As long as we perceive ourselves traveling down this continuous tunnel, we cannot set out in a new direction. The walls hem us in, forcing us to go the way we *have* gone. We are imprisoned. We cannot be born again.

Yet time doesn't really work this way. Past, present, and future are not continuous. We have seen them that way to give ourselves the illusion that we are locked in that tunnel, when the truth is that we are not in the tunnel at all. Time has a continuity, but it is a whole other *kind* of continuity, and we will see what that is as we proceed.

> 5.   The miracle enables you to see your brother <u>without</u> his past, and so perceive him as born again. His errors <u>are</u> all past, and by perceiving him <u>without</u> them you are <u>releasing</u> him. And since his past is yours, you <u>share</u> in this release. Let no dark cloud out of <u>your</u> past obscure him from you, for truth lies <u>only</u> in the present, and you <u>will</u> find it if you seek it there. You have looked for it where it is <u>not</u>, and therefore have not found it. Learn, then, to seek it where it <u>is</u>, and it <u>will</u> dawn on eyes that see. Your past was made in anger, and if you use it to <u>attack</u> the present, you will <u>not see</u> the freedom that the present holds.

Application: Pick someone you started out loving, but whose loveliness and worth were slowly blocked out by the gradual accumulation of misdeeds. Then say,

> *The miracle allows me to see [name] without his past,*
> *and so perceive him as born again.*

Now imagine this person as truly born again, without all the chains of the past that he has been dragging around, free of all past mistakes. Realize that he has always been free of these past chains. Only the cloud of guilt in your own mind, which you superimposed on him, obscured this fact.

Now realize that by seeing him as free of the past, you are free, too. The past that you have been superimposing on him was a past you made in anger, and it's been imprisoning *you*. By freeing him, now you are free.

> 6.   Judgment and condemnation [the anger with which you made your image of the past] are <u>behind</u> you, and unless you bring them <u>with</u> you, you <u>will</u> see that you are free of them. Look lovingly upon the present, for it holds the <u>only</u> things that are forever true. All healing lies within it because <u>its</u> continuity is real. It extends to <u>all</u> aspects of the Sonship [Ur: of consciousness] <u>at the same time</u>, and thus enables

them to <u>reach each other</u>. The present is before time <u>was</u> [an allusion to "Before Abraham was, I am"—John 8:58], and <u>will be</u> when time is no more. In it are all things that are eternal, and they <u>are</u> one. <u>Their</u> continuity is timeless and their communication is unbroken, for they are <u>not separated</u> by the past. Only the past <u>can</u> separate, and it is <u>nowhere</u>.

Just as your brother's mistakes are in the past, so your judgments of your brother's mistakes are also in the past. Unless you haul these judgments with you into the present, you will see that they are gone and you are free.

Now we see what time's real continuity is. It is the continuity of the *present*: "All healing lies within it [the present] because its continuity is real." The current moment is a clean birth, unconditioned by the past. It is not an effect of past events. In it, we are free to choose whatever we want. Nothing of the past constrains us. The next moment is also a clean birth, in which we are also free to make new choices. *That* is time's continuity. It is a continuous flow of the present moment, in which each moment is unconditioned freedom, freedom to leave the past and set out in a new direction.

Think about how different this is from the other notion of time's continuity. In one, the past rolls forward, constantly reproducing itself in the present and future. In the other, the present rolls forward, offering us one moment after another of potential pure freedom.

In fact, there is really only *one* present moment. This present moment—right now—is actually the same moment as it was 10,000 years ago, when mammoths walked the earth. It only seems different because different scenery occupies it. Think of it this way. As I write this, it is 11:23 AM, Sunday morning. The scene in front of me is my computer screen on my desk in my office. Now, all of you are experiencing this same present moment (11:23 AM), but you are obviously seeing different scenes in front of you. Different scenes are thus occupying the exact *same* moment. Now imagine that this is true of all the scenes that have been in your individual life. They were all different, but just like the different scenes we as a group are experiencing at 11:23, all of the scenes in your life occupied the exact same present moment.

In this single present, says our paragraph, all things can reach each other. All things are *continuous*. We often think it would be nice to talk to someone from the past or future, to sit down and chat with William

Shakespeare or with someone from 1,000,000 A.D. Yet it seems like we can't, because time separates. Yet if there is only one present moment, then we really *can* reach these people. Similarly, it seems like we can't even talk to some of the people in the present, because the painful past we shared with them has separated us. Yet again, if there is only one present moment, then there really is nothing standing between us. In the continuity of the present, all beings are continuous.

> 7.   The present offers you your brothers in the light that would unite you <u>with</u> them, and free <u>you</u> from the past. Would you, then, hold the past <u>against</u> them? For if you do, you are choosing to remain in the darkness <u>that is not there</u>, and refusing to accept the light that is offered you. For the light of perfect vision is freely given as it is freely received, and can be accepted only <u>without limit</u>. In this one, still dimension of time [the present] that does not change, and where there is no sight of what you <u>were</u>, you look at Christ and call His witnesses [your brothers] to shine on you *because you called them forth*. And <u>they</u> will not deny the truth in you, because you looked for it in them and <u>found</u> it there.

Time seems to have three dimensions: past, present, and future. Yet it there is really only *one*: the present. Activity seems to take place within it, yet the space of the present itself is still; it never changes. "In this one, still dimension of time," our brothers are offered to us in light, a light that would join us with them and free us "from the past." In the present, we could call them to take the stand as witnesses to the Christ in us, and they would gladly do so. Why wouldn't they, when we testified to the Christ in *them*? The only possible reason we would not call on these witnesses is if we still wanted to hold the past against them. And we would only hold the past against them if we ourselves were "choosing to remain in the darkness that is not there."

> 8.   Now [the present] is the time of salvation, for <u>now</u> is the release from time. Reach out to all your brothers, and touch them with the touch of Christ. In timeless union <u>with</u> them is <u>your</u> continuity, unbroken because it is wholly shared. God's guiltless Son is <u>only</u> light. There is no darkness in him <u>anywhere</u>, for he is whole. Call all your brothers to witness to his wholeness, as I am calling you to join with me. Each voice has a part in the song of redemption, the hymn of gladness and

thanksgiving for the light to the Creator of light. The holy light that shines forth from God's Son is the witness that his light is of his Father.

While we each feel trapped in our own imprisoning tunnel of past-flowing-to-future, we all seem separate, for we are all trudging through different tunnels. Yet when we realize that time is truly one continuous present moment, we can realize our *own* true continuity. We can realize that we are continuous with *each other*. Then we will see that our own continuity, like time's, is unbroken, extending out to infinity.

Because we are continuous with our brothers, we can reach out and "touch them with the touch of Christ." We can remind them of the light in them. We can tell them they are free of the darkness of their past mistakes. This is our individual part in the great song of redemption—to set our brothers free from their past.

This in turn calls them to take up *their* part in the song of redemption. Now they can dedicate themselves to touching still more brothers with the touch of Christ. As we all lift our voices in this song, we are really singing in two directions at once. We are singing to our brothers about the light in them, calling them to remember, and we are singing to God, thanking Him for creating us all in a light that can never be dimmed.

> 9.   Shine on your brothers in remembrance of your Creator, for [Ur: and] you <u>will</u> remember Him as you call forth the witnesses to His creation [your brothers]. Those whom you heal bear witness to <u>your</u> healing, for in <u>their</u> wholeness you will see your own. And as your hymns of praise and gladness rise to your Creator, He will return your thanks in His clear Answer to your call. For it can never be that His Son called upon Him and remained unanswered. His call to you is but your call to Him. And in Him you are answered by His peace.

This is our part in the redemption: to lay aside the darkness of the past, which would condemn everyone we see, and instead shine on our brothers, in acknowledgment of the light God placed in them. As we shine on them, they will remember their wholeness and be healed. And they will then become witnesses to the wholeness in us, for their healing wouldn't exist without the wholeness in us.

Our shining on our brothers is simultaneously our hymn of praise and gladness to God, and this hymn is simultaneously a call to Him, a call that asks for His Answer. How could He not answer us with His peace?

Application: Speak these words silently to at least three people in your life,

My part in the redemption is to shine on you,
*in acknowledgment of the holy light that shines **in** you,*
and in remembrance of the One Who created us in light.

10.   Child of light, you know not that the light is in you. Yet [Ur: And] you will find it through its witnesses [the brothers you heal], for having given light to them <u>they will return it</u>. Each one you see <u>in</u> light brings <u>your</u> light closer to your awareness. Love always leads to love. The sick, who <u>ask</u> for love [see 12.II.1-2], are grateful for it, and in their joy they shine with holy thanks. And this they offer you who <u>gave</u> them joy. They are your guides to joy, for having received it <u>of</u> you they would keep it [by giving it]. You have established them as guides to peace, for you have made it manifest in them. And <u>seeing</u> it, its beauty calls you home.

I believe this is one of the most important statements in the Course of the process by which we are saved. Let's picture it in a concrete way.

You find yourself depressed on a particular day, because you don't believe the light is in you. And then you discover that a friend of yours is sick. She has the love in her that would heal her, yet she doesn't think she deserves this love, because of her past mistakes. You, however, don't see her past. You see only the light in her, shining so brightly that you can't imagine why she feels undeserving of love. You radiate such conviction about the light in her that she begins to see herself through your eyes. And as she does, she is healed.

But it doesn't stop there. Having received this holy gift from you, she is filled with joy. And in her joy, she shines with holy thanks. Everything about her attitude exudes gratitude. She is brimming over with a vision of the holy light in *you*, a vision which, in spite of false humility, you can't resist. Thus, she returns to you the gift you gave. As you were her guide to healing, she becomes your guide to joy.

Now you are no longer depressed, for now you know the light is in you.

11.   There is a light that this world cannot give. Yet <u>you</u> can give it, as it was given <u>you</u>. And <u>as</u> you give it, it shines forth to call you <u>from</u> the world and follow it. For this light will attract you as nothing in this world can do. And you will lay aside the world and find another [the real world]. This other world is bright with love <u>which you have given it</u>. And here will everything remind you of your Father and His holy Son. Light is unlimited [in the real world], and spreads across this world in quiet joy. All those you brought <u>with</u> you will shine on you, and you will shine on them in gratitude because they brought you here. Your light will join with theirs in power so compelling, that it will draw the others out of darkness as you look on them.

We can see this paragraph as a sort of reinterpreted Exodus, in which we are the Moses-figure. We begin our journey in a world without light. Yet there is a light in us, and as it shines on our brothers in love, we see it. This light attracts us like nothing else. It illumines the path ahead of us, pointing the way to the promised world—a world without darkness.

So we leave the familiar world and set out to follow our light to its home world. As we travel, we bring with us all those who were healed by the light in us. Yet paradoxically, because they carry the light that is leading us onward, they will in some sense lead *us*.

Once we have arrived, we will find a land flowing with light and joy. There, the light is unlimited, and spreads across the land in quiet joy. Those who came with us will shine on us, as we will shine on them in gratitude for bringing us here. And out of this mutual shining will come a single light, in which we all are joined. This light will be so powerful and so compelling that it will shine back on those still in the world of darkness, causing wave upon wave of new Exoduses to the promised land of light.

12.   Awaking unto Christ is following the laws of love [as you give so shall you receive] <u>of your free will</u>, and out of quiet recognition of the truth in them. The attraction of light must draw you willingly, and willingness is signified by <u>giving</u>. Those who accept love <u>of</u> you become your willing witnesses to the love you gave them, and it is <u>they</u> who hold it out to <u>you</u>. In sleep you are alone, and your awareness is narrowed to yourself. And that is why the nightmares come. You dream of isolation <u>because</u> your eyes are closed. You do not <u>see</u> your brothers, and in the darkness you cannot look upon the light you <u>gave</u> to them.

The journey sketched in the previous paragraph is how we awaken unto Christ. We give the light of our love to our brothers, and they then become our witnesses, testifying to the love in us. After hearing enough testimony from them, even we, harsh judges of ourselves that we are, will admit that the defendant—ourselves—is innocent of all charges.

The process, then, is driven by truly seeing our brother. Yet right now we are asleep, and when you are asleep, you do not see your surroundings. You are aware of nothing but the interior of your own mind. That is why we feel so isolated; "that is why the nightmares come." Waking up means opening our eyes and seeing our brothers as they really are.

> 13. And yet the laws of love are not suspended because you sleep. And you have followed them through all your nightmares, and have been faithful in your giving, for you were <u>not</u> alone. Even in sleep has Christ protected you, ensuring the real world <u>for</u> you when you awake. In <u>your</u> name He has given <u>for</u> you, and given <u>you</u> the gifts He gave. God's Son is still as loving as his Father. Continuous <u>with</u> his Father, he has no past <u>apart</u> from Him. So he has never ceased to be his Father's witness <u>and his own</u>. Although he slept, <u>Christ's vision did not leave him</u>. And so it is that he can call unto himself the witnesses that teach him that he never slept.

Yet even in our sleep, the Christ in us has given for us. Therefore, we *have* followed the law of love (as you give so shall you receive) even in our most self-centered days. Because Christ has given for us, we are still innocent, we are still our Father's Son, and the real world awaits us. We have no reason to stay in the prison cell of the past. Nothing is preventing us from walking out into the world of light.

VII. Attainment of the Real World
Commentary by Robert Perry

1.   Sit quietly and look upon the world you see, and tell yourself: "The real world is not like this. It has no buildings and there are no streets where people walk alone and separate. There are no stores where people buy an endless list of things they do not need. It is not lit with artificial light, and night comes not upon it. There is no day that brightens and grows dim. There is no loss. Nothing is there but shines, and shines forever."

Application: This paragraph is already an exercise, so please take a couple of minutes and do what it says.

The overriding impression I get from doing this exercise is that there is a whole alternative world to the world that my eyes look upon. Everything I see involves separateness, varying shades of light and darkness, and the potential for loss. Yet the real world has none of these things. It is a world composed of pure light, always shining, free of all boundaries and loss. Can there really be a world like that? Could I live in that world? These are the thoughts that come to my mind

2.   The world you see <u>must be denied</u>, for sight of it is costing you a different kind of vision. *You cannot see both worlds*, for each of them involves a different kind of seeing, and depends on what you cherish. The sight of one is possible because you have <u>denied the other</u>. Both are not true, yet either one will seem as real to you as the amount to which you hold it dear. And yet their power is <u>not</u> the same, because their real attraction to you <u>is</u> unequal.

The world I see with my physical eyes seems to be a fact. Yet I could see the real world all around me, right now, if I were willing to open an inner set of eyes. To do this, all I need do is change what I value. I see this world simply because I have denied the real world and cherished the physical world. Yet I could withdraw value from this world and cherish the real world instead, and then I would see it.

Each world, in other words, is only as real to me as the value I put on it. Yet in the end, I really am more attracted to the real world than this world, and therefore "their power [for me] is not the same."

> 3.   You do not really want the world you see, for it has disappointed you since time began. The homes you built have never sheltered you [see T-22.In.2:8 and W-pl.182.3:3]. The roads you made have led you nowhere [see T-31.IV.2:7-14], and no city that you built has withstood the crumbling assault of time. Nothing you made but has the mark of death upon it. Hold it not dear, for it is old and tired and ready to return to dust even as you made it. This aching world has not the power to touch the living world at all. You could not give it that, and so although you turn in sadness from it, you cannot find in it the road that leads <u>away</u> from it into another world.

This paragraph always gives me a sense of Jesus looking over vast stretches of time. He sees our attempts to find happiness in this world. He sees our hopes rise as we build a new home, a new road, or a new city. And then he sees our disappointment, as it slowly sinks in that life hasn't really changed. He sees us trying to suck happiness out of these forms, even as they begin to crumble and return to the dust from which they were made, until the home has been razed, the road lies overgrown with weeds, and the city is covered by sand. He sees us do this again and again, as the centuries and eons pass by, always seeking but never finding. And so he knows, as we look about us in the exercise from paragraph 1, that we do not really love the city we look upon. We have been there, we have done that, and we are not satisfied.

We keep hoping that somewhere in this world there is a road that will take us to a magical place, where, without changing our mind at all, we can be in paradise. Yet paradise is the real world, and it is not a place. It is an all-pervasive reality that we can see from *any* place.

> 4.   Yet the <u>real</u> world <u>has</u> the power to touch you even here, <u>because you love it</u>. And what you call with love <u>will</u> come to you. <u>Love always answers</u>, being unable to deny a call for help, or not to hear the cries of pain that rise to it from every part of this strange world you made but do not want. All that you need [Ur: The only effort you need make,]

to give this world away in glad exchange for what you did <u>not</u> make is willingness to learn <u>the one you made is false</u>.

This world cannot touch the real world, yet the real world can touch us "even here." While we sit in this world feeling utterly let down by it, our desires go out to another world, in which our longings can be satisfied. Our heart calls out to the real world, which hears our call and answers. And so the real world does touch us here. It graces us with brief intimations that somewhere there exists paradise. Yet to really give away this world and gain the real world, we need to do more than long for it. We need to accept the underlying basis of the world's inability to satisfy; we need to accept its insubstantiality. It is not real-but-sinful. It is not real and spiritual. It is simply not real. Are we willing to learn that?

> 5. You <u>have</u> been wrong about the world because you have misjudged <u>yourself</u>. From such a twisted reference point [misjudging yourself], what <u>could</u> you see? All seeing starts <u>with the perceiver</u>, who judges what is true and what is false. And what he judges false <u>he does not see</u>. You who would <u>judge</u> reality <u>cannot</u> see it, for whenever judgment enters reality has slipped away. The out of mind *is* out of sight, because what is denied is <u>there</u> but is not recognized. Christ is still there, although you know Him not. His Being does <u>not</u> depend upon your recognition. He lives within you in the quiet present, and waits for you to leave the past behind and enter into the world He holds out to you in love.

Perception of world flows from perception of self. We see the wrong world because we have believed in the wrong self. We look within and see a false self, and then look without and see its reflection everywhere. As a result, we see the physical world as real, and we judge the real world to be unreal, thus making it invisible to us.

To see the real world, we need to step out of the judge's seat. When we think we can decide what is real and what is not, we blind ourselves to reality, whose very nature is that *it is not up to us*. Yet when we do that, reality doesn't disappear. It is still there. The Christ in us is still there. And He is waiting for us to accept Him as our real Self, so that from this true reference point we can look out upon the real world.

6.   No one in this distracted world but has seen some glimpses of the other world about him. Yet while he still lays value on his own, he will <u>deny</u> the vision of the other, maintaining that he loves <u>what he loves not</u>, and following not the road that love points out. Love leads so gladly! As you follow Him [Christ/love], <u>you</u> will rejoice that you have found His company, and learned of Him the joyful journey home. You wait but for <u>yourself</u>. To give this sad world over and exchange your errors for the peace of God is but *your* will. And Christ will <u>always</u> offer you the Will of God, in recognition that you share it <u>with</u> Him.

That first sentence is so important. When you read that we must see a world our eyes can't see, it can sound impossible. Yet *every* single one of us has seen glimpses of this other world. It happens whenever we get a sense that there is some lovely, radiant meaning in a person, an event, or a situation that goes beyond what our eyes can see.

Yet ironically, even in the face of these glimpses, we stubbornly maintain that we love this world more. Our current lover (the world) has treated us like crap for years, while here in front of us stands the Christ, silently pointing out the road to paradise. Yet we stay put, staunchly defending the wonderful qualities of our abusive lover. We are only waiting for ourselves. We are only waiting to follow our own will. Once we do, and begin to walk along the road with Christ, we will be overjoyed that we have found His company and that with Him we are going *home*.

Application: Think of some glimpse you've had of the real world, some instance in which you felt you glimpsed the eternal in a person, in an object, in an event, in a situation, in yourself. Then ask yourself, "If I could live in a world in which everything was like this, could the physical world realistically offer me anything that could compare?"

7.   It is God's Will [a will you share with Him] that nothing touch His Son except Himself, and nothing else comes nigh unto him [an allusion to Psalm 91: "A thousand shall fall at thy side, and ten thousand at thy right hand; but it shall not come nigh thee"]. He is as safe from pain as God Himself, Who watches over him in everything. The world about him shines with love because God placed him in Himself where pain is not, and love surrounds him without end or flaw. Disturbance of his peace can never be. In perfect sanity he looks on love, for it is all about

him and within him. He <u>must</u> deny the world of pain the instant he perceives the arms of love around him. And from this point of safety he looks quietly about him and recognizes that the world is one with him.

Application: This paragraph is a beautiful description of being in the real world. Yet its beauty can easily escape us because it is addressed to the third person. Let's read it again, making it a series of first person statements. Read it slowly and above all, imagine each line as being true:

It is God's Will that nothing touch me except Himself, and nothing else comes nigh unto me

I am as safe from pain as God Himself, Who watches over me in everything.

The world about me shines with love because God placed me in Himself where pain is not, and love surrounds me without end or flaw.

Disturbance of my peace can never be.

In perfect sanity I look on love, for it is all about me and within me.

I must deny the world of pain the instant I perceive the arms of love around me.

And from this point of safety I look quietly about me and recognize that the [real] world is one with me.

8.   The peace of God [which we find in the real world] passeth your understanding <u>only</u> in the past. Yet here it *is*, and you <u>can</u> understand it *now*. God loves His Son forever, and His Son <u>returns</u> his Father's Love forever. The real world is the way that leads you to remembrance of the one thing that is wholly true and <u>wholly yours</u>. For all else you have <u>lent</u> yourself in time, and it <u>will</u> fade. But this one thing is <u>always</u> yours, being the gift of God unto His Son. Your <u>one</u> reality was <u>given</u> you, and <u>by</u> it God created you as one with Him.

Everything in this world is just a temporary loan. One day we'll have to give it all back as it crumbles in our hands. Yet the real world is not like that; it gives us gifts that last forever. The real world is still a realm of perception, yet perceiving it is how we at last return to that which never passes away: God's eternal love for us, and our eternal love for Him.

The Course has a slight issue with that biblical line about the peace of God which passeth understanding (Philippians 4:7). What cannot be understood must remain beyond our grasp, forever a mystery, forever out of reach. Earlier, in the Urtext, Jesus says that this peace passeth only *human* understanding. Here, he says that the peace of God passed our understanding only in the past, in which we were mired in this world. Yet in the real world this peace can be understood—and thus laid hold of—*now*.

> 9.   You will first <u>dream</u> of peace [the peace of the real world], and <u>then</u> awaken to it. Your first exchange of what you made for what you want is the exchange of nightmares [the world] for the happy dreams of love [the real world]. In these lie your true perceptions, for the Holy Spirit corrects the world of dreams, where <u>all</u> perception is. Knowledge needs <u>no</u> correction. Yet the dreams of love lead <u>unto</u> knowledge. In them you see nothing fearful, and <u>because</u> of this they are the welcome that you <u>offer</u> knowledge. Love waits on welcome, <u>not</u> on time, and the real world is but your welcome of what always was. Therefore the call of [Heaven's] joy is in it, and your glad response is your awakening to what you have not lost.

What strikes me about this paragraph is that the way I permanently awaken to Heaven is that I live in the real world. The real world is still perception (though not physical perception) and therefore it is ultimately illusory. Yet seeing it represents my welcome to the eternal. It is a condition that is free of fear, and thus it represents my welcome to everlasting love. ("The real world is but your welcome of what always was"). It is a condition in which I experience the call of Heaven's joy, and so it compels me to respond by leaping into Heaven. ("Your glad response is your awakening to what you have not lost.").

What I find interesting, then, is that what brings on my final awakening to eternity is not a specific decision that I make. It does not happen in a particular meditation. It is not any specific event in time. What invites my final awakening is my living in a certain state, the state the Course calls the real world (or happy dream—which is a happy state in the dream, not happy *events* in the dream). Thus, my invitation to eternity is not a specific act or decision; it is an overall, stable state in which I live. My willingness to abide in that state is my invitation to be with God once and for all.

Remaining Commentary by Greg Mackie

10.   Praise, then, the Father for the perfect sanity of His most holy Son. Your Father knoweth that you have need of nothing. In Heaven this is so, for what could you need in eternity? In your world you do need things. [Ur: because] It is a world of scarcity in which you find yourself *because* you are lacking. Yet can [Ur: But *can*] you find yourself in such a world? Without the Holy Spirit the answer would be no. Yet because of Him the answer is a joyous *yes!* As Mediator between the two worlds, He knows what you have need of and what [Ur: *which*] will not hurt you. Ownership is a dangerous concept if it is left to you. The ego wants to have things for salvation, for possession is its law. Possession for its own sake is the ego's fundamental creed, a basic cornerstone in the churches it builds to itself. And at its altar it demands you lay all of the things it bids you get, leaving you no joy in them.

This section has spoken of the attainment of the real world, which we will inevitably choose because we are inherently sane. Now Jesus shifts into a discussion of *needs*, which includes a fascinating discussion of *things*. When he speaks of "things" here, Jesus means earthly things, in particular material possessions. In Heaven we need nothing (the second sentence here is a reversal of Luke 12:30, "Your Father knoweth that ye have need of these things"). But on earth we do temporarily need earthly things. How, then, can we meet our earthly needs in a way that supports our journey from the world we do not want to the real world we do want?

If we didn't have the Holy Spirit to guide us, our situation would be hopeless, because we'd be forever serving the ego's needs at our expense. In the ego's view, possession of things for its own sake is the way to salvation; as the saying goes, "He who dies with the most toys wins." Indeed, conspicuous consumption is the world's religion; like Gordon Gecko in the movie *Wall Street*, we're all chanting "Greed is good." But while we tell ourselves that following the religion of acquisition is the golden road to happiness, all we're doing is increasing the *ego's* happiness, not ours. As we lay our possessions at the ego's altar, we're like Scrooge in *A Christmas Carol*, with a full bank account but an empty soul. As we identify with our possessions, we chain ourselves to this world and lose sight of who we really are.

Fortunately, however, we *do* have the Holy Spirit to guide us. He knows which things we actually need while we're here and which things are just sacrificial trophies for the ego. As Mediator between the worlds, He knows how to provide for our earthly needs in a way that doesn't chain us to this world but instead facilitates our journey to the real world. He knows how to give us things in a way that enables us to rediscover who we really are even here. *Yes!*

> 11.   Everything the ego tells you that you need will hurt you. For although the ego urges you again and again to get, it leaves you nothing, for what you get it will demand of you. And even from the very hands that grasped it, it will be wrenched and hurled into the dust. For where the ego sees salvation it sees separation, and so you lose whatever you have gotten in its name. Therefore ask not of yourself what you need, for you do not know [Ur: *for you know not*], and your advice to yourself will hurt you. For what you think you need will merely serve to tighten up your world against the light, and render you unwilling to question the value that this world can really hold for you.

Dedicating our lives to acquiring the earthly things the ego says we need will always hurt us, because while we tell ourselves we will gain, in truth we will lose. We will lose because the ego demands that we use everything we acquire to inflate *it*, leaving us with nothing that would make *us* truly happy. We will lose because we literally lose all earthly things eventually. "You can't take it with you"; even if he who dies with the most toys wins, he still *dies*. The greatest loss, though, is not losing our toys when we die but losing sight of the light of the real world, binding ourselves more tightly to a painful world we don't even really want. To alleviate this pain, the first step is to stop asking ourselves what we need, in recognition of the fact that we don't really know.

> 12.   Only the Holy Spirit knows what you need. For He will give you all things that do not block the way to light. And what else could you need? In time, He gives you all the things that you need have, and will

renew them as long as you have need of them. He will take nothing <u>from</u> you as long as you have <u>any</u> need of it. And yet He knows that <u>everything</u> you need is temporary, and will but last [Ur: and need but last] until you step aside from <u>all</u> your needs and realize that all of them <u>have been</u> fulfilled. Therefore He has no investment in the things that He supplies, except to make certain that you will <u>not</u> use them on behalf of lingering in time. He knows that you are not at home there, and He wills no delay to wait upon your joyous homecoming.

We don't really know what earthly things we need, but the Holy Spirit *does* know and will happily provide them for us. Many Course students believe the Holy Spirit does not give us earthly things, but this section makes it clear this is not so. He gives us everything we need to live in this world, will renew it as long as we need it, and will never take away anything we truly need.

The difference between this and the ego's religion of greed is that the Holy Spirit gives us things to serve *His* goal. The ego goads us into acquiring things to sacrifice at its altar; the Holy Spirit gives us only things that facilitate our journey to the real world. The ego has a huge investment in possessions since its very salvation lies in them; the Holy Spirit has no investment in them except to make sure we don't use them "on behalf of lingering in time." The ego acquires things for their own sake; the Holy Spirit acquires them merely as means to help us meet temporary worldly needs while we journey toward the recognition we have no real needs at all.

Here, then, is the Course's answer to that perennial question "Does the Holy Spirit give you parking spaces?": Yes, *if* it serves His goal of leading you to your joyous homecoming.

> 13.   Leave, then, your needs to Him. He will supply them with no emphasis at all upon them. What comes to you of Him comes safely, for He will ensure it never can become a dark spot, hidden in your mind and kept to hurt you. Under His guidance you will travel light and journey lightly, for His sight is ever on the journey's end, which is His goal. God's Son is not a traveller through <u>outer</u> worlds. However holy his perception may become, no world <u>outside</u> himself holds his inheritance. Within <u>himself</u> he <u>has</u> no needs, for light needs nothing but to shine in peace, and from <u>itself</u> to let the rays extend in quiet to infinity.

The first two sentences here sum up the attitude the Holy Spirit takes (and wants us to take) toward earthly needs. Spiritual seekers often swing between two extremes: the idea the Holy Spirit is a divine Butler who serves up whatever goodies we want to live the "good life" on earth (much "prosperity" teaching fits this description), and the idea the Holy Spirit is so "pure" and removed from the world that He has nothing to do with our earthly needs. (Some Course students believe He doesn't act in the world at all.) In the first extreme, you have both supply and emphasis on it; in the second, neither supply nor emphasis on it.

The Course, however, offers the best of both worlds: supply with no emphasis on it. I find both of these elements immensely reassuring. Yes, we do have earthly needs, and it is reassuring that the Holy Spirit will supply them for us. Yes, we do face the painful temptation of acquiring things for our egos, and it is also reassuring that He will help undo this temptation by placing no emphasis on the things He supplies. I think it takes both of these elements for us to truly "travel light and journey lightly." Only by both having the provisions we need on the journey *and* keeping our emphasis on the journey's goal will we journey lightly to the recognition that our only need is to shine our light in peace.

14.   Whenever you are tempted to undertake a useless [Ur: foolish] journey that would lead <u>away</u> from light, remember what you <u>really</u> want, and say:

The Holy Spirit leads me unto Christ, and where else would I go? What need have I but to awake in Him?

15.   Then follow Him in joy, with faith that He will lead you safely through all dangers to your peace of mind this world may set before you. Kneel not before the altars to sacrifice, and seek not what you will surely lose. Content yourself with what you will as surely <u>keep</u>, and be not restless, for you undertake a quiet journey to the peace of God, where He would have you be in quietness.

Application: Bring to mind some physical thing you currently think you need to bring you happiness, some thing that tempts you to take a "foolish journey" away from light. Apply the following words to this thing:

I will not ask of myself what I need, for I do not know, and my advice to myself will hurt me.

What I think I need will merely serve to tighten up my world against the light, and render me unwilling to question the value that this world can really hold for me.

Only the Holy Spirit knows what I need.

I will leave, then, my needs to Him.

He will supply them with no emphasis at all upon them.

What comes to me of Him comes safely, for He will ensure it never can become a dark spot, hidden in my mind and kept to hurt me.

He will lead me safely through all dangers to my peace of mind this world may set before me.

For He meets my earthly needs only to serve my real need: to awaken to Christ.

The Holy Spirit leads me unto Christ, and where else would I go? What need have I but to awake in Him?

16.   In me you have already overcome every temptation that would hold you back. We walk together on the way to quietness that is the gift of God. Hold me dear, for what except your brothers can you need? We will restore to you the peace of mind that we must find together. The Holy Spirit will teach you to awaken unto us and to yourself. This is the only real need to be fulfilled in time. Salvation from the world lies only here. My peace I give you. Take it of me in glad exchange for all the world has offered but to take away. And we will spread it like a veil of light across the world's sad face, in which we hide our brothers from the world, and it from them.

What do we hold dear? If we're honest, we have to admit that most of the time we hold the things of the world dear. But here, Jesus asks us to hold *him* dear—what a beautiful thought! Why should we do this? One reason is that he has already overcome all the temptations we're currently struggling with; as he is reported to have said in the gospels, "Be of good cheer; I have overcome the world" (John 16:33). By holding him dear, we partake of the peace he is so eager to share: "My peace I give unto you: not as the world giveth, give I unto you" (John 14:27). He

248

wants nothing more than to free us from the chains of valuing the world's shabby gifts.

Finally, holding him dear is a way of holding all of our brothers dear, and this is our only real need in this world: to join with our brothers and awaken to our shared Identity as Christ. By letting the Holy Spirit teach us to fulfill this need, we will help everyone overcome the world just as Jesus did.

> 17. We cannot sing redemption's hymn alone. My task is not completed until I have lifted every voice with mine. And yet it is <u>not</u> mine, for as it is my gift to you, so was it the Father's gift to me, given me through His Spirit. The sound of it will banish sorrow from the mind of God's most holy Son, where it cannot abide. Healing in time <u>is</u> needed, for joy cannot establish its eternal reign where sorrow dwells. You dwell not here, but in eternity. You travel but in dreams, while safe at home. Give thanks to every part of you that you have taught how to <u>remember</u> you. Thus does the Son of God give thanks unto his Father for his purity.

Let's face it, the world is a sad place. We keep telling ourselves that if we just acquire enough we will be happy, but even the richest people on earth are terribly sad if they don't have the peace of God. Jesus has come to save us from this. He is singing the hymn of redemption from sorrow and calls us all to join him. This song "will banish sorrow from the mind of God's most holy Son, where it cannot abide." It is the song of healing the world needs to hear, a song we are called to sing to every brother we meet. By extending healing to all, by offering the gift of gratitude to all the holy brothers we have taught to remember the truth of who we are, we will recognize that our true home is with our Father in Heaven—a home where we have no needs, a home we never really left.

VIII. From Perception to Knowledge
Commentary by Greg Mackie

> 1.   All healing [Ur: therapy] is release from the past. That is why the Holy Spirit is the only Healer [Ur: therapist]. He teaches that the past does not exist, a fact which belongs to the sphere of knowledge, and which therefore no one in the world can know [Ur: *no-one in the world knows*]. It would indeed be impossible to be in the world with this knowledge. For the mind that knows this unequivocally knows also it dwells in eternity, and utilizes no perception at all. It therefore does not consider where it is, because the concept "where" does not mean anything to it. It knows that it is everywhere, just as it has everything, and forever.

The major theme of this section is the relationship between perception and knowledge, and how we get from one to the other. The way we get from perception to knowledge, the section will tell us, is to extend healing by seeing everyone without the past. But strictly speaking, we're not the healers; the Holy Spirit heals *through* us. Only He can release from the past, because only He *knows* the past does not exist.

We ourselves cannot know this, because "It would indeed be impossible to be in the world with this knowledge." What an amazing statement! Many spiritual teachers in this world claim to be fully enlightened, but according to this paragraph they can't be, because if they were *fully* enlightened they wouldn't be here. The mind of a fully enlightened being is beyond perception entirely; it "knows that it is everywhere, just as it has everything, and forever." Who in this world can unequivocally say that?

Keep an eye on that trio of everywhere/everything/forever. We will see variations on it in the next few paragraphs.

> 2.   The very real difference between perception and knowledge becomes quite apparent if you consider this: There is nothing partial about knowledge. Every aspect is whole, and therefore no aspect is separate. You are an aspect of knowledge, being in the Mind of God, Who knows you. All knowledge must be yours, for in you

250

<u>is</u> all knowledge. Perception, at its loftiest, is <u>never</u> complete. Even the perception of the Holy Spirit, as perfect as perception <u>can</u> be, is without meaning in Heaven. Perception can reach <u>everywhere</u> under His guidance, for the vision of Christ beholds <u>everything</u> in light. Yet no perception, however holy, will last <u>forever</u>.

This paragraph introduces the word "aspect," which we'll see a lot in this section. When the Course speaks of "aspects" (as in "aspects of reality" in the next paragraph), it usually means individual Sons of God, parts of the Sonship. We see that in this paragraph where you, an individual Son of God, are an aspect of knowledge.

Though it is impossible to have knowledge in this world, in Heaven we not only *have* knowledge, we *are* knowledge. We *have* knowledge because in us is all the knowledge of God. We *are* knowledge because we ourselves are in the Mind of God. Each of us is part of knowledge, and since there is nothing partial about knowledge, each of us is also the whole of knowledge. In short, knowledge is all-encompassing. It is totally unified. It is everywhere, everything, and forever.

Even the loftiest perception falls short of this exalted state. Yes, the Holy Spirit's perception can reach everywhere, and the vision of Christ sees everything in the light of holiness. But it is not complete because, unlike knowledge, it is temporary: It will *not* last forever.

3. Perfect perception, then, has many elements <u>in common</u> with knowledge [both perfect perception and knowledge extend everywhere and encompass everything], making transfer <u>to</u> it possible. Yet the last step must be taken by God, because the last step in your redemption, which <u>seems</u> to be in the future, <u>was</u> accomplished by God in your creation. The separation has <u>not</u> interrupted it. Creation cannot <u>be</u> interrupted. The separation is merely a faulty formulation of reality, <u>with no effect at all</u>. The miracle, without a function in Heaven, <u>is</u> needful here. <u>Aspects</u> of reality can still be seen, and they will replace aspects of <u>unreality</u>. Aspects of reality can be seen <u>in everything</u> <u>and</u> <u>everywhere</u>. Yet only God can gather them together, by crowning them <u>as one</u> with the final gift of eternity.

Here is a full picture of the journey from perception to knowledge. When we separated our minds from God, we seemed to interrupt creation. Yet we did not, because creation cannot be interrupted. All we did was make a false perception, "a faulty formulation of reality." Now we make the journey from false to true perception. The vehicle that takes us on this journey is the miracle, which enables us to see aspects of reality—our fellow Sons of God—as they truly are, freed from the past. Finally, we reach "perfect perception," which is so close to knowledge that transfer to knowledge is at last possible.

But only God can make that transfer, because only He *knows* that creation has never been interrupted. In fact, that very transfer, God's "last step," is simply His affirmation that creation was in the beginning, is now, and always will be. He takes the aspects of reality seen everywhere and in everything, and lifts them into the forever that has always been.

> 4.   Apart from the Father and the Son, the Holy Spirit has no function. He is not separate from either, being in the Mind of Both, and knowing that Mind is one. He is a Thought of God, and God has <u>given</u> Him to you because He has <u>no</u> Thoughts He does not share. His message speaks of timelessness in time, and that is why Christ's vision looks on everything with love. Yet even Christ's vision is not His reality. The golden <u>aspects</u> of reality that spring to light under His loving gaze are partial glimpses of the Heaven that lies beyond them.

To make this journey from perception to knowledge, we need the Holy Spirit, because He has a foot in both camps, so to speak. He is in the Mind of the Father, so He knows of timelessness. He is also in the mind of the Son, so He can also speak "of timelessness in time" to us. He is thus the One who brings us to the "perfect perception" described in the last paragraph. He gives us Christ's vision, which "looks on everything with love." He reveals our brothers as they truly are: golden aspects of reality shining in the light of love. He brings us to the gate of Heaven, where God can take the final step and restore us to the knowledge that the Mind of Father and Son is one.

> 5.   This is the miracle of creation; *that it is one forever.* Every miracle you offer to the Son of God is but the true perception of one <u>aspect</u> of the whole. Though every aspect *is* the whole, you cannot <u>know</u> this until you <u>see</u> that every aspect <u>is the same</u>, perceived in the <u>same</u> light and <u>therefore</u> one. Everyone seen <u>without</u> the past thus brings you nearer to the end of time by bringing healed and healing sight into the

darkness, and <u>enabling the world to see</u>. For light must come into the darkened world to make Christ's vision possible even here. Help Him to give His gift of light to all who think they wander in the darkness, and let Him gather them into His quiet sight that makes them one.

We make the journey described in these paragraphs by performing miracles for our brothers, by helping Christ bring His gift of light to all who think they wander in darkness. Each miracle is the true perception of one brother, one aspect of the whole. The miracle enables us to see that brother without his past, which brings healing. The more miracles are extended, the closer we are brought to the end of time. Eventually, we see that every aspect is the same, and therefore all are one. This perfect perception makes us ready for God's final step, through which we will come to know that each aspect *is* the whole.

Application: Bring to mind someone you know who seems to be wandering in the darkness, perhaps a person who feels bound by his or her past in some way. In your mind, say the following to this person:

> *I offer you a miracle, [name].*
> *To you who think you wander in the darkness,*
> *I offer Christ's gift of light.*
> *You are completely free of the past.*
> *You are one with me and with all our brothers.*
> *All of us are beautiful and equal in our holiness.*
> *Our shared light enables the world to see.*

6.   They are all the same; all beautiful and equal in their holiness. And He will offer them unto His Father as they were offered unto Him. There is <u>one</u> miracle, as there is <u>one</u> reality. And every miracle you do contains them all, as every aspect of reality you see blends quietly into the one Reality of God. The only miracle that ever was is God's most holy Son, created in the one Reality that is his Father. Christ's vision is His gift to you. His Being is His Father's gift to Him.

Though the Course's usual definition of "miracle" is a divine healing of perception (either within your mind or extended to the mind of another), it has another definition that was alluded to in the last paragraph's reference to "the miracle of creation." According to that definition, God's creation of His Son was a miracle. That is the "one miracle"; that is "the only miracle that ever was."

The miracles we do on earth are reflections of that one miracle, affirmations of the miracle that is the purity, holiness, and oneness of God's Son. They are part of a divine gift exchange that goes like this:

1. God gives Christ's Being to Him.
2. Christ gives His vision to us.
3. Through Christ's vision we extend miracles, and thus give our brothers to Christ.
4. Christ gives our brothers (and ourselves) to God.

> 7. Be you content with healing, for Christ's gift you <u>can</u> bestow, and your Father's gift you <u>cannot</u> lose. Offer Christ's gift to everyone and everywhere, for miracles, offered the Son of God through the Holy Spirit, attune <u>you</u> to reality. The Holy Spirit knows your part in the redemption, and who are seeking you and where to find them. Knowledge is far beyond your individual concern. You who are part of it and all of it need only realize that it is of the Father, <u>not</u> of you. Your role in the redemption <u>leads</u> you to it by re-establishing its oneness in your mind [Ur: minds].

Many spiritual seekers hanker for knowledge—blowout experiences of direct union with God. But here we are told, "Be you content with healing." The focus of the Course's path is not blowout enlightenment experiences, which are useful but can often leave the ego totally intact. Instead, its focus is on the egoless extension of miracles to our brothers. Knowledge is really not our concern on this path; instead, our job is to take our part in the redemption by offering Christ's gift of true perception to everyone everywhere. If we simply devote ourselves to healing, we can trust we will ultimately be led to a more permanent awareness of knowledge and union with God than any brief experience could give us.

Application: Let's make a commitment to that function of healing.

Holy Spirit, let me be content with healing.

Let me offer Christ's gift of miracles to everyone and everywhere.
Let me know who are seeking me and where to find them.
Let me fulfill my role in the redemption,
which leads me to knowledge by re-establishing its oneness in
my mind.

8.   When you have seen your brothers as yourself you will be <u>released</u> to knowledge, having learned to <u>free</u> yourself through Him Who knows of freedom. Unite with me under the holy banner of His teaching, and as we grow in strength the power of God's Son will move in us, and we will leave no one untouched and no one left alone. And suddenly time will be over, and we will all unite in the eternity of God the Father. The holy light you saw <u>outside</u> yourself, in every miracle you offered to your brothers, will be <u>returned</u> to you. And <u>knowing</u> that the light is <u>in</u> you, <u>your</u> creations will be there <u>with</u> you, as you are in your Father.

This section has traced in many ways the path from perception to knowledge. Here is another version, which reminds me of a social movement like the civil rights movement. (I'm also reminded of the "great crusade" imagery of T-1.III.1:6.) First, we unite with Jesus "under the holy banner of [the Holy Spirit's] teaching." Uniting under this banner means offering miracles to our brothers, extending true perception to them. As we do this, more and more brothers join under the Holy Spirit's banner—the miracle workers' movement grows in strength. (I can almost hear everyone singing "We Shall Overcome.") The power of God's Son works through the growing movement, extending miracles to everyone everywhere.

Finally, *everyone* is joined under the banner, united as one Son of God. And then, suddenly, time is over. Joining is complete. The miracles everyone has given are returned. We all see our brothers as ourselves. "We Shall Overcome" becomes Beethoven's "Ode to Joy." And with this we are released to knowledge, fully joined with one another and our creations in God our Father.

9.   As miracles in this world join you to your brothers, so do your creations establish your fatherhood in Heaven. <u>You</u> are the witness to the Fatherhood of God, and He has given you the power to create

the witnesses to <u>yours</u>, which is as <u>His</u>. Deny a brother here, and you deny the witnesses to your fatherhood in Heaven. The miracle that God created is perfect, as are the miracles that <u>you</u> established [Ur: created] in His Name. They need no healing, nor do you, when you accept them [Ur: know *them*].

The last two paragraphs bring in the word "witness," an important term in the Course. To be a "witness" means to provide evidence for something, to testify to its existence. We are the witnesses to the Fatherhood of God—we are the evidence of His Fatherhood. In like manner, our creations in Heaven are the witnesses to *our* fatherhood. These creations are "miracles" in the sense I referred to earlier: Just as God's creation of His Son was a miracle, so our creation of our "sons" was a miracle.

But when we deny a brother on earth—when we see anyone as anything less than a perfect Son of God—we deny our heavenly creations (especially since, as it says elsewhere in the Course, these creations were created by the Sonship as a whole, including this brother). The only way out of this is to extend a miracle to the brother we are denying—a miracle in the usual Course sense of true perception. By extending a miracle, we undo our denial of our brother and join with him. This undoes our denial of our heavenly creations, and thus reconnects us to the witnesses to our fatherhood in Heaven.

> 10. Yet in this world your perfection is unwitnessed. God knows it, but <u>you</u> do not, and so you do not <u>share</u> His witness <u>to</u> it. Nor do you witness unto Him, for reality is witnessed to as one. God waits your witness to His Son and to Himself. The miracles you do on earth are lifted up to Heaven and to Him. They witness to what you do not know, and as they reach the gates of Heaven, God will open them. For never would He leave His Own beloved Son outside them, and beyond Himself.

In Heaven, God knows our perfection, and it is also witnessed to by our creations, which are as perfect as we are. But here on earth, our perfection is *un*witnessed because we've denied it. Again, the way to undo this denial is to extend miracles to our brothers. Seeing our brothers with true perception witnesses to the knowledge that we threw away, including knowledge of our perfection. Seeing everyone with true perception enables God to take the last step Himself. At the end of the journey, He will throw open the gates of Heaven and, like the father of the prodigal welcoming his beloved son home, He will joyously bring us in and restore the knowledge we have forgotten but never truly lost.

IX. The Cloud of Guilt
Commentary by Greg Mackie

1.   Guilt remains the only thing that hides the Father [see T-13.In.1:7 and T-13.II.1:2], <u>for guilt is the attack upon His Son</u>. The guilty <u>always</u> condemn, and <u>having</u> done so they <u>will</u> still condemn, linking the future to the past as is the ego's law. Fidelity to this law lets no light in, for it <u>demands</u> fidelity to darkness and <u>forbids</u> awakening. The ego's laws are strict, and breaches are severely punished. Therefore give no obedience to its laws, for they <u>are </u>laws of punishment. And those who follow them believe that <u>they</u> are guilty, and so they <u>must</u> condemn. Between the future and the past the laws of God must intervene, if you would free yourself [Ur: yourselves]. Atonement stands between them, like a lamp shining so brightly that the chain of darkness in which you bound yourself [Ur: yourselves] will disappear.

As we've seen in previous sections, the ego's law is that the future is linked to the past. We've condemned ourselves for our sins in the past, and this guarantees future condemnation in the form of punishment. Isn't this what life feels like? Our past misdeeds weigh us down more and more as we trudge through our days. As we age, life becomes increasingly painful (physically if nothing else) until at last we receive the death penalty. If the past determines the future, there's really no way out of this, no way for any light to come in and dispel the darkness.

In the laws of God, though, the *present* is linked to the future. If we accept the Atonement in the present—God's affirmation of our perfect innocence—we bring God's light into the darkness. It will shine away the past and set us free from the long trudge to death. Don't we all yearn to be released from our chains? Release is there for the asking; all we must do is stop obeying the ego's law and let the laws of God intervene.

2.   Release from guilt is the ego's whole undoing. *Make no one fearful,* for his guilt is yours, and by obeying the ego's harsh commandments you bring its condemnation on yourself, and you will not escape the punishment it offers those who obey it. The ego rewards fidelity to it with pain, for faith in it *is* pain. And faith can be rewarded only

258

in terms of the belief in which the faith was placed. Faith <u>makes</u> the power of belief, and <u>where</u> it is invested determines its reward. For faith is <u>always</u> given what is treasured, and what is treasured <u>is</u> returned to you.

We all yearn to be innocent, and accepting the Atonement is the way to recognize our inherent innocence. The ego wants no part of this, however, because release from guilt is its doom. So, it offers us its own plan for preserving our innocence: make *someone else* guilty and fearful of the punishment guilt entails. A later Course passage speaks of how "your accusing finger points to him, unwavering and deadly in its aim" (T-31.V.6:4). We all love to point the finger, don't we? This is an extremely clever plan, for it seems to give us what *we* want—innocence—but actually gives the ego what *it* wants: confirmation of our guilt. To test this out, think of how you really feel when you try to make someone else guilty. Do you truly feel clean and pure inside, or do you feel mean, grimy, tainted—in a word, *guilty*?

This awful feeling is exactly what the ego wants, and as long as we identify with it, so do we. We have joined the cult of the ego, a masochistic cult that rewards its followers with pain. Like the villain in *The Da Vinci Code*, we are extremely devoted to self-flagellation. As we tell ourselves we're relieving our pain by dumping our guilt onto someone else, secretly we're taking a beating from the ego and saying, "Thank you, sir, may I have another?" All the while, Jesus is calling to us from outside the cult compound, saying: "*Make no one fearful.* Can't you see what projecting your guilt is doing to you?"

> 3.   The world can give you <u>only</u> what you gave it, for being nothing but your own projection, it <u>has</u> no meaning apart from what you found in it and placed your faith in. Be faithful unto darkness and you will <u>not</u> see, because your faith <u>will</u> be rewarded as you <u>gave</u> it. You *will* accept your treasure, and if you place your faith in the past, the future <u>will</u> be like it. Whatever you hold dear <u>you think is yours</u>. The power of your <u>valuing</u> will make it so.

It seems to us that the pain we experience is inflicted on us by the world against our will—it's so unfair! But in truth, the only reason the world hurts us is because we've projected our belief in our own sin upon the world, and that projection returns to us in the form of punishment. Our membership in the cult of the ego leads us to *treasure* past sins, and this leads inevitably to the "reward" of future pain. How can we see what is really there when we're projecting the darkness of sin everywhere we look?

> 4.   Atonement brings a re-evaluation of <u>everything</u> you cherish, for it is the means by which the Holy Spirit can <u>separate</u> the false and the true, which you have accepted into your mind [Ur: minds] <u>without distinction</u>. Therefore you cannot value one without the other, and guilt has become <u>as true for you as innocence</u>. You do <u>not</u> believe the Son of God is guiltless because you see the past, and see <u>him</u> not. When you condemn a brother you are saying, "I who <u>was</u> guilty choose to <u>remain</u> so." You have denied <u>his</u> freedom, and by so doing you have denied the witness unto <u>yours</u>. You could as easily have <u>freed</u> him from the past, and lifted from his mind the cloud of guilt that binds him <u>to</u> it. And in <u>his</u> freedom would have been your <u>own</u>.

When we condemn others to free ourselves from guilt, we are telling ourselves that guilt and innocence are both valuable: "My innocence is valuable, and your guilt is also valuable because it *preserves* my innocence." Underneath this, as we've seen, our real motivation for projecting guilt onto others is to hold onto our own guilt, which we cherish. The Atonement, however, enables us to reconsider our membership in the cult of the ego. Perhaps a cult that rewards us with pain isn't so hot after all. Perhaps seeing the innocent Son of God instead of the sinful past will be a happier choice. When we choose the Atonement, the Holy Spirit shows us that guilt is wholly false and innocence is wholly true, and therefore innocence is the only thing of value. He shows us the wholly innocent Son of God in the brother we were condemning, which frees him from guilt and thus frees us as well.

Application: Bring to mind someone you are currently seeing as guilty, someone who seems to make you feel "innocent" in comparison. Say the following to this person:

> *When I condemn you, [name], I am saying, "I who **was** guilty choose to **remain** so now and in the future."*

I have denied your freedom, and by so doing I have denied the witness unto mine.
I choose instead to free you from the past, and lift from your mind the cloud of guilt that binds you to it, because I know that in your freedom is my own.

5.   Lay not his guilt upon him, for <u>his</u> guilt lies in his secret thought [Ur: in his secret that *he* thinks] that <u>he</u> has done this unto <u>you</u>. Would you, then, teach him he is <u>right</u> in his delusion? The idea that the guiltless Son of God can attack himself and <u>make</u> himself guilty <u>is</u> insane. In <u>any</u> form, in <u>anyone</u>, *believe this not.* For sin and condemnation are the same, and the belief in one is faith in the other, calling for punishment <u>instead</u> of love. <u>Nothing</u> can justify insanity, and to call for punishment <u>upon yourself must</u> be insane.

When we make other people feel guilty, we attack ourselves and make ourselves feel guilty. Moreover, we reinforce whatever guilt they already have, for their guilt stems from the fact that they've been playing the same game. But it is sheer insanity to believe that we, wholly innocent Sons of God, could *truly* attack ourselves and make ourselves *truly* guilty. Jesus implores us to give up this nutty idea entirely: "In any form, in anyone, *believe this not.*" Why have faith in something that offers punishment instead of love? Why keep calling for punishment on ourselves?

6.   See no one, then, as guilty, and you will affirm the truth of guiltlessness <u>unto yourself</u>. In every condemnation that you offer the Son of God lies the conviction of your <u>own</u> guilt. If you would have the Holy Spirit make <u>you</u> free of it, accept His offer of Atonement for <u>all</u> your brothers. For so you learn that <u>it is true for you</u>. Remember always that it is impossible to condemn the Son of God <u>in part</u>. Those whom you see as guilty become the witnesses to guilt <u>in you</u>, and you <u>will</u> see it there, for it *is* there until it is undone. Guilt is <u>always</u> in your mind, <u>which has condemned itself</u>. Project it not, for while you do, it cannot <u>be</u> undone. With everyone whom you release from guilt great is the joy in Heaven [a reference to Luke 15:7 and 15:10], where the witnesses to your fatherhood rejoice.

This paragraph is a good summary of the two choices that confront us. We think we can condemn the Son of God in part—that we can see another as guilty to preserve our own innocence. But in truth, when we see our brothers as guilty we preserve our own guilt, because what we're seeing in them *is* our own guilt, projected from our minds. They become witnesses to our own guilt. And as long as we keep projecting our guilt onto them, we won't see that it's ours, and thus it can't be undone.

We have another choice, however: to accept the Holy Spirit's offer of Atonement for everyone. We can choose to withdraw our projection of guilt from our brothers, to "see no one…as guilty." Seeing them as guiltless affirms our own guiltlessness. They become witnesses to our freedom. As we release them, we release ourselves, and all of Heaven— including our own creations, the witnesses to our fatherhood—celebrates the glad tidings of release.

> 7.   <u>Guilt makes you blind</u>, for while you see one spot of guilt within you, <u>you</u> <u>will not see the light</u>. And by projecting it the <u>world</u> seems dark, and shrouded in <u>your</u> guilt. You throw a dark veil over it, and cannot see it <u>because you cannot look within</u>. You are afraid of what you would see there, but it is <u>not</u> there. *The thing you fear is gone.* If you would look within you would see only the Atonement, shining in quiet and in peace upon the altar to your Father.

The last two paragraphs of this section (this one and the following one) speak of looking within. We are utterly convinced that we are horribly guilty, that at the core of our being is a dark, stinking lump of sin that can never be undone. This is so fearful that we can't bear to look at it. Instead, we project our guilt onto the world, making the *world* seem dark. We are blind to the light of the world, because we are blind to the light within us. The good news, though, is that the dark, stinking lump of sin isn't really within us. *"The thing you fear is gone."* The Atonement has shined it away. If we will just look within, we will see a shining altar to our Father where we thought we would see a bloody altar to the ego.

> 8.   Do not be afraid to look within. The ego tells you all is black with guilt within you, and bids you <u>not to look</u>. Instead, it bids you look upon your brothers, <u>and see the guilt in them</u>. Yet this you cannot do <u>without remaining blind</u>. For those who see their brothers in the dark [Ur: those who see their brothers dark], and guilty in the dark in

which they shroud them, are too afraid to look upon the light within. Within you is <u>not</u> what you believe is there, and what <u>you</u> put your faith in. Within you is the holy sign of perfect faith <u>your Father</u> has in you. <u>He</u> does not value you as you do. He knows Himself, and knows the truth <u>in you</u>. He knows <u>there is no difference</u>, for He knows not of differences. Can <u>you</u> see guilt where God <u>knows</u> there is perfect innocence? You can <u>deny</u> His knowledge, but you <u>cannot</u> change it. Look, then, upon the light He placed within you, and learn that what you feared was there <u>has been</u> replaced with love.

Application: Jesus says to us, "Do not be afraid to look within." So let's do that now.

Imagine yourself approaching a large door to the innermost chamber of a castle.
You realize this is the door to what is within *you.*
You are afraid to open it, because you hear the ego warning you to back away:
"Don't look in there!
Don't you realize this chamber is full of terrible demons, the spawn of your black, bottomless guilt?
Think of all the sins you've committed, all the hateful thoughts you've had, the mean things you've said to others, the rotten things you've done to them.
You don't really want to face those demons, do you?
The only way you can feel better about yourself is to forget all about what's behind that door.
See the guilt in other people instead and you'll never have to face the terrible demons within this chamber."

But now you hear the voice of Jesus reassuring you:
"Do not be afraid to look within.
Within this chamber is not what you believe is there.
God knows what is within you.
For He knows Himself, He knows the truth in you, and He knows there is no difference between them.
Within you is the holy sign of perfect faith your Father has in you.

Within you is perfect innocence.
Within you is not a den of demons, but a choir of heavenly angels.
Look, then, upon the light God placed within you, and learn that what
  you feared was in this chamber has been replaced with love."

With this reassurance from Jesus,
Open the door and look within.

X. Release from Guilt
Commentary by Greg Mackie

This section's major theme is that as long as we keep displacing our guilt, we will see it as real and thus be afraid to look within. But if we stop displacing it and acknowledge its actual source, we will see it as insane and thus be able to look within, where it will be dispelled by the Atonement and we will see the innocent Son of God we really are.

> 1. You are accustomed to the notion that the mind can see the source of pain where it is not. The doubtful service of such displacement is to hide the <u>real</u> source of guilt, and <u>keep</u> from your awareness the full perception <u>that it is insane</u>. Displacement <u>always</u> is maintained by the illusion that the source of guilt, from which attention is diverted, <u>must be true</u>; and <u>must be fearful</u>, or you would not have displaced the guilt onto what you believed to be <u>less</u> fearful. You are therefore willing [Ur: with little opposition] to look upon all kinds of "sources," [Ur: underneath awareness] provided they are not the deeper source to which they bear no real relationship at all.

As psychologists, Helen and Bill were very familiar with displacement, which a psychology textbook of mine defines as "the transfer of emotion from the person or object causing the emotion to another person or object considered 'safer.'" Here, Jesus says we do that with guilt. The actual source of our guilt is the belief that we have truly killed God's Son (see T-13.II.3:1-2) and have thus turned ourselves into murderous monsters. This is so terrifying to contemplate that we displace the guilt onto bogus, "safer" sources. Earlier, Jesus spoke of us ascribing our guilt to failing our "ego ideals" (T-13.II.2:4). Here (in the Urtext version), we ascribe it to the unconscious "sources" uncovered in psychoanalysis.

We need to stop playing this game and look squarely at the "deeper source" of our guilt. After all, "The idea that the guiltless Son of God can attack himself and make himself guilty is insane" (T-13.IX.5:3). If we really recognized that the source of our guilt is an utterly false belief, we would have no need to displace it.

2.   Insane ideas <u>have</u> no real relationships, for that is why they <u>are</u> insane. No real relationship can rest on guilt, or even hold one spot of it to mar its purity. For all relationships that guilt has touched are used but to avoid the person *and* the guilt. What strange relationships you have made for this strange purpose! And you forgot that real relationships are holy, and cannot be used by <u>you</u> at all. They are used <u>only</u> by the Holy Spirit, and it is that which <u>makes</u> them pure. If you displace <u>your</u> guilt upon them, the Holy Spirit cannot use them. For, by pre-empting <u>for your own</u> ends what you should have given <u>Him</u>, He cannot use it [Ur: them] for <u>your</u> release. No one who would unite in <u>any</u> way with <u>anyone</u> for his individual [Ur: his *own*] salvation will find it in that strange relationship. It is not shared, and so it is not real.

Our relationships with other people are another apparently "safe" place to displace our guilt. We tell ourselves that dumping our guilt onto others is our salvation from having to look at the monsters we've become. But we're just putting our heads in the sand. When we project guilt onto a relationship partner, we are both avoiding the guilt without really undoing it and avoiding the *partner* because we no longer see who he or she really is. If all you're seeing in a relationship partner is your own guilt, how can that even be called a relationship?

These are "strange relationships" indeed—what the Course will eventually call special relationships. If we want real relationships with others, we must stop using them as dumping grounds for our guilt and let the Holy Spirit use them for His purpose. He will replace our special relationships with holy relationships, relationships dedicated to *undoing* guilt rather than perpetuating it. Uniting with others in holy relationships is the Holy Spirit's true means for our salvation.

3.   In any union with a brother in which you seek to lay <u>your</u> guilt upon him, or share it <u>with</u> him or perceive his own, *you* will feel guilty [Ur: *you will feel guilty*]. Nor will you find satisfaction and peace with him, because your union with him <u>is not real</u>. You will see guilt in that relationship <u>because you put it there</u>. It is inevitable that those who suffer guilt <u>will</u> attempt to displace it, because they <u>do</u> believe in it. Yet though they suffer, they will not look within <u>and let it go</u>. They cannot know they love, and cannot understand <u>what loving is</u>. Their main concern is to perceive the source of guilt <u>outside</u> themselves, <u>beyond</u> their own control.

X. Release from Guilt

As we've seen, the root of the whole game of displacement is our belief that our guilt is real. As long as we believe we've truly become monsters, we will attempt to get rid of our guilt by seeing it outside ourselves. We see other people as guilty. We blame them for our own guilt feelings. We wallow in guilt with them, hoping to lighten the burden by sharing it. But the end result of all this is that *we still feel guilty*. Since the whole point of displacement in our eyes is to get rid of guilt, it is an utter failure. In the end, the only way out is to recognize our guilt isn't real, to look within and see that "what you feared was there has been replaced with love" (T-13.IX.8:13). Indeed, love is the *only* thing that has ever been there.

> 4.   When you maintain that you are guilty but the source of your guilt lies in the past, you are not looking inward. The past is not *in* you [Ur: The past is *not* in you]. Your weird associations to it have no meaning in the present. Yet you let them stand between you and your brothers, with whom you find no real relationships at all. Can you expect to use your brothers as a means to "solve" the past, and still to see them as they really are? Salvation is not found by those who use their brothers to resolve problems that are not there. You wanted not salvation in the past. Would you impose your idle wishes on the present, and hope to find salvation now?

Another false "source" onto which we try to displace our guilt is the past. We think we're guilty for all the rotten things we think we've done in this life, all the ways we've been unloving. (I still feel guilty over my childhood memory of stealing Halloween candy from a group of younger children.) We try to use our brothers to "solve" the past by projecting our guilt onto them in various ways. One way, discussed in earlier sections and suggested by that reference to "weird associations" (see also T-17. III.2:5), is to project our "shadow figures" from the past, images of those who were "guilty" of not giving us the special love we wanted. But if you see your wife as your mother or your husband as your father, you are relating to a ghost, not a person. How can salvation be found in that?

All of this is simply another ruse to keep us from looking within. The past is *not* in us. It is gone. We didn't want salvation in the past, but we can have it in the present if we stop imposing the past *on* the present.

5.   Determine, then, to be <u>not</u> as you were. Use no relationship to hold you to the past, but with each one each day be born again. A minute, even less, will be enough to free you from the past, and give your mind in peace over to the Atonement. When everyone is welcome to you as you would have <u>yourself</u> be welcome to your Father, you will see no guilt in you. For you will have <u>accepted</u> the Atonement, which shone within you all the while you dreamed of guilt, and would not look within and <u>see</u> it.

The first sentence here is a reference to a line in the previous section, which said that when we condemn a brother, we are saying to ourselves, "I who *was* guilty choose to *remain* so" (T-13.IX.4:4, Urtext version). The way to be not as we were—guilty—is to stop using relationships to chain us to the past, "but with each one each day be born again."

Application: Choose a current relationship in your life, especially one onto which you have been projecting guilt (blaming the other person for problems, etc.). Take a minute now to be born again in this relationship by saying the following silently to your relationship partner:

I will not use my relationship with you, [name], to hold me to the past.
Instead, with our relationship this day, I choose to be born again.
I choose to use our relationship to free me from the past, and give my mind in peace over to the Atonement.
When you, [name], are as welcome to me as I would have myself be welcome to my Father,
I will see no guilt in me.
For I will have accepted the Atonement, which shone within me all the while I dreamed of guilt, and would not look within and see it.

6.   As long as you believe that guilt is justified in <u>any</u> way, in <u>anyone</u>, <u>whatever</u> he may do, [Ur: in *any* way, in *anyone*, *whatever* he may do] you will not look within, where you would <u>always</u> find Atonement. The end of guilt will never come as long as you believe <u>there is a reason for it</u>. For you must learn that guilt is <u>always</u> totally insane, and <u>has</u>

no reason. The Holy Spirit seeks not to dispel <u>reality</u>. If <u>guilt</u> were real, <u>Atonement</u> would not be. The purpose of Atonement is to dispel illusions, <u>not</u> to establish them as real and <u>then</u> forgive them.

Again, all the displacement we're doing is based on the conviction that our guilt is real. This belief is so pervasive that even when we acknowledge that the Holy Spirit can dispel guilt, we think this means dispelling *real* guilt. For instance, consider traditional Christianity. It says emphatically that sin is real, yet God magically wiped it away through Jesus' Atonement on the cross. Yet this is really just another displacement, in which we dump our guilt onto Jesus by saying he paid the *penalty* for our guilt. This simply cannot work: If our guilt were real, Atonement of any kind would be impossible.

We must come to recognize that guilt is not real "in *any* way, in *anyone, whatever* he may do." Think about that. Hitler is not guilty. Jeffrey Dahmer is not guilty. Osama bin Laden is not guilty. That person you're thinking about right now is not guilty. Only by learning that there is *never* a legitimate cause for guilt will we look within and accept the Atonement.

> 7. The Holy Spirit does not <u>keep</u> illusions in your mind to frighten you, and show them to you fearfully to demonstrate what He has saved you <u>from</u>. <u>What He has saved you from is gone</u>. Give <u>no</u> reality to guilt, and see <u>no</u> reason for it. The Holy Spirit does what God would have Him do, and has <u>always</u> done so. He has <u>seen</u> separation, but <u>knows</u> of union. He <u>teaches</u> healing, but He also <u>knows</u> of creation. He would have you see and teach as He does, and through Him. Yet what He knows you do <u>not</u> know, though it is yours.

The first sentence again reminds me of traditional Christianity. I've heard Christian evangelists go on and on about how horribly sinful we are and how deserving we are of hell, in order to scare us into accepting Jesus: "Look what he has saved you from!" But the Holy Spirit does not work this way. He knows that guilt is totally baseless. He sees that we feel guilty over our apparent separation from God, but He knows it is baseless because we are still one with God. He teaches us how to heal the guilt that stems from our apparent rift with God, but He knows that it is baseless because there is no real rift: Creation is unchanged. Though we don't know this yet, we can learn it if we "see and teach as He does, and through Him." He wants us to see no reason for guilt, and teach everyone the glorious truth that what the Holy Spirit has saved us from is *gone*.

> 8.   *Now* it is given you to heal and teach, to make what will be *now* [Ur: *will be*, now]. As yet it is not now. The Son of God believes that he is lost in guilt, alone in a dark world where pain is pressing everywhere upon him from without. When he has looked within and seen the radiance there, he will remember how much his Father loves him. And it will seem incredible that he ever thought his Father loved him not, and looked upon him as condemned. The moment that you realize guilt is insane, wholly unjustified and wholly without reason, you will not fear to look upon the Atonement and accept it wholly.

This world is a bitter place; even believers in God have not hesitated to call it a "vale of tears." It certainly seems like we are hopeless, godforsaken sinners in a dark land, condemned to suffer countless pains and indignities until death takes us at last. This is how life feels *now* for most of us, but the Course promises that we *will be* released.

How are we released? By fulfilling our function on earth, which is "to make what *will be,* now." We do this through healing our brothers, withdrawing our displacement of guilt upon them, refusing to use our relationships with them to bind us to the past, teaching them in thought, word, and deed that "guilt is insane, wholly unjustified and wholly without reason." When we do this, we will accept the Atonement within ourselves, and the idea that we could ever be forsaken by God will seem as strange as believing that "the sun could choose to be of ice; the sea elect to be apart from water, or the grass to grow with roots suspended in the air" (W-pI.156.3:3).

> 9.   You who have been unmerciful to yourself [Ur: yourselves] do not remember your Father's Love. And looking without mercy upon your brothers, you do not remember how much you love Him. Yet it is forever true. In shining peace within you is the perfect purity in which you were created. Fear not to look upon the lovely truth in you. Look through the cloud of guilt that dims your vision, and look past darkness to the holy place where you will see the light. The altar to your Father is as pure as He Who raised it to Himself. Nothing can keep from you what Christ would have you see. His Will is like His Father's, and He

offers mercy to every child of God, as He would have <u>you</u> do.

Here we are given the same message in different words. Our condemnation of ourselves and others—our belief in guilt—has blinded us to God's Love for us and ours for Him. But if we offer mercy to our brothers in place of condemnation, we will recognize the mercy God has for us. Then we will no longer be afraid to look within and accept the Atonement.

Application: Think of a brother whom you have been unmerciful toward. Say the following to this person:

> *I who have looked without mercy upon you, [name], now offer mercy to you, as Christ would have me do.*

Now that you have offered mercy to your brother, you are ready to look within.

Remember how much your Father loves you, and how much you love Him.

In shining peace within you is the perfect purity in which you were created.

Fear not to look upon the lovely truth in you.

Look through the cloud of guilt that dims your vision, and look past darkness to the holy place where you will see the light.

The altar to your Father is as pure as He Who raised it to Himself.

Nothing can keep from you what Christ would have you see.

His Will is like His Father's, and He offers mercy to every child of God, including you.

10. <u>Release</u> from guilt as you would <u>be</u> released. There is no other way to look within and see the light of love, shining as steadily and as surely as God Himself has always loved His Son. *And as His Son loves Him.* There is no fear in love, for love is guiltless. You who have <u>always</u> loved your Father can have no fear, for <u>any</u> reason, to look within and see your holiness. You <u>cannot</u> be as you believed you <u>were</u>. Your guilt is without reason because it is not in the Mind of God, where <u>you</u> are. And this *is* reason, which the Holy Spirit would <u>restore</u> to you.

> He would remove <u>only</u> illusions. All else He would have you see. And in Christ's vision He would show you the perfect purity that is forever within God's Son.

The first three lines in this paragraph are a good summary of the entire section's teaching: If we release our brothers from the guilt we have displaced onto them, we will be able to look within and see the love that is truly there. We are not the guilty monsters we thought we were because we are in the Mind of God, and nothing monstrous can possibly be there.

The Holy Spirit yearns to show us this, yet we are incredibly afraid of looking within. We are so convinced of our sin that when He implores us to look within, we think He means: "Get real! Take a look at what a miserable sinner you really are!" Some Christian spiritual practices, especially in the monastic tradition, focus on looking within to see how depraved we are, so we will be moved to repentance. But He's not trying to get us to realize what poisonous snakes we are. He's not trying to make us face real demons. All He wants to do is remove illusions and show us what is really there: "the perfect purity that is forever within God's Son."

> 11.   You cannot enter into <u>real</u> relationships [Ur: relationship] with <u>any</u> of God's Sons unless you love them all and <u>equally</u>. Love is not special. If you single out <u>part</u> of the Sonship for your love, you are imposing guilt on <u>all</u> your relationships and <u>making</u> them unreal. You can love <u>only</u> as God loves. Seek not to love <u>unlike</u> Him, for there <u>is</u> no love apart from His. Until you recognize that this is true, you will have no idea <u>what love is like</u>. No one who condemns a brother can see <u>himself</u> as guiltless and in the peace of God.

We return to the earlier theme of real relationships, and the Course gives us one of its "hard teachings": The only way to have a real relationship with *anyone* is to love *everyone* equally, whether it be our spouse or Saddam Hussein. Singling out a special person on whom to bestow our love is a special relationship, and as we saw in paragraph 2, special relationships are premium dumping grounds for our guilt. Indeed, singling out particular individuals for special love imposes guilt on *all* of our relationships. It is an attempt to love unlike God. It is an attack, because it cuts off the "loved" one from the rest of the Sonship and condemns the "unloved" ones as unworthy of love. How could we not feel guilty?

Loving everyone equally doesn't mean that we can't have relationships with particular individuals. We can't give an equal amount of time and attention to everyone, so the Holy Spirit assigns specific people to be our relationship partners (see, for instance, M-3.1). But though the *form* of our relationships varies, the *content* of each is meant to be the same: pure, limitless love. We can extend this love in a momentary encounter with a grocery store clerk as easily as we can with the person we spend our lives with.

If he is guiltless and in peace and sees it not, he is delusional, and has not looked upon himself. To him I say:

Behold the Son of God, and look upon his purity and be still. In quiet look upon his holiness, and offer thanks unto his Father that no guilt has ever touched him.

12. No illusion that you have ever held against him has touched his innocence in any way. His shining purity, wholly untouched by guilt and wholly loving, is bright within you. Let us look upon him together and love him. For in love of him is your guiltlessness. But look upon yourself, and gladness and appreciation for what you see will banish guilt forever. I thank You, Father, for the purity of Your most holy Son, whom You have [Ur: Thou hast] created guiltless forever.

Application: As we come to love all of our brothers equally, as God loves them, we will be prepared to look within and see what is really there. As we stop condemning our brothers with special love, we will recognize that *we* are guiltless and at peace. Now, hear these words as a personal invitation from Jesus to look within and see your own guiltlessness. I recommend inserting your own name at various points:

Behold the Son of God, and look upon his purity and be still.
In quiet look upon his holiness, and offer thanks unto his Father that
no guilt has ever touched him.
No illusion that you have ever held against him has touched his
innocence in any way.

His shining purity, wholly untouched by guilt and wholly loving, is
bright within you.
Let us look upon him together and love him.
For in love of him *is* your guiltlessness.
But look upon yourself, and gladness and appreciation for what you
see will banish guilt forever.
I thank You, Father, for the purity of Your most holy Son, whom You
have created guiltless forever.

13. Like you, my faith and my belief are centered on what I treasure.
The difference is that I love *only* what God loves <u>with</u> me, and because
of this I treasure you beyond the value that you set on yourself [Ur:
yourselves], even unto the worth that God has placed upon you. I love
all that He created, and all my faith and my belief I offer unto it. My
faith in you is as strong as all the love I give my Father. My trust in you
is without limit, and without the fear that you will hear me not. I thank
the Father for your loveliness, and for the many gifts that you will let
me offer to the Kingdom in honor of its wholeness that is of God.

Jesus wants us to see ourselves the same way he sees us, and it is
a beautiful vision indeed. The previous section said that our faith and
belief are invested in the ego's view of us as sinful and deserving of
punishment (see T-13.IX.2-3). Identified with the ego, we actually
treasure this twisted view of ourselves. But Jesus' faith and belief are
invested in who we really are—beautiful, loving, infinitely worthy Sons
of God—and *this* is what *he* treasures. Because he knows the truth about
us, he trusts us completely to hear his message and give his priceless
gifts to the Kingdom. For those of us who feel like we'll never get the
Course or be the miracle worker it is training us to be, Jesus' faith in us
is good news indeed.

14. Praise be to you who make the Father one with His Own Son.
Alone we are all lowly, but together we shine with brightness so intense
that none of us alone can even think of it. Before the glorious radiance
of the Kingdom guilt melts away, and transformed into kindness will
never more be what it was. Every reaction you experience will be so
purified that it is fitting as a hymn of praise unto your Father. See only

praise of Him in what He has created, for He will never cease His praise of <u>you</u>. United in this praise we stand before the gates of Heaven where we will surely enter in our sinlessness [Ur: blamelessness]. God loves you. Could I, then, lack faith in you and love Him perfectly?

The word that jumps out for me in this final paragraph is *praise*. Jesus begins by praising us. Alone everyone is lowly (even Jesus!), but together we are infinitely praiseworthy, shining "with brightness so intense that none of us alone can even think of it." The fruit of this radiant joining is that guilt will be transformed into kindness toward everyone, which is the way we praise God on earth (see T-4.VII.8). Our reactions to our brothers will become "fitting as a hymn of praise unto your Father." As we praise God's creation through kindness, we will learn that God has never ceased His praise of us. And finally, united in this praise, we will all enter into Heaven, free at last from guilt and fully awakened to the Love we share with God.

XI. The Peace of Heaven
Commentary by Greg Mackie

This chapter has taken us on a grim tour through the horrors of guilt. In this final section, Jesus assures us that we *will* overcome guilt and find the peace of Heaven because it is God's will that we do so. "There is no chance that Heaven will not be yours, for God is sure, and what He wills is as sure as He is."

> 1.   Forgetfulness and sleep and even death become the ego's best advice for dealing with the perceived and harsh intrusion of guilt on peace. Yet no one sees himself in conflict and ravaged by a cruel war unless he believes that <u>both</u> opponents in the war are real. Believing this he must escape, for such a war would surely end his peace of mind, and so destroy him. Yet if he could but realize the war is between [Ur: forces that are] real and <u>unreal</u> powers, he could look upon himself and <u>see</u> his freedom. No one finds himself ravaged and torn in endless battles if he himself perceives them as wholly without meaning [Ur: battle, which he *himself* perceives as wholly without meaning].

We do feel caught in an endless battle with guilt. Our days are filled with what Robert calls the "redemption cycle": feeling guilty and then trying to find some way to redeem ourselves. We try to be "good," make amends, make excuses, blame others, ascribe our guilt to "safer" sources (displacement), try to forget about it, numb ourselves, and even hope that death will release us from it: "Rest in peace."

But the only way to really find peace is to recognize that there *is* no battle. As long as we believe guilt is real, peace of mind is impossible. But if we see that the invading force of guilt is no more real than the Klingons of *Star Trek*, we will be free. We will not be afraid to look within and see the peace that has always been there. If peace is the only reality, what could we have *but* peace of mind?

> 2.   God would not have His Son embattled, and so His Son's imagined "enemy" [Ur: which he made] is totally unreal. You are but trying to escape a bitter war from which you *have* escaped. The war is gone. For

you have heard the hymn of freedom rising unto Heaven. Gladness and joy belong to God for your release, because <u>you</u> made it not. Yet as you made not freedom, so you made not a war that could <u>endanger</u> freedom. Nothing destructive ever was or will be. The war, the guilt, the past are gone as one into the unreality from which they came.

I've heard stories about old Japanese soldiers found on isolated islands in the Pacific, who thought that World War II was still going on years after it ended. Like them, we're fighting a war that was over long ago. It is over because long ago we heard the hymn of freedom (a reference, I believe, to T-13.X.14). This joyous hymn tells us that the war is over because there never *was* a war. The "opponent" is and always was unreal, so the whole war was just a bad dream. Freedom is ours because freedom has *always* been ours.

3.   When we are all united in Heaven, you will value <u>nothing</u> that you value here. For nothing that you value here do you value wholly, and so you do not value it at all. Value is where God placed it, and the value of what God esteems <u>cannot be judged</u>, for it <u>has been established</u>. It is <u>wholly</u> of value. It can merely be appreciated <u>or not</u>. To value it partially is <u>not to know its value</u>. In Heaven is everything God values, and nothing else. Heaven is perfectly unambiguous. Everything is clear and bright, and calls forth <u>one</u> response. There is no darkness and there is no contrast. There is no variation. There is no interruption. There is a sense of peace so deep that no dream in this world has ever brought even a dim imagining of what it is.

Let that first sentence really sink in: When we wake up in Heaven we will value *nothing* that we value here. That really puts some perspective on all the stuff we cling to and obsess about here, doesn't it? The only things worth valuing are things of absolute value, and all values here are relative. For example, a couple of sections ago, Jesus talked about how we value both innocence and guilt. We value our own innocence, and we value other people's guilt because it seems to *preserve* our innocence. We see both as real, so we "cannot value one without the other" (T-13.IX.4:2). We value both innocence and guilt, but we don't value either wholly.

In Heaven, though, everything is of absolute value and thus wholly of value. The thing that stands out most for me in this description of Heaven is its total *one-sidedness*. There are no opposites (like innocence and guilt) competing with one another for value. Heaven has only one meaning and calls forth only one response. There is no contrast or variation or interruption: It is all one seamless whole. The inevitable result of this is *deep peace*. If there is no conflict between opposites, what else could there be?

Application: Bring to mind some earthly thing you value, something you find difficult to give up. Now tell yourself: *"When I am united with my brothers in Heaven, this will have no value for me. For I do not value this wholly, and so I do not really value it at all."*

4. Nothing in this world can give this peace, for nothing in this world is wholly shared. Perfect perception can merely show you what is <u>capable</u> of being wholly shared. It can also show you the <u>results</u> of sharing, while you still remember the results of <u>not </u>sharing. The Holy Spirit points quietly to the contrast, knowing that you will finally let Him judge the difference <u>for</u> you, allowing Him to demonstrate which <u>must </u>be true. He has perfect faith in your final judgment, because He knows that <u>He will make it for you</u>. To doubt this would be to doubt that His mission will be fulfilled. How is this possible, when His mission is of God?

Only in the state of heavenly knowledge can things be *wholly* shared, because only there can total, unmediated joining occur. In perception there is always some distinction between subject and object, which is a barrier to absolute joining. However, perfect perception does show us what *can* be wholly shared—things of absolute value like love, joy, and peace—while we're in a world where the opposites of those things are painfully apparent. This contrast is key to the whole process of awakening: The Holy Spirit shows us this contrast, and once we see how stark the difference really is, we have all the incentive in the world to say to Him, "Choose for me!" The great news is that this means we cannot fail. Our final decision for God is inevitable because the very Voice for God will make it for us.

5.   You whose mind is [Ur: minds are] darkened by doubt and guilt, remember this: God gave the Holy Spirit to you, and gave <u>Him</u> the mission to <u>remove</u> all doubt and every trace of guilt that His dear Son has laid upon himself. <u>It is impossible that this mission fail.</u> Nothing can prevent what God would <u>have</u> accomplished from accomplishment. Whatever your reactions to the Holy Spirit's Voice may be, whatever voice you choose to listen to, whatever strange thoughts may occur to you, God's Will *is* done. You <u>will</u> find the peace in which He has established you, because <u>He</u> does <u>not</u> change His Mind. He is invariable as the peace in which you dwell, and of which the Holy Spirit reminds you.

Who among us is not wracked by doubt and guilt? As we walk the path of the Course, we all have that voice within us saying, "You're worthless and weak. You'll never make it. Give up now!" Jesus' words to us here are the perfect antidote to the sickness of despair.

Application: Think about your own doubt and guilt, your nagging belief that someone as inadequate as you will never make it back to Heaven. Now say these reassuring words to yourself:

> *My mind has been darkened by doubt and guilt, but whatever my reactions to the Holy Spirit's Voice [think of some of those reactions],*
> *whatever voice I choose to listen to [think of times you've listened to the ego], whatever strange thoughts may occur to me [think of some strange thoughts you've had],*
> *God's Will **is** done.*
> *The Holy Spirit's mission is to remove all doubt and every trace of guilt that I have laid upon myself.*
> ***It is impossible that this mission fail.***
> *Nothing can prevent what God would have accomplished from accomplishment.*
> *I will find the peace in which He has established me, because He does not change His Mind.*

6.   You will not remember change and shift in Heaven. You have need

of contrast only here. Contrast and differences are necessary teaching aids, for by them you learn what to avoid and what to seek. When you have <u>learned</u> this, you will find the answer that makes the need for <u>any</u> differences disappear. Truth comes of its <u>own</u> will unto its own. When you have learned that you <u>belong</u> to truth, it will flow lightly over you without a difference of <u>any</u> kind. For you will <u>need</u> no contrast to help you realize that <u>this is what you want</u>, and <u>only</u> this. Fear not the Holy Spirit will fail in what your Father has given Him to do. <u>The Will of God can fail in nothing</u>.

We return to a theme from paragraph 4: the need for contrast and differences while we're here. This is a need I think many Course students tend to minimize. I can think of many times where I've made a distinction between different things in a class and someone objected because "the Course says we shouldn't see differences." Obviously, there are certain types of differences the Course doesn't want us to see. But there are other differences we *must* see, especially the difference between the false and the true, which tells us what to avoid and what to seek. We have to learn this with the Holy Spirit's help, because only when do will we find the answer that brings us back to Heaven, where no differences exist.

7.   Have faith in only this one thing, and it will be sufficient: God wills you be in Heaven, and nothing can keep you <u>from</u> it, or <u>it</u> from you. Your wildest misperceptions, your weird imaginings, your blackest nightmares all mean nothing. They will not prevail against the peace God wills for you. The Holy Spirit <u>will</u> restore your sanity because insanity is <u>not</u> the Will of God. If that suffices Him, it is enough for you. You will <u>not</u> keep what God would have removed, because it breaks communication with you with whom He would communicate. His Voice *will* be heard.

Application: We just did a similar application in paragraph 5, but we can't remind ourselves enough that our return to Heaven is inevitable. So, again bring to mind your doubts and your guilt and say these reassuring words to yourself:

God wills I be in Heaven, and nothing can keep me from it, or it from me.

My wildest misperceptions, my weird imaginings, my blackest nightmares all mean nothing.
They will not prevail against the peace God wills for me.
The Holy Spirit will restore my sanity because insanity is not the Will of God.
*His Voice **will** be heard.*

8.   The communication link that God Himself placed within you, joining your mind [Ur: minds] with His, <u>cannot</u> be broken. You may believe you <u>want</u> it broken, and this belief <u>does</u> interfere with the deep peace in which the sweet and constant communication God would <u>share</u> with you is known. Yet His channels of reaching out [us, His Sons] <u>cannot</u> be wholly closed and separated <u>from</u> Him. Peace will be yours because His peace still flows to you from Him Whose Will <u>is</u> peace. <u>You have it now.</u> The Holy Spirit will teach you how to <u>use</u> it, and by extending it, to learn that it <u>is</u> in you. God willed you Heaven, and will <u>always</u> will you nothing else. The Holy Spirit knows <u>only</u> of His Will. There is <u>no</u> chance that Heaven will not be yours, for God is sure, and what He wills is as sure as He is.

God's Voice will be heard because communication with Him is forever unbroken. In this paragraph (with ideas from elsewhere in the Course added in), I see the following sequence:

1. In the separation, we tried to break communication with God. "The separation was not a loss of perfection, but a failure in communication" (T-6.IV.12:5).
2. To make sure communication was not broken, God established the Holy Spirit as the communication link between Him and His separated Sons.
3. We still think we want this communication link to be broken. We refuse to listen to the Holy Spirit. This does block the deep peace that comes from open communication with God.
4. But this communication link cannot be broken. We who are God's channels of reaching out cannot be totally closed off. Communication with God is still going on.
5. For this reason, we have peace *now*, and will inevitably rediscover

it.

6. We rediscover peace by choosing to listen to the Holy Spirit, Who will teach us how to communicate it to our brothers. By extending it, we learn that peace is in us.

7. We *will* do this, for it is God's Will. There is no chance that Heaven will not be ours.

> 9. You will learn salvation because you will learn <u>how to save</u>. It will not be possible to <u>exempt yourself</u> from what the Holy Spirit wants to teach you. Salvation is as sure as God. His certainty suffices. Learn that even the darkest nightmare that disturbs the mind of God's sleeping Son holds no power over him. He <u>will</u> learn the lesson of awaking. God watches over him and light surrounds him.

It is through saving others, through letting the Holy Spirit teach us how to extend peace to our brothers, that we will recognize that we are saved. Do you want to end the nightmare of guilt, to learn that it has no power over you, to learn that God watches over you and light surrounds you? Give peace to that person you've been resenting—yes, *that* one— and you will receive the peace you gave.

> 10. Can God's Son lose himself in dreams, when God has placed <u>within</u> him the glad call to waken and be glad? He cannot separate himself from what is <u>in</u> him. His sleep will not withstand the call to wake. The mission of redemption will be fulfilled as surely as the creation will remain unchanged throughout eternity. You do <u>not</u> have to know that Heaven is yours to <u>make</u> it so. It *is* so. Yet to <u>know</u> it, the Will of God must be accepted <u>as</u> your will.

Application: Since Jesus is so determined to let us know that our awakening is certain, let's relieve our doubt and guilt by repeating the reassuring words he gives us one more time:

> *God has placed within me the glad call to waken and be glad.*
> *I cannot separate myself from what is in me.*
> *My sleep will not withstand the call to wake.*
> *The mission of redemption will be fulfilled as surely as the*

creation will remain unchanged throughout eternity.
I do not have to know that Heaven is mine to make it so.
It is so.

11.   The Holy Spirit will [Ur: *cannot* fail to] undo <u>for</u> you everything you have learned that teaches that what is <u>not</u> true must be <u>reconciled</u> with truth. This is the reconciliation the ego would substitute for your reconciliation to sanity and to peace. The Holy Spirit has a very different kind of reconciliation in His Mind for you, and one <u>He will effect</u> as surely as the ego will <u>not</u> effect what it attempts. Failure is of the ego, <u>not</u> of God. From Him you <u>cannot</u> wander, and there is no possibility that the plan the Holy Spirit offers *to* everyone, for the salvation *of* everyone, will not be perfectly accomplished. You <u>will</u> be released, and you will <u>not</u> remember anything you made that was not created <u>for</u> you and <u>by</u> you in return. For how can you remember what was never true, or <u>not</u> remember what has always been? It is this reconciliation with truth, and <u>only</u> truth, in which the peace of Heaven lies.

The reason we don't experience the peace of Heaven right now is that we're frantically trying to reconcile what is not true with what is true. This is what happens when we don't see the contrast the Holy Spirit wants us to see. We try to mix everything together, to reconcile opposites: God and ego, Heaven and earth, love and hate, spirit and body, life and death, innocence and guilt. This attempt is doomed to fail, but this failure is the best thing that can happen to us. It opens the door for the Holy Spirit, Whose plan for our redemption *cannot* fail to be perfectly accomplished. In the end, we will forget all of our futile attempts to reconcile the false and the true, and side entirely with the truth of God's creation. This absolute commitment to the true side of the war that never was *is* the peace of Heaven.

About the Circle's
TEXT READING PROGRAM

An Unforgettable Journey through the Text in One Year

The Text is the foundation of *A Course in Miracles*, yet many students find it hard going. This program is designed to guide you through the Text, paragraph by paragraph, in one year.

Each weekday, you will receive an e-mail containing that day's Text section, along with commentary on each paragraph, written by Robert Perry or Greg Mackie. The readings contain material edited out of the published Course as well as exercises for practical application. This is the material that has been presented now in book format in our series *The Illuminated Text*.

By signing up for our online program, you will also receive:

- Weekly one-hour class recordings led by Robert Perry and Greg Mackie that summarize that week's sections and answer students' questions
- An online forum for sharing with others in the program
- Related articles on key Text sections e-mailed directly to you
- Your personal web archive, with access to all your commentaries and class recordings
- An unlimited "pause feature" for pausing your program while you're away

Want to learn more? Call us today on 1-888-357-7520, or go to www.circleofa.org, the largest online resource for *A Course in Miracles*!

We hope that you will join us for this truly enlightening program!

ABOUT THE AUTHORS

Robert Perry has been a student of *A Course in Miracles* (ACIM) since 1981. He taught at Miracle Distribution Center in California from 1986 to 1989, and in 1993 founded the Circle of Atonement in Sedona, Arizona. The Circle is an organization composed of several teachers dedicated to helping establish the Course as an authentic spiritual tradition.

One of the most respected voices on ACIM, Robert has traveled extensively, speaking throughout the U.S. and internationally. In addition to contributing scores of articles to various Course publications, he is the author or co-author of nineteen books and booklets, including the hugely popular *An Introduction to A Course in Miracles*. Robert's goal has always been to provide a complete picture of what the Course is—as a thought system and as a path meant to be lived in the world on a daily basis—and to support students in walking along that path.

Robert has recently authored his first non-ACIM book, *Signs: A New Approach to Coincidence, Synchronicity, Guidance, Life Purpose, and God's Plan*, available on Amazon sites internationally.

Greg Mackie has been a student of *A Course in Miracles* since 1991. He has been teaching and writing for the Circle of Atonement since 1999, and has written scores of articles for A Better Way, the newsletter of the Circle of Atonement, as well as other ACIM publications. He is the author of *How Can We Forgive Murderers?* and co-taught, along with Robert Perry, the Text Reading Program and the Daily Workbook Program, which consisted of 365 recordings.

CPSIA information can be obtained at www.ICGtesting.com
Printed in the USA
267745BV00002B/1/P